The
Man
Who
Pardoned
Nixon

by Clark R. Mollenhoff

Game Plan for Disaster: An Ombudsman's Report
     on the Nixon Years
Strike Force: Organized Crime and the Government
The Pentagon
Despoilers of Democracy
Tentacles of Power
Washington Cover-Up

The Man Who Pardoned Nixon

Clark R. Mollenhoff

a Giniger Book
published in association with
St. Martin's Press, Inc.   New York
St. James Press   London

Published in association with The K. S. Giniger Company, Inc.,
225 Park Avenue South, New York, N.Y. 10003.

Published simultaneously in U.K. by St. James Press
for information, write:
St. James Press Ltd.
3 Percy Street
London W1P 9FA
SBN   900997 89 3

Contents

"I think the President has to be a person of great truth and the American people have to believe that he is truthful."

Gerald Ford, November 5, 1973

"The code of ethics that will be followed will be the example I set."

Gerald Ford, August 28, 1974

Introduction

I HAVE BEEN a reporter for thirty-five years, and have been a Washington reporter for more than twenty-five years. In that capacity I have known Gerald R. Ford since shortly after he arrived in Washington, and I have had a good personal relationship with him.

During most of that period of time, I have been registered as a political independent and have engaged in investigations of corruption and mismanagement in government under both Democratic and Republican administrations, but have tried to avoid involvement in the politics of any administration.

However, I have accepted appointments from two administrations, one Democratic and the other Republican. In 1962, I was appointed by President John F. Kennedy to a three-year term as a member of the U.S. Advisory Commission on Information Policy, a non-paying advisory role overseeing the work of the United States Information Agency. In 1969, I was appointed by President Richard M. Nixon as Deputy Counsel to the President and four months later became Special Counsel to the President, in a newly-created ombudsman role with the assignment to gather evidence of wrongdoing and to recommend corrective action.

During the eleven months I was on the White House staff, I became disillusioned with President Nixon's lack of action against potential problems, and resigned to return to newspaper work. In that role, I pursued the Watergate scandals and cover-up with a diligence that displeased Mr. Nixon and some of his supporters.

Because I had worked for President Nixon and had high hopes for what his administration might have achieved, I felt particularly let down by the Watergate affair and was relieved and pleased when Gerald Ford became president. My relationship with Ford had remained pleasant throughout Watergate and, even though I did not agree with his position, I understood that, as House Republican leader, he could not be expected to lead an assault on the president of his own party. But, aware of the weaknesses in his background and some questionable political actions, I hoped that he would rise above those limitations and be another Harry Truman.

I have set out my experiences as Special Counsel to President Nixon and during the Watergate affair in a recently published book, *Game Plan for Disaster,* which focused on the corrupting influence of excessive secrecy in government as demonstrated in Mr. Nixon's misuse and abuse of "executive privilege."

This book is an effort to take a similar hard critical look at Gerald Ford's background and first nineteen months in the White House and examine his record on many of the same crucial issues of credibility and performance.

CLARK R. MOLLENHOFF
Washington, D.C.
March 15, 1976

1. A Disappointing Record

RICHARD M. NIXON, not the American people, put Gerald R. Ford, Jr., in the White House. Some men might have risen above these circumstances; others would have plodded along trying to meet the challenge. But Ford's first nineteen months as President have given us little to praise and much that is highly vulnerable to criticism.

This should have been expected because, in all of Gerald Ford's political life, he has demonstrated no commitment except to the Republican Party and within that party only to the extent that it did not entail any risk for his only longtime political goal: to be Speaker of the House of Representatives.

He was less irritating than other ambitious politicians because he was a professional "nice guy" trying to captivate everyone in the same manner he did as an athletic hero through high school, college, law school and a four-year tour in the Navy. It is significant that Ford, despite a degree from the prestigious Yale Law School, preferred the role of athletic director during his Navy service.

While Gerald Ford undoubtedly has the capacity to understand the issues if he feels impelled by personal benefit, he has prevailed by avoiding convictions or commitments except to the Republican House organization and even then with the adroit flexibility that marked his denying his role in ousting House Republican leaders Joseph Martin in 1959 and Charles Halleck in 1965 though he was the major beneficiary of those revolts.

Gerald Ford has learned thoroughly over the years the doctrine of "plausible deniability" and to use other people to do the unpleasant political jobs often referred to as "dirty work."

Thus, Representative Melvin Laird and others took the heat and made the enemies by ousting Joe Martin, but it was Gerald Ford who moved up the House leadership ladder.

Again, Melvin Laird, and then Representatives Donald Rumsfeld, Robert Griffin and Charles Goodell, took the hazardous front line position in ousting Charlie Halleck, but it was Gerald Ford who became House Republican Leader.

As he rose in the ranks of House Republican leaders, Ford adapted easily to speaking with enthusiasm for either ultraliberals or ultraconservatives. When he appeared in Indiana as the main speaker at Charles Halleck Day, Ford denied the charge that he was seeking to unseat Halleck as House Republican Leader with the same kind of evasive rhetoric we now recognize as his hallmark as President. He found no problem of conscience in speaking for and acting against the man who stood in his way.

Gerald Ford's public life has been a study in amiability; he has played the Republican establishment game, reserving to himself enough flexibility to dart in any direction when expediency beckoned. Friends of the President in Congress, preparing for Lincoln Day addresses in 1976, searched long and diligently for any legislation carrying his name or the stamp of his character. There was nothing.

The only time he flourished his cape in the arena was in 1970 when he was pushed to the fore by the Nixon Administration in the unsuccessful effort to oust Supreme Court Justice William O. Douglas in political retaliation against the defeat of Nixon's Supreme Court nominees, Judge Clement Haynsworth and Judge Harrold Carswell. Even so, he operated mainly through Representative Edward Hutchinson, another Michigan Republican, who was a high-ranking member of the House Judiciary Committee. Hutchinson was the same man he later used to carry out his Republican strategy of stall and evade in the Nixon impeachment inquiry in 1974.

Criticism of Justice Douglas because he accepted money from the Albert Parvin Foundation, whose funds came from a Las Vegas gambling club linked with organized crime, could be justified. However, the timing and tenor of Ford's moves to depose Douglas were strict partisan politics of a retaliatory nature.

The losing fight to discredit Justice Douglas was clumsy and ineffective, with valid criticism lost in a maze of ideological and partisan recriminations. It was the only time when Jerry Ford issued statements in his own name, attacked an adversary in his own name and, as the tool of the Nixon Administration, lost the "plausible deniability" of the professional "nice guy."

Although most political observers were aware of Ford's past operations as a pragmatic Republican machine politico, able to compromise on any issue or principle, they hoped he could emerge as another Harry Truman when it became apparent Nixon would be forced to resign or be impeached. They were willing to overlook his last-ditch stand for Nixon as an "innocent man" long after the first Nixon-edited White House tapes lost the support of the *Chicago Tribune*, the *Omaha World-Herald*, and even Senate Republican Leader Hugh Scott.

They were willing to forget that House Republican Leader Gerald Ford had led the fight to kill the Patman committee's investigation of the Watergate affair in September and October of 1972, although they knew the manner in which he had pulled the strings on a junior Michigan Republican Congressman, Garry Brown, to successfully sidetrack Patman until after the election. They were willing to disregard his less than forthright answers to the Judiciary Committee during his vice-presidential confirmation hearings when he denied the lead role in killing the Patman probe, if only he would demonstrate that he had broken with the past and had no obligations to Richard Nixon or others of the Nixon White House gang to contaminate his future decisions.

With full knowledge of those past operations, insiders were misled for several weeks by President Gerald Ford's talk of candor, openness and the importance of integrity and truth in government. They wanted to believe a new Ford was emerging to meet the country's needs, as Harry Truman had emerged despite his ties with Kansas City's Pendergast machine.

The full and complete pardon for Richard Nixon was the shock that awakened the country to the fact there was no new Gerald Ford, that this was the same politician who had known and admired Richard Nixon for twenty-five years and who still felt political loyalty to him and his gang despite the disgrace Watergate had brought to the Republican Party and the nation.

Month after month since then, Ford has demonstrated that the Nixon pardon was no temporary political aberration but was as callously calculated as was Nixon's commutation of the prison term of Teamster's Union boss James R. Hoffa. Both were done with the understanding that there would be some degree of public outrage, but with the belief it would be forgotten before the next election.

Ford's record for duplicity has matched and, for the time period involved, surpassed Nixon's. The press and public, wrung out by the wearying months of Nixon outrages, were too often exhausted to do more than whimper protests.

Ford spoke of openness and vetoed a Freedom of Information law. He spoke of candor and weasled away from his seeming promise not to pardon Nixon. He spoke of cooperation with Congress and the need to be accountable, but used "executive privilege" to cover up for Secretary of State Henry A. Kissinger's evasions and falsehoods.

Ford promised farmers fair prices and fair profits and vetoed a farm bill increasing target prices on corn and wheat. He promised labor he would sign a common situs picketing bill and vetoed it. He shilly-shallied on a tax cut, on an energy program and on aid to New York City and only demonstrated that he had no well-thought-out program or resolve on any of those issues but was playing for political effect rather than solutions.

In the international field, Ford talked of the glories of detente and defended the Soviets against charges of violating arms control agreements. He then complained because

Congress and the public did not respond to the urgency of his requests to counter Soviet assistance in Angola and in other parts of the world.

Ford denounced the political use of the Central Intelligence Agency and then appointed George Bush, a former Republican National Committee chairman without intelligence experience, to run that agency. He castigated the Congress for cutting his defense budget and then fired Defense Secretary James Schlesinger for his forthright dedication to assuring congressional acceptance of the need for greater defense spending.

Ford spoke of the importance of proper administration and enforcement of the laws and yet disregarded evidence of massive mismanagement and corruption in many agencies of government. While he expressed varying degrees of concern over corruption and "conflicts of interest," he has done absolutely nothing to demonstrate that he intends to take action other than promoting the culprits—the proven liars, power abusers and mismanagers who had the right political connections.

On the basis of better than a year and a half as President, Gerald Ford has continued to project a pleasant, professional "nice guy" image and little else. But even that image will not stand close scrutiny, for he allowed his political campaign manager, Howard (Bo) Callaway, to undercut Vice President Nelson A. Rockefeller while praising Rocky and denying personal responsibility for Callaway's campaign.

In the same way, President Ford has tried to remain above assaults on former California governor Ronald Reagan and has stood by while Rockefeller and others have carried the attack in New Hampshire and Florida. But first he tried to neutralize Reagan with offers of Cabinet posts.

Ford's answer to Nixon efforts to misuse the Central Intelligence Agency is greater presidential control of the CIA, relying on a three-man intelligence-oversight committee appointed by the president and subject to removal by the president. His answer to CIA and FBI abuses exposed by the press and by Congressional committees is to propose legislation putting a tighter lid on government secrets with new laws for jailing those who would leak classified documents to the press or to Congress. If these laws had been in force at the time of Watergate, Nixon would probably be in office today.

His record number of vetoes has been more for political effect than for moving the nation forward, and his own estimate of his "greatest success" in his more than nineteen months in office is the movement of the country out of the recession of 1975. While this bread-and-butter issue is of great importance to the nation, the only Ford Administration actions were the fumbling nonactions of vetoing a wide assortment of Democratic programs. "Success" was obviously more luck than economic planning.

President Ford remains unwilling to criticize Richard Nixon, even though Nixon's moving into the limelight by his visit to China was an embarrassment to Ford in the New Hampshire primary. It is well to remember that Ford, for some reason still unknown to the public, feels an obligation to Nixon and has indicated that Nixon might yet emerge with an active role in public life.

Gerald Ford is not our first duplicitous president and will not be our last, but his record is made hypocritical by his repeated assertions that his would be an administration "of openness and candor" in contrast to the "long nightmare" of deceptions and falsehoods of the last two years of Richard Nixon's regime.

Regardless of what happens in the 1976 election, Ford is insulated from the economic and political realities most citizens must face by the assurance of a $60,000-a-year presidential pension for life, plus personal staff expenses of $100,000 a year in addition to the miscellaneous fringe benefits that go with Secret Service protection. These are luxuries that could not have been assured by even a million-dollar legacy; Gerald Ford must remember that he owes it all to Richard Nixon.

Some critical political observers refer to Gerald Ford as "Richard Nixon's revenge on the American people." It is indisputable that Gerald Ford is Richard Nixon's hand-picked successor, and so far he has not let his mentor down.

2. Up from Grand Rapids

GERALD FORD WAS born Leslie Lynch King on July 14, 1913, in Omaha, Nebraska, the son of Leslie King, a wool dealer, and Dorothy Gardner King. J. F. terHorst, in his comprehensive biography of Ford, says, "little is known" about Ford's first two years, except that "the marriage foundered" from the start. His mother returned to the home of her parents in Grand Rapids, Michigan, where she met and married a young paint salesman named Gerald R. Ford, who later adopted the two-year-old youngster, renamed him Gerald R. Ford, Jr., and reared him as his own son.

With the exception of those two years, Ford lived the normal life of a boy in an upper-middle-class home in Middle America, apparently unaware until his last years in high school that he was the adopted son of Gerald Ford, Sr., and the half brother of Thomas, Richard and James Ford.

There is no indication that the unusual events of his first two years, or the later discovery that Gerald Ford was not his real father, had any adverse impact upon the development of the strong and athletic youth who played basketball, baseball and football at South High in Grand Rapids. Ford played center on the high school football team for three years and was All-State center the last two years. In his senior year, South High won the state championship.

Although athletics were the moving force in his high school days, he was an Eagle Scout and, according to ter-Horst, "received good grades, some A's, mostly B's, and a C or two" in four years of high school.

Recruited by the University of Michigan on a football scholarship in part subsidized by Grand Rapids alumni, Ford maintained a B average while playing varsity football and washing dishes at the Delta Kappa Epsilon fraternity house. Although awarded the Most Valuable Player honor in his senior year, he had the misfortune of spending most of his sophomore and junior years on the bench when he played behind All-American center Chuck Bernard on a Big Ten championship team.

The Michigan team lost seven of its eight games in Ford's senior year, but Ford was an outstanding enough player to be selected for the annual East-West Shrine Game in San Francisco and for the College All-Stars in the traditional game against the championship professional football team.

Ford turned down professional football contracts offered by the Green Bay Packers and the Detroit Lions and accepted a $2,400-a-year job as assistant line coach at Yale University, where he hoped to enter law school, though Phi Beta Kappa students dominated the accepted list. Despite problems getting accepted as a full-time student while working as an assistant football coach, Ford managed to graduate in the top third of his class with an LL.B. degree in 1941.

He returned to Grand Rapids for a brief fling at a law partnership with Philip Buchen, a friend from University of Michigan days, but joined the Navy on April 20, 1942 —a few months after the Pearl Harbor disaster.

Athletics dominated Ford's four years of service rather than law. Commissioned an ensign, he was assigned to the Navy physical-training unit headed by former boxing champion Gene Tunney, and finished his Navy service as director of physical training and assistant navigational officer on the light aircraft carrier *Monterey* with the U.S. Third Fleet in the Pacific. After two years of combat duty, with ten battle stars and the rank of lieutenant commander, Ford was discharged in late 1945 to again enter the practice of law in Grand Rapids. His ratings by his superiors in the Navy had been excellent, and according to the terHorst biography, Capt. L. T. Hundt of the *Monterey* gave Ford a maximum rating of four with the comment that he was an "excellent leader . . . resourceful . . . steady."

After less than two years in law practice with the firm of Butterfield, Keeney and Amberg, Ford decided to challenge the four-term Republican Congressman from Michigan's Fifth District, Bartel J. Jonkman, in the primary. The popular Ford won handily in the Republican primary fight in September and married Elizabeth Bloomer Warren in October, and in November his victory over the Democratic candidate was automatic and by a large margin.

His marriage to a divorcée was politically timed to avoid its being an issue in the tough 1948 Republican primary test in western Michigan, where opposition to divorce by

many older voters might be a decisive factor in a close
election.

In 1949, the year he entered the House, Ford was selected by the U.S. Junior Chamber of Commerce as one
of the nation's ten outstanding young men, and he began
his steady climb up the political ladder toward his admitted ambition to become the Republican Speaker of
the House.

In 1956, when Harold E. Stassen, Eisenhower's dis-
armament chief, launched a "dump Nixon" movement,
Gerald Ford was part of the group of House members
who banded together to keep Nixon on the ticket as a
vice-presidential candidate. The core of this group was
the membership of the Chowder and Marching Club, the
social-political Republican group that Nixon helped Ford
organize in 1949.

In 1959, he joined with others in unseating House
Speaker Joseph Martin, the aging Massachusetts conservative, and replacing him with Representative Charles Halleck, an equally conservative but more aggressive Indiana
Republican. In 1961, Ford received the American Political
Science Association's distinguished congressional service
award, and in 1963 he was the front man for a "young
Turks" warning revolt against Halleck's stern discipline
and was chosen chairman of the House Republican Conference in place of Halleck's choice, Representative
Charles Hoeven of Iowa.

In 1960, Ford permitted the Michigan Republicans to
start a "Ford for Vice President" drive at the Republican
Convention. Though he had no real hope of landing the
number-two spot, he was pleased when Nixon rejected
him with this compliment: "I don't know of anyone
whose views on domestic and foreign policy are more con-

sonant with mine than Jerry here, but if I'm elected, I'll need him in the House."

Nixon picked Henry Cabot Lodge as his running mate, as a compromise with the liberal Republican forces. The ticket was defeated and Nixon returned to California, but Ford was re-elected and continued his quest for power in the House.

When Halleck was ousted in January 1965, with Representative Mel Laird providing the savvy and political muscle, Ford was a co-conspirator and the obvious choice for minority leader.

Jerry Ford never moved prematurely and rarely telegraphed his punches. Little advance notice was served to Halleck in 1965 when Ford ousted him and became the House Republican Leader. In fact, Jerry Ford had denied he was a party to the planned coup when he went to Warsaw, Indiana, on October 28, 1964, a few days before the election, to be the major speaker at Charlie Halleck Day.

Ford responded to Indiana reporters who questioned whether he was a member of the intrigue: "At a time when Republicans are fighting against overwhelming odds, it is completely inappropriate to discuss a change in our House Leader or to undercut our congressional leadership. . . . No case, thus far, has been made for a change." Only a few weeks after the election, Ford was front man for the cabal that ousted Halleck as Republican leader by a vote of 73 to 67.

From 1965, when he assumed the House Republican leadership post, until 1968, Ford spent much time speaking for Republican congressional candidates in all parts of the country. It was action that solidified his own political base in the House and also projected him as a force to help his longtime friend Nixon, who was on the same circuit as part of his big comeback effort.

While Ford kept to the middle ground in the Gold-water-Rockefeller fights in 1968, there was no doubt that his allegiance was with Nixon that year and had been from the time he helped organize House Republicans for Nixon with the aid of other members from the 1949 Chowder and Marching Club.

The election of Richard Nixon to the White House pushed House Republican Leader Ford into a position of closeness to the presidency that he had never known. It was an exhilarating experience even when Ford had little or no part in policymaking but was simply the obedient Republican who would take the marching orders from Haldeman, Ehrlichman or Nixon and relay them without challenge to the Republicans in the House.

It infuriated such conservatives as H. R. Gross, John Ashbrook and Phil Crane when Ford returned from the White House to tell them they were to support Nixon's Family Assistance Plan, especially since he himself accepted the completely misleading claims that it would take people off welfare rolls and put them on payrolls when all of the incentives propelled them in the opposite direction.

There were other foreign relations and domestic issues regarding which Ford's ready acceptance of anything that came from the Nixon White House caused grumbling, but the Republicans were in a minority and not in much position to bolt.

Burned badly by letting his hand show in the Douglas impeachment effort, Jerry Ford reverted to a behind-the-scenes role in letting someone else take the front position.

When the District of Columbia Police Department arrested five men in the Democratic National headquarters in the Watergate apartment and office complex on June 17, 1972, it became quickly apparent why any Republican with an eye to the future should stand far back from the affair and let the White House handle control of the FBI investigation under acting FBI Director Pat Gray. Attorney General Richard Kleindienst, a conservative Republican from Arizona, appeared to be equally reliable to take White House instruction with regard to prosecution in what the White House had characterized as a "third rate burglary."

Although Senator William Proxmire and Representative Wright Patman had indicated some immediate interest in tracing the more than $5,000 in new hundred-dollar bills found on the burglars, the possibility of a congressional investigation was not taken seriously at first.

But that did not take into account the ingenuity of irascible and irrepressible old Wright Patman and his crew of investigators. They were able to see that the presence of James McCord, Jr., an employee of the Nixon re-election committee, caught with four other burglars meant some Nixon committee involvement. Putting that together with the early public knowledge of the involvement of E. Howard Hunt, a former Nixon White House consultant, and G. Gordon Liddy, a former White House aide and a lawyer for the Nixon re-election committee, they had the framework for a political conspiracy to burglarize Democratic headquarters.

Patman's committee saw immediately that tracing the new hundred-dollar bills and all other funds to the committee would be an almost certain way to expose the connection to the Nixon re-election committee, still vehemently denied at the White House.

In July and August, the Patman investigators went about their business, quietly interviewing witnesses and pulling records together, and neither the White House nor House Leader Gerald Ford took the effort seriously until late July, when Patman's investigators asked to interview former Commerce Secretary Maurice Stans, who was finance chairman for the Nixon re-election committee. It was then that the effort to block Patman's probe assumed a new importance and became top priority for the Nixon White House. The importance of the role played by then House Republican Leader Gerald R. Ford in that successful cover-up would be difficult to overstate.

That Ford had a role is undisputed, but he has made every effort to minimize his involvement and to reject suggestions by some Democrats that Nixon's decision to name him Vice President was in any respect a payoff for the successful prevention of a full investigation and public hearing in October 1972.

Hindsight reveals now just how important it was to Richard Nixon and the White House to prevent Patman's efforts to obtain subpoena power and authority for the House Banking and Currency Committee to conduct hearings.

During hearings on his nomination for Vice President in late 1973, Ford acknowledged meeting twice with the Republican members of the House Banking and Currency Committee and having conversations with various Democratic and Republican members of that committee to support the Nixon White House effort to halt the investigation. But Ford has contended that he had no discussions with President Nixon, former Commerce Secretary Stans or anyone else from the White House or the Nixon re-election committee on the political need to end the investigation.

Ford's position has been that he and other Republicans on the committee were not trying to obstruct a legitimate investigation but were genuinely concerned that public hearings would cause unnecessary delays in the trial of the seven men initially indicted on September 15, 1972, in connection with the June 17, 1972, burglary and bugging.

Testimony and public statements in various Watergate-related hearings establish the following chronology of events concerning the Patman committee:

In late June 1972, immediately after the Watergate burglary, Representative Wright Patman and Senator William Proxmire made separate inquiries regarding the source of the new hundred-dollar bills found on the person of the Watergate burglars and in hotel rooms occupied by them.

Dissatisfied by lack of response from the Federal Reserve Board and from the Justice Department, Chairman Patman assigned Joseph C. (Jake) Lewis, an able and aggressive professional staff member, and Chief Investigator Curtis A. Prins to follow up inquiries on the Watergate matter within the jurisdiction of the House Banking and Currency Committee.

Senator Proxmire, then ranking member of the Senate Banking and Currency Committee, assigned his administrative assistant Howard E. Shuman and legislative aide Richard A. Wegman to investigate and coordinate their information with Patman's staff.

Hampered by lack of subpoena power, Patman's staff launched a quiet investigation in early July, talking to friendly sources and accumulating records and documents in a thorough but discreet manner not immediately apparent to the Republican members of the committee or to Republican staff members.

By mid-August, however, the Nixon White House was warned of possible political problems resulting from Patman's investigation. "The White House concern was twofold," Dean related in testimony before the Senate Watergate Committee in June 1973. "First, the hearings would have resulted in more adverse pre-election publicity regarding the Watergate, and second, they just might stumble into something that would start unraveling the cover-up."

Initially, Maurice Stans and Kenneth Parkinson, a prominent Washington lawyer serving as counsel for the Nixon re-election committee, were assigned to handle the Patman committee's investigation of the dispersal of the funds of the Committee to Re-elect the President. Stans, as finance chairman, was responsible for those funds.

However, as the intensity of the investigation increased, Stans and some Texas oil men were requested to submit to staff interviews. The former Commerce Secretary then asked for political assistance and advice for the White House. Advisers there were aware that Patman investigators had numerous conversations with Parkinson and had interviewed Stans at the Republican National Convention in Miami Beach, Florida, on August 25, 1972.

Upon Stans' return from the convention he was requested to meet with Patman's staff on August 30. Although accompanied by Parkinson, Stans was upset by the necessity to subject himself to an interview by the Patman committee investigators with the possibility of being subpoenaed to testify under oath at a later date.

The morning meeting was held at Stans' office, with

bitter and unsatisfactory exchanges as Prins and Lewis attempted to review Stans' procedures for handling big cash political contributions, specifically, the cash disbursed through Deputy Campaign Director Jeb S. Magruder and the committee's legal counsel, G. Gordon Liddy, in the weeks just preceding the Watergate burglary.

Stans and Parkinson objected to continuation of the interview unless a Republican staff member was present. Lewis responded that there would be no objection to a Republican staff member being present at the afternoon meeting scheduled at the Rayburn House Office Building. Stans and Parkinson went to the White House for lunch, while Lewis and Prins returned to the Rayburn Building to notify Graham Northrup, the minority staff member, of Stans' request.

Northrup contacted Representative William B. Widnall, the ranking Republican member who was out of the city, and was informed that Widnall was concerned about the involvement of the White House in the Watergate affair and anxious to avoid having the minority staff participate.

Northrup so told Jake Lewis, who dutifully informed Stans and Parkinson of the hitch and told them where they could contact Congressman Widnall. Sometime between that conversation and the meeting in mid-afternoon, Stans obtained reluctant agreement from the New Jersey Republican to permit the minority staff member to sit in on the interview with Stans.

The afternoon meeting was hardly more satisfactory than the morning one because of Stans' reluctance to cooperate and because of interruptions by two telephone calls—one from President Nixon. Stans was permitted to take the twelve-minute call from the President in privacy during the middle of the interview. Presumably a White House tape of the Nixon-Stans conversation exists, but the content of that conversation has never been made public.

A short time later Representative Ben Blackburn, a Republican Committee member from Georgia, called from a pay phone in his home state to protest Stans' being interviewed by the Patman staff. Though the staff was unaware of any press notice, Representative Blackburn learned of the interview from a radio news report.

In a statement read by Graham Northrup, Blackburn directed Stans not to answer any further questions until the full Banking and Currency Committee had passed on the need for the investigation and determined whether it had proper jurisdiction.

The Blackburn call effectively blocked efforts to interview Stans, and it was immediately apparent that a concerted White House and Republican endeavor to cripple or kill the Patman committee investigation would be made by attacking the authority of Chairman Patman to force production of witnesses or documents. Clearly, efforts to conduct further interviews of Stans or other witnesses controlled by the Nixon White House would be of limited value.

House Republican Leader Ford did not immediately take a sufficiently active role as far as the White House was concerned. But his Michigan protégé, Representative Garry Brown, a Republican member of the House Banking Committee, speedily maneuvered to thwart further investigations or public hearings.

John Dean testified about the White House staff effort to sound out Republican members of the Banking and Currency Committee "to determine who would be most helpful on the committee, and Brown indicated his willingness to assist."

On September 8, Representative Brown sent a letter to Attorney General Richard Kleindienst asking for his view on whether it would be "inappropriate or improper" for Stans to testify before the Banking and Currency Committee with respect "to his knowledge of the financial aspects of the Watergate incident."

Brown's letter called attention to "the embargo which had been placed by [U. S. District] Judge [Charles] Richey on his [Stans'] testimony by a deposition which has been taken in the civil suit arising out of the Watergate incident."

The Michigan Congressman also raised the question of Stans' testifying in view of a federal grand jury investigation and the possibility of the return of criminal indictments.

"Would it be inappropriate or improper for Mr. Stans to testify before our committee with respect to this matter because of the impact publicizing of such testimony might have on the ultimate trial of any or all of those indicted as a result of the grand jury action, especially insofar as such publicity might be used as a basis for a claim that the accused, or any of them, may have been prejudiced?" Representative Brown asked the Attorney General, his letter indicating the kind of answer he wanted.

Though the Michigan Republican's interest was apparent, he disclaimed knowledge of the position Stans would take with respect to Chairman Patman's request for testimony. "I ask these questions only for the purpose of being better informed should a confrontation arise and should I be called upon as a member of the committee to support or oppose whatever position is taken by Mr.

Stans on the Chairman's request for his appearance," Representative Brown wrote.

"I hasten to add that although this inquiry relates only to Mr. Stans' testimony, it is equally relevant to whomever else, similarly situated, the Chairman might feel prompted to call as a witness should this investigation be expanded."

John Dean later testified that this letter "was, in fact, drafted by Mr. Parkinson for Congressman Brown." Brown answered that he "unequivocally denied the charge." Regardless of who drafted it, the Garry Brown letter of September 8 became the focal point for arguments against granting Chairman Patman the subpoena power he and his staff contended they needed to compel production of documents and witnesses on the Watergate financing.

To contest the White House and the House leadership drive to stop his committee, Chairman Patman had his staff prepare a detailed report on facts the investigation had established from a standpoint of documented improprieties and illegalities in the Watergate affair within the jurisdiction of the House Banking and Currency Committee.

That eighty-page report was circulated to the thirty-seven members of the House Banking and Currency Committee on September 12, 1972, four days after Garry Brown's letter to Kleindienst and three days before federal grand jury indictments were returned against seven Watergate burglars, including two former White House aides, E. Howard Hunt and G. Gordon Liddy. Rumors of the impending indictments circulated for several weeks, and Ronald Ziegler, the White House press secretary, took the position that when the indictments were returned, they would include some former White House personnel, thus rationalizing it would "prove" the investigation "was not a cover-up."

The carefully documented Patman staff report demonstrated beyond a doubt the need for hearings and the necessity to investigate more thoroughly the highly unusual manner in which $700,000 in Texas oil money—much of it in cash—had been rushed to Washington on April 5, 1972, just two days before the new campaign disclosure law took effect.

The source of the information in the staff report included GAO reports, police sources, public records and interviews conducted by the congressional committee staff of business people, including Texas oil men, Mexican businessmen and lawyers who had some role in "laundering" part of the money through a Mexican bank.

In the course of my work as a Washington investigative reporter, I had the Patman report in my possession when on September 14 I went to the offices of the Committee to Re-elect the President to interview Stans for my newspaper—the same date initially scheduled for his appearance before the Patman committee. That particular date was strictly a coincidence, because I had been trying since mid-July to question Stans. As finance chairman of the Nixon re-election committee, he was obviously the key figure in tracing money links between the Nixon reelection committee and the Watergate burglars.

Stans simply did not return my calls, and since my relations with him had always been good, I was certain he did not wish to see me because he did not have a credible story. I goaded DeVan Shumway and Powell Moore, both in the Nixon committee press office, about Stans' unavailability.

"Stans just isn't seeing anyone," Shumway said. "I'm sure that he will see you as soon as he sees anyone, but this Watergate matter is extremely sensitive and he doesn't want to take a chance of upsetting things," Shumway continued. He added that he felt certain Stans was not the kind who would knowingly take part in the financing of a burglary, and that eventually a good explanation would be made for the mysterious money transactions.

In late August, I increased the frequency of my calls to Stans' office, but had nearly conceded defeat despite constant assurances that he would see me "at the right time." Then, on September 12, I received a call that Stans hoped to see me in a few days; and within twenty-four hours I was given an 8:00 A.M. appointment for Wednesday, September 14, but with the possibility that it might have to be later in the day. I was sure it was just another attempt to string me along, and was surprised to have it confirmed that afternoon.

In preparation for the interview, I had carefully reviewed the still-secret report by the Patman committee staff containing the history of a $25,000 check from Kenneth Dahlberg, a finance committee representative from Minneapolis. It had been traced to the Miami bank account of one of the Watergate burglars, Bernard Barker.

I was also very much interested in the explanation Stans would give to clarify the intricate legal problems connected with $89,000 in Texas oil money "laundered" through a Mexico city lawyer and bank and then channeled to the Nixon re-election committee in cash. The General Accounting Office had questioned the legality of the re-election committee's failure to report the $25,000 Dahlberg check, and I wondered whether Stans was aware of all of the circumstances of the transfers to Mexico when he agreed to accept the money for the committee.

Even if the transactions were technically legal, I wanted to ask Stans whether he had discussed with President Nixon the ethical questions involved in such deliberate violations of the spirit of the new law requiring public accounting for the sources of political funds.

When I reached Stans' office in the First National Bank Building, I was surprised to find Richard Moore, a gray-haired and grandfatherly White House staff man, in the outer office. Moore, a California public relations man and lawyer, said he was there at Nixon's request. While President Nixon wanted Stans to tell me all the facts, there must be due regard for "executive privilege" in order to protect the presidency, Dick Moore explained.

Though Stans gave me his version of part of the facts, he balked at revealing his conversations with President Nixon on the events prior to Watergate or the aftermath of the Watergate burglary. Stans disagreed with the GAO judgment on the illegality of the contributions handled through the Mexican bank, as well as the late delivery of $25,000 from Dahlberg. He declared he had a legal opinion from White House Counsel John W. Dean III to support him on this point.

It was indeed peculiar that the finance chairman of the Nixon re-election committee was receiving legal opinions from the White House Counsel at odds with the GAO and, in one instance, with the Justice Department. That itself was a story because President Nixon had said in an August 29, 1972, press conference, during which he rejected the suggestion that a Special Watergate Prosecutor be named, that John Dean was coordinating all Watergate investigations for the White House.

Stans' comments indicated to me that Dean was active in the effort to whitewash the White House role in Watergate. In addition to arousing my suspicion that Dean was in charge of the cover-up for the Nixon White House, Stans inadvertently corroborated reports I had heard from House Republicans that killing the Patman committee investigation was a major goal of the cover-up.

Stans believed some Watergate indictments would be returned "within a few days" and that this would nullify Watergate as a political issue because former White House officials would be included. Stans also expressed confidence that the House Republican leadership (specifying House Republican Leader Gerald Ford and Representative Garry Brown) could block Patman from obtaining subpoena power until after the 1972 election.

Stans was not accusatory in his comments or intending to inform on Gerald Ford or Garry Brown. He was simply citing the facts as he saw them to support his belief that the Patman committee probe could be stopped and that he would not be required to testify under oath on the embarrassing questions that were unanswered. It was also in line with what others in the White House as well as Republicans in the House and Senate were repeating to quiet fears of a Watergate hearing before the election.

This provided the solution to his problem, Stans told me, because he would not volunteer to go before the committee unless subpoenaed. Most of the Republicans would stick together and enough Democrats on the committee were opposed to Democratic candidate George McGovern to make it possible for Patman to be defeated in his own committee, Stans explained.

I countered that even if Patman were stopped, the Office of Federal Elections and the GAO were still regarded as nonpartisan by the public. Dick Moore interjected that neither the Office of Federal Elections nor the GAO had subpoena power and that they "have to go through the Justice Department," which was under a Nixon appointee.

In the course of the questioning, Stans referred to a legal memorandum describing the chronology of the Dahlberg check for $25,000, but he resisted giving me a copy until I pressed the issue.

"I want to be sure I have it accurately, and I don't want to have you complain later that I gave a wrong impression because I wasn't precisely accurate on matters of sharply differing legal opinion," I said. Moore protested that they could hardly give me a copy of the same memorandum they had refused to give the Patman committee.

I retorted, "If the memorandum is accurate, there is no reason you shouldn't give it to me for use in writing my story. If you've given me an inaccurate story, I want to have something concrete to come back here and raise hell about if I've been used." Stans assured me that his story and the memorandum were indeed accurate, and Dick Moore nodded his assent. Stans handed me a copy and I left the office.

As I returned to the National Press Building, I mulled over what I had learned:

White House Counsel John Dean, heading an investigation requested by President Nixon, was providing legal opinions to Stans and others who were responsible for the irregular and perhaps illegal handling of huge cash contributions.

President Nixon had consulted with Stans, had some knowledge of the Mexican maneuver and had expressed no criticism of Stans or of the manner in which the re-election committee was being run.

Stans was relying on Republican Congressmen, including Gerald R. Ford and Garry Brown, to block Chairman Patman from obtaining the subpoena power necessary to conduct effective hearings on Watergate before the November election.

Through Attorney General Richard Kleindienst, Stans and Moore were confident they could prevent either the GAO or the Office of Federal Elections from obtaining subpoenas for crucial records or testimony before the election.

The return of indictments against those directly involved in the Watergate burglary was expected to appease the public demand for effective action. Clearly the indictment of the burglars was part of the Watergate cover-up.

On September 15, 1972, a federal court grand jury returned an eight-count indictment to the court of Chief United States District Judge John J. Sirica. Named in the indictment were the five men arrested at gunpoint at Democratic headquarters on June 17, 1972, and the "big fish" promised by the administration, G. Gordon Liddy and E. Howard Hunt.

According to the line House Leader Gerald Ford was passing to Republicans in the House, the naming of Liddy, a forty-two-year-old White House lawyer who had been financial counsel at the Nixon committee, and Hunt, a fifty-four-year-old former White House consultant and a former CIA employee, was to demonstrate that the

Nixon Administration would take action against its own.

A few days later, Ron Ziegler asked me if the indictment of Hunt and Liddy had not convinced me that the
Watergate investigation "was no whitewash." "It is a
cover-up," I declared, "and anyone familiar with investigations can see it is, for they haven't made a serious effort to
use the immunity laws to crack Liddy, Hunt and other
witnesses who could tell how it was financed."

Had Ziegler been present in the Oval Office that late
afternoon of September 15, he would have understood
more clearly that the indictments themselves and the drive
to stop Patman's House investigation were an integral
part of the Watergate cover-up.

3. Killing Patman's Probe

ON THE DAY the indictments were returned, President Nixon considered the battle half won. John Dean was to be congratulated for his three-month effort to keep the lid on the Watergate investigation, but now House Leader Gerald Ford must become more active in the effort to stop the Patman committee investigation that was still threatening the Nixon Administration's election game plan.

White House Chief of Staff H. R. (Bob) Haldeman arranged for Dean to come to the Oval Office a few hours after the return of the indictments against Hunt and Liddy and the five men arrested at Watergate.

It was the sweet smell of success to President Nixon, who greeted Dean: "Well you had quite a day today, didn't you? You got Watergate on the way, huh?"

"Quite a three months," Dean said. Then, in response to a question from Haldeman, he said, "The press is playing it just as we expected," explaining that the newspapers were concentrating on the fact that "two White House aides" were among the seven indicted.

The President eventually turned the discussion with Dean to "your other investigations," and Dean noted that "the other area we are going to [have] some publicity on in the coming weeks" was the Patman hearings.

"Whether we will be successful or not in turning that off, I don't know," Dean replied. "We've got a plan whereby [Henry B.] Rothblatt [attorney for the Miami five] and [William O.] Bittman [Hunt's attorney], attorneys for the seven that were indicted today, are going to go up and visit every [House committee] member and say, 'If you commence hearings you are going to jeopardize the civil rights of these individuals in the worst way and they'll never get a fair trial.' "

Dean explained further to the President and Haldeman the plans to use civil rights pleas to block Patman: "We've got somebody approaching the ACLU [American Civil Liberties Union] for these guys, and have them go up and exert some pressure because we just don't want Stans up there in front of the cameras with Patman and Patman asking all these questions."

The young counsel warned that if the Patman committee hearings started, "it's just going to be the whole thing, the press going over and over and over again." Another suggestion he made to stop Patman was that "[former Texas governor John] Connally is close to Patman and, probably, if anybody could talk turkey to Patman, Connally might be able to."

Then Dean complained that "Jerry Ford is not really taking an active interest in this matter that is developing" and suggested that Maurice Stans "go see Jerry Ford and try to brief him and explain to him the problem he's got."

"What about Ford?" the President asked, and Dean

replied, "If Ford can get the minority members together on that one, it's going to be a lot."

The President replied with a complaint against the ranking Republican member of the committee, William Widnall: "They've got a very weak man in Widnall, unfortunately." But, in a plug for Representative Margaret Heckler, he added that she was "all right."

President Nixon suggested that Jerry Ford could talk to Widnall. "Put it down, Jerry should talk to Widnall and, uh, just brace him, tell him I thought it was [unintelligible] start behaving."

"That would be very helpful, to get our minority side at least together on the thing," Dean replied, and the President added: "Jerry has really got to lead on this. He's got to really be [unintelligible].

"They ought to raise hell about this—these hearings are jeopardizing the [civil rights]," Nixon said. "I don't know as the counsel [for the defendants] calling on the members of the committee will do much good . . . I was thinking that they really ought to blunderbuss in the public arena. It ought to be publicized."

Dean responded, "Right," and Haldeman followed it with "Good."

Then Dean concluded that "if Patman pulls the string off, that's the last forum" in which the Watergate matter might be aired before the November election.

Nixon commented philosophically: "The worst may happen, but it may not. So you just try to button it up as well as you can and hope for the best . . . and remember that basically the damn thing is just one of those unfortunate things, and we're trying to cut our losses."

Dean agreed, "That's right, and certainly it had no effect on you. That's the . . . good thing."

Haldeman added, "It really hasn't. It has been kept away from the White House almost completely and from the President totally. The only tie to the White House has been the [Charles] Colson effort they keep trying to haul in."

"The game has to be played awfully rough," President Nixon said, and he instructed Haldeman: "Now, you, you'll follow through with Ford on how it's going to operate."

Haldeman suggested "getting [John] Mitchell" into the effort, and Dean commented, "I don't really think that would be good. I think Maury [Stans] can talk to Ford if that will do any good, but it won't have the same impact, because he's the one directly involved, but I think Maury ought to brief Ford at some point on, on exactly what his whole side of the story is."

The President added that "maybe [John] Ehrlichman should talk to him [Ford]. Ehrlichman understands the law, and the rest, and should say, 'Now God damn it, get the hell over with this.'"

"Is that a good idea?" Haldeman asked, and Nixon continued, "I think maybe that's the thing to do. . . . This is, this is big, big play. I'm getting into this thing. So that he [Ford], he's got to know that it comes from the top . . . that's what he's got to know."

"Right," Haldeman replied, and Nixon continued,

"I can't talk to him myself—and he's got to get at this and screw this thing up while he can, right?"

Dean interjected that "if we let that slide up there with the Patman committee, it'd be just, you know, just a tragedy to let Patman have a field day up there."

"What's the first move?" President Nixon asked. "When does he call his witnesses?"

Dean replied that Patman had not yet taken the vote of his committee "on whether he can call hearings," and explained that was why they planned to have the attorneys for the Watergate defendants at the doorstep of the committee members on Monday "to tell him what he's doing if he proceeds."

Dean then informed the President that Representative Garry Brown had already written Kleindienst a letter pushing civil rights arguments and asking, "If the Chairman [Patman] holds committee hearings on this, isn't this going to jeopardize your criminal case?"

"Brown's a smart fellow," President Nixon commented admiringly. "He's from, he's from Michigan . . . and some tie to Ford."

"Good lawyer, and he's being helpful," Dean added. "He's anxious to help."

"Right," the President said. "Just tell . . . Ehrlichman to get Brown in and Ford in and they can all work out something. But they ought to get off their asses and push it—no use to let Patman have a free ride here."

Stopping Patman was the first order of business as the Oval Office meeting broke up, and the very businesslike Haldeman had a list of chores to do for the President.

With Dick Cook, the White House liaison with the House, he noted: "Ford—brace Widnall re Patman hearings."

Under "E" for Ehrlichman he noted: "Must get minority together—raise hell re jeopardizing defendants. P [for President] can't talk to you —but it must be done."

A separate note under "E" regarding Ehrlichman's responsibilities was: "Get Garry Brown & Ford in. . . ."

Between September 15 and the vote of the Patman com-

mittee on October 3, House Leader Gerald Ford met twice
with the Republican members of the committee and with
some of the Democratic members who were willing to
play ball with the Nixon Administration because of their
disenchantment with Senator McGovern, the Democratic
presidential nominee. What was said at those meetings
has never been disclosed, but Ford has denied that he took
part in them as part of the White House game plan to
stop the Patman committee.

Although the Democrats had a 22 to 15 majority in the
Banking and Currency Committee, a switch of only four
Democrats would defeat Patman if all the Republicans
stayed firm behind the Nixon White House position.
Chairman Patman hoped one or two of the more independent-minded Republicans would back him because
of the forceful case his staff members had made in the
report.

One they expected to persuade was Representative
Margaret Heckler, of Massachusetts, who had defeated
former House Speaker Joe Martin in 1966. I had been
impressed with her as intelligent, independent and genuinely interested in honest government, and I tried to determine whether there was any possibility she would vote
with the Democrats in the showdown meeting initially
scheduled for September 27.

The week before the final vote she deplored Watergate and the evidence indicating it had been financed out
of Nixon campaign funds. Heckler was bitterly critical of
the White House gang for ignoring the Republican National Committee and the senatorial and congressional
candidates except in a few isolated cases. When I asked
her how she was going to vote on the subpoena-power

issue, she turned her wrath on Patman, characterizing him as "a tyrant" who was going to use the committee to try to elect George McGovern.

"Why not let the full truth come out?" I asked, suggesting she vote for subpoena power. She replied that fair trials for the seven Watergate defendants had to be considered and that, in addition, Patman and his staff could be expected to distort the record. "That's the White House line being peddled by Garry Brown to block public questioning of Stans and Mitchell," I said. "It's as bad a cover-up as the Bobby Baker case, and they are using a lot of the same tricks." I proposed that she read the eighty-page Patman staff report for herself and not rely on Brown. I explained that Brown's letter to the Department of Justice was an attempt to push Assistant Attorney General Henry Petersen, a Democrat, into fronting for a delay on the hearings until after the election.

Heckler told me that she had not had time to examine all of the evidence Patman's staff had accumulated but that House Republican Leader Gerald Ford had told her it was one of the most obviously partisan investigations he had seen in his years in Congress. He had said that the White House had assured him that Watergate was simply "a caper" perpetrated by Liddy, Hunt and some irresponsible Cuban-Americans. He had declared that no higher officials at the White House or the Nixon re-election committee were involved and that Patman was engaged in "a political witch hunt."

"I think you should read the staff report," I remonstrated, but she was obviously committed to a position.

She said that Petersen, who she had been told was a Democrat and a veteran career employee of the Department of Justice, had written a letter asking for a delay in congressional hearings until after the criminal trials, which would be after the election. She asked me whether I believed Petersen would be a part of a Republican cover-up, and I had to say that I didn't believe he would willingly take any action that was political unless specifically directed to do so by the Attorney General. The Petersen letter was the Republican trump card, and I did not want to challenge his credibility even though I believed it was a serious mistake in judgment for him to have signed the letter when he must have known how it would be used.

After a week of heavy Republican lobbying by Ford and Brown, Chairman Patman brought the subpoena-power issue to a vote on October 3. The vote was 20 to 14 against him, with all Republicans, including Widnall and Heckler, opposed. Four southern Democrats and two other Democrats joined the Republicans to give Nixon his victory over Patman.

Garry Brown, proud of his role for the White House, acknowledged that he was a key figure in the defeat of Patman and had cooperated with the Justice Department and House Republican Leader Gerald Ford. Ford was unavailable for comment on his role in the White House victory, and I assumed he did not wish to answer questions in which he would be challenged to distinguish between the Watergate cover-up and the cover-ups of various Democratic administrations he had so freely criticized.

Patman predicted that eventually "the facts will come out, and when they do I am convinced they will reveal why the White House was so anxious to kill the committee's investigation. The public will fully understand why this pressure was mounted."

Democratic Chairman Lawrence O'Brien termed it "a

victory for the Nixon Administration . . . a victory for
secrecy, suppression and skulduggery."

The victory endeared Gerald Ford to the Nixon White
House on a crucial issue, in a crucial time when some of
Nixon's aides did not believe he was being as helpful as
a House Republican political leader should be for his
longtime friend and political ally of more than twenty
years. He could not have projected then the payoff for
his political loyalty, but then no one could have forecast
Vice President Agnew's disgraceful and hurried exit from
public office.

The vote to deny subpoena power to the Patman committee squelched the last effective Watergate investigation,
at least until after the election. That was sufficient in
October 1972, because the polls showed Nixon with a
lopsided lead over George McGovern, and Nixon was
assumed to have "Four More Years" to force revenge on
his Watergate pursuers and to quietly stifle the Watergate
investigation in an FBI headed by a Nixon appointee and
in a Justice Department dominated by an attorney general of Mr. Nixon's choice.

Whether they had acted on instruction from the White
House or whether they were simply following the normal
instincts of partisan Michigan Republicans, Gerald Ford
and Garry Brown had accomplished their mission to
"screw things up" for Chairman Patman.

4. The Nixon Loyalist

THE 1972 PRESIDENTIAL election gave Richard Nixon and his Chief of Staff, H. R. Haldeman, confirmation of their belief that the end had justified the means. The Nixon-Agnew ticket won in forty-nine states, while the McGovern-Shriver ticket won only in Massachusetts (by a 55 percent majority) and the District of Columbia (by a 79 percent majority).

The American people had endorsed the behind-the-scenes activities of the Nixon re-election committee and had given them a mandate to continue on their "glorious quest" for world peace and domestic stability. To these men and others in their corner, including House Republican Leader Ford, the overwhelming landslide of November 7 indicated that the American people were never going to allow a "third rate burglary" by some "overzealous Cubans" to divert them from the "real hard choices" that had to be made for the security of the Republic.

With the Patman hearings squelched, the election won

and Dr. Kissinger's assurance that "peace is at hand" in Vietnam, Richard Nixon and Bob Haldeman felt comfortable that the worst was over. The Nixon White House and their Republican allies in Congress closed their eyes and ears to the truth as they knew it to be, as if the American people had seen all the facts clearly and yet re-elected the Nixon-Agnew team.

In fact, the American people had not seen the tip of the iceberg, and Gerald Ford, re-elected by a substantial margin in the Fifth District of Michigan, had a vested interest in preventing any of this hydra-headed monster from rearing up again.

Because House Republican Leader Gerald Ford had done his job well, there was virtually no possibility of an effective hearing being launched against the ruthless White House gang now safely entrenched for four more years. The House, with all its members limited to two-year terms, had little stomach for a tough confrontation with an administration willing to use or misuse any of its powers of investigation, harassment or prosecution. Men like House Speaker Carl Albert and House Ways and Means Committee Chairman Wilbur Mills had no resolve to uncover anything.

The United States Senate, with its six-year staggered terms, was a different story. Freed from the pressure of seeking election every two years, two-thirds of the Senators could risk considerable independence from time to time and were less susceptible to the iron-handed control of committee chairmen. Senate Democratic Leader Mike Mansfield, of Montana; Assistant Senate Democratic Leader Robert Byrd, of West Virginia; and Senator Sam Ervin, an articulate constitutional law expert from North Carolina, formed the strong backbone of resolve to unveil Watergate with a Senate investigation as soon as the trial of the seven burglars was concluded.

Republican Leader Ford rightly declined discussions of Watergate pending the outcome of the trial before Chief United States Judge John J. Sirica, which was scheduled to begin in January 1973. Most of the press and responsible Democratic critics of the Nixon Administration recognized the need to defer action on the other aspects of Watergate at this time.

President Nixon, H. R. Haldeman, John Ehrlichman, John Dean and others who knew the inside story scurried around in November and December before the trial started, making payments of nearly $300,000 to the Watergate burglars and their lawyers to continue the obstruction of justice. It gave John Dean and Jeb S. Magruder, Deputy Director of the Committee to Re-elect the President, time to coordinate the perjury with Herbert (Bart) Porter, Magruder's assistant, on the nearly $200,000 in cash paid to the burglars through G. Gordon Liddy.

The respite from press and Democratic pressure was deceptive to Nixon and his bevy of White House connivers because they believed if they could keep the lid on the criminal-trial testimony, they could avoid involvement of higher-ups and the Watergate ordeal would be behind them. They moved ahead with their plans, shuffling tried and tested members of the White House team to get better control of positions in the Cabinet, departments and agencies and making only limited concessions to the fact that Watergate might come apart.

Haldeman comforted a nervous Magruder with a post on the Nixon Inaugural Committee and, following that, a promise of the highest post available not requiring confirmation by the Senate and its inevitable prying questions. Egil (Bud) Krogh was another White House staffer who couldn't be moved until the Watergate trial was completed.

The White House scrutinized Judge Sirica's conservative Republican background and assumed he retained political loyalties guaranteeing the trials would be routine and that pleas of guilty could be entered by key defendants, jail terms and fines meted out and Watergate swept under the rug. But Judge Sirica was an unusual judge. He recognized the potential for cover-up and perjury and took unusual steps to assure that "the truth" would come out. He rejected pleas of guilty by any of the seven defendants unless they would plead guilty to all counts and state under oath that they were indeed guilty of the charges; also, that they were under no pressures of physical fear or pay-offs and had received no promises.

Even with those severe restrictions, White House pressures and promises resulted in five of the defendants pleading guilty during the trial.

Only James W. McCord, Jr., an electronics expert who had worked for the Nixon re-election committee, and G. Gordon Liddy, a lawyer for the Nixon committee, maintained their innocence throughout the trial and were finally convicted by the jury on January 30, 1974. Sentencing of the defendants was deferred until the third week of March.

The tempo of the Senate investigation increased immediately after the trial, and on February 7 the Senate, by a 70 to 0 vote, adopted a resolution to establish a seven-member select committee of four Democrats and three Republicans. The committee was to be headed by Senator Ervin, and its duty was to probe all aspects of the

Watergate burglary and bugging and other reported attempts at political espionage in the 1972 election campaign. Senate Republican Leader Hugh Scott, of Pennsylvania, lost a drive to gain equal membership with the Democrats and to extend the probe to cover the 1964 and 1968 election campaigns, in which it was contended Democrats had used unethical and illegal methods of espionage.

In Oval Office conferences and other meetings, President Nixon and his staff discussed ways of influencing or controlling the Republican members of the committee. Senator Howard Baker, of Tennessee, Senator Edward J. Gurney, of Florida, and Senator Lowell Weicker, Jr., of Connecticut, were the diverse group selected. In addition to Ervin, the Democrats were a varied aggregate of mixed talents, with unproven records in regard to investigations of problems of political ethics. They were Senator Joseph M. Montoya, of New Mexico, Senator Herman E. Talmadge, of Georgia, and Senator Daniel Inouye, of Hawaii.

From the outset, Chairman Ervin recognized the possibility that the Nixon White House would try to claim "executive privilege" as a cover-up device in the Watergate investigation, but it first became a serious issue in the confirmation hearings on the nomination of Pat Gray to be permanent Director of the Federal Bureau of Investigations.

Gray, a retired Navy captain and a former assistant attorney general, had been acting director of the FBI during the Watergate cover-up. Tapped to use the power of the FBI to obstruct the investigation, he had cooperated with the White House by keeping John Dean and others posted on the status of the investigation throughout the summer and fall of 1972. Though a reluctant participant in the cover-up, Gray had supplied the White House with FBI

agents' reports unbeknown to Attorney General Richard
Kleindienst and Assistant Attorney General Henry E.
Petersen in the same time frame that House Leader
Gerald Ford and Congressman Garry Brown were stop-
ping the Patman committee.

President Nixon apparently depended on the assurance
of Senate Judiciary Committee Chairman James O. East-
land, of Mississippi, and Senator Roman Hruska, the ranking Republican member from Nebraska, that the Gray
nomination could be pushed through without opening up
Watergate. But the persistent questioning of Senators
Ervin, Robert Byrd, John Tunney of California and Phil
Hart of Michigan opened the first cracks in the dam of
information. Senator Byrd, initially favorable to the Gray
nomination, asked the questions that ultimately wrecked
Gray and led to the withdrawal of his nomination in early
April and his ultimate resignation a few weeks later.

Gerald Ford remained silent throughout the development of evidence that Gray had been peddling confidential FBI information to the Nixon White House, and
he was strangely unprotesting of the most extreme claims
of executive privilege. How could Ford, outspoken critic
of excessive secrecy and executive privilege in Democratic
administrations, remain quiet while the Nixon White
House carried these practices to extremes? This was the
same Gerald Ford who, in October 1966, had said: "We
have strayed from the rule of law. Our government leaders, by dealing in half-truths and misinformation, led us
to believe that honor and justice are just words. The
measure is that the end justifies the means."

Apparently that criticism of the Johnson Administration was only his means to a highly partisan political end,
as was his comment on March 2, 1967, when he declared:

"Any analysis of today's political picture in America of necessity revolves about a single phrase—four words—'a crisis of confidence.'. . . The American people are constantly engaged in a search for truth—for political truth, for moral truth, truth in government, for verities in our international relations . . . the credibility gap continues, the crisis of confidence grows."

And certainly the crisis of confidence in the Nixon Administration was growing in March and early April as the White House stonewalled and Attorney General Kleindienst shocked the Congress on April 10 by stating that military force could implement the exercise of executive privilege—the ultimate claim of presidential power. The Attorney General told a stunned Senate subcommittee that the President could bar Congress or the courts from any document in the executive branch and could direct any executive branch official to refuse to testify even if criminal acts were involved. This power could be invoked even in an impeachment hearing, Kleindienst said, and he observed that the Capitol police and the United States marshals were a puny physical force against the miltary power at the disposal of the Commander in Chief.

The premise that the Congress and the courts had to take into account the military power at the disposal of the President before challenging his authority to withhold documents or witnesses was as shocking to most Republicans as it was to Democrats. Senator Barry Goldwater was among the first to denounce this thesis for "hiding of evidence from Congress." Representative John Anderson, an Illinois Republican who headed the House Republican Conference Committee, accused the Attorney General of making an "unnecessarily provocative and contemptuous statement that contained such an alarming and dangerous notion of executive privilege" that Congress could not ignore it.

Congressman Anderson arranged to appear before the same Senate subcommittee the next day to state: "The Attorney General has thrown down the gauntlet. If this Congress is to preserve even a semblance of integrity and independence, it must act immediately to nullify the sweeping claim of executive power asserted by the Attorney General." Other Republicans, conservative and liberal alike, commented angrily as the certainty of a cover-up now emerged. Representative William Scherle, an Iowa Republican, said that President Nixon, by shrouding his staff with a curtain of secrecy, had "endowed them with the arrogance of nobility or royalty."

But Gerald Ford, the advocate of candor and truth for Democratic administrations, remained silent for a week. When he spoke, he told a GOP gathering that Nixon White House officials should "go before the Senate Committee, take an oath and deny it [the cover-up] publicly."

From that time on, with the unfolding of every new development, Jerry Ford's remarks treated each fresh shock as the beginning of the closing chapter of Watergate, which the nation should put behind it and proceed with more important business. There is no record that he commented at all on the sudden resignation of Pat Gray, whose nomination he had supported. Senator Lowell Weicker, initially a Gray supporter, withdrew his backing and revealed that Gray admitted he had, at the suggestion of the Nixon White House, destroyed evidence taken from John Dean's safe.

When forced resignations of Haldeman, Ehrlichman and Dean were announced on April 30, Ford responded that it was "a first step to clearing the air" of the Watergate mess. The House Republican Leader avoided criticism of Nixon or of the White House figures involved and simply scrambled to adjust his rhetoric to new and better political ground. He continued on his political-stone-walling course throughout the shocking testimony by James McCord on the White House pressure tactics used to persuade the burglars to plead guilty on promises of pay-offs and eventual pardons, and throughout the testimony by John Dean on the conspiracy from inside the Oval Office and the Executive Office Building.

Jerry Ford probably was no better prepared than anyone else who had visited in the Oval Office for Alexander P. Butterfield's startling testimony that essentially all of President Nixon's official conversations had been recorded. Late in the afternoon of Monday, July 16, 1973, Butterfield, then Administrator of the Federal Aviation Administration, was called to the witness chair by Chief Counsel Sam Dash. Dash commented only that "some very significant information" had been obtained from Butterfield.

He turned the questioning over to Minority Counsel Fred Thompson, who established for the record that Butterfield had been on the White House staff as a Deputy Assistant to the President under Bob Haldeman from January 21, 1969, until noon on March 14, 1973, when he became head of FAA.

"Mr. Butterfield, are you aware of installation of any listening devices in the Oval Office of the President?" Thompson asked, and Butterfield replied, "I was aware of listening devices, yes, sir."

Under instructions from White House Chief of Staff Haldeman, Butterfield had supervised the installation of a system in which the taping devices were triggered automatically by the Secret Service as President Nixon moved

from room to room in the White House and to the hide-
away office in the Executive Office Building.

"It was voice actuated," Butterfield explained, which
ment that unless there were technical difficulties, the conversations of all Mr. Nixon's official and unofficial visitors
were recorded.

Every lawyer who became aware of Butterfield's testimony immediately understood the significance of those
White House tapes in corroborating or destroying John
Dean as a witness. Former White House Counsel Dean
had testified that he believed some of his conversations
with Nixon, Haldeman and Ehrlichman might have been
recorded even though he had no knowledge of the super-
secret taping system.

And every lawyer in the Senate and House—including
Jerry Ford—recognized the potential for possible embarrassment to visitors unaware that Nixon was recording
their most confidential comments and advice.

It was a certainty that as long as Richard Nixon held
control of the White House tapes, he had a whip hand
over anyone who had been careless in his confidences.
Who possessed a power of recall sufficient to be certain
he had not uttered a few culpable phrases?

5. Zig-Zag Course on Watergate

ONLY GERALD R. FORD knew the extent of his surprise, shock and anger as he digested the testimony of Alexander Butterfield in late July of 1973. Richard Nixon, his friend for twenty-five years, had kept him in the dark about many moves in the past, and he had displayed no public resentment. Jerry Ford, the blind defender, was expected to switch course and rally behind Nixon policies and programs, often making it plain that he had only scant knowledge of their provisions or purposes.

Jerry Ford, as well as many congressional leaders of both parties and other presidential intimates, must have wondered what unwitting comments, asides or even cajoling profanities, not uttered unguardedly by public people, his good friend had recorded for posterity. From that moment on, any competent lawyer had to realize that the White House tapes unraveled the whole skein as far as any relevant conversations with President Nixon were concerned. If the tapes supported Dean, then the President of the United States and many of the President's men were involved in a criminal obstruction of justice. Those in Congress who had taken part in a conspiracy to stop the Patman investigation would be included if they had knowledge that they were covering up criminal acts. The recorded Oval Office tapes could be conclusive on that score or they could be ambiguous as to guilty knowledge.

But, for defenders of the Nixon White House, the existence of the tapes offered a glimmer of hope that a few of the recordings would demonstrate that John Dean had testified falsely or was substantially inaccurate—and thus be used to destroy his credibility. Bracing for future shock, Nixon authorized Bob Haldeman to listen to some of the crucial tapes the last week in April when it became apparent that John Dean was talking to prosecutors Seymour Glanzer and Earl Silbert. Nixon himself listened to some key tapes in early June to prepare a counterstrategy and concoct defensible explanations of certain vague and unclear contents.

Shortly after John Dean's devastating five days before Senator Ervin's panel, President Nixon called Haldeman back from California in July to audit the crucial tapes again in order to probe for a weakness, seek a discrepancy, in Dean's testimony—anything to attack his credibility. This time Haldeman removed those pertinent tapes from the White House to the home he maintained in Georgetown so that he could monitor them, take notes and make a confidential report to the President.

Whether or not Jerry Ford recognized the critical predicament presented by John Dean's dry, monotonic barrage, Richard Nixon and Bob Haldeman, with full knowledge, refreshed by careful dissection, knew the tapes gave substantial corroboration to Dean's testimony that, in crucial conversations in the Oval Office on September 15, 1972, on March 13, 1973, and on March 21, 1973, discussions took place on the need for a million-dollar payoff fund for E. Howard Hunt and the other convicted Watergate burglars to keep them quiet.

Ford's Michigan protégé, Representative Garry Brown, who had been so proud of his part in killing the Patman probe, now recognized that Dean's testimony on the September 15 Oval Office meeting changed things. What had been a partisan political chore by which the junior Michigan Congressman ingratiated himself with Ford, ten years his senior and the House Leader, could become a criminal obstruction of justice if either he or Ford had knowledge of the White House involvement in the Watergate crimes at the time they took the lead in squelching Patman's investigation. Nearness to House Leader Ford—something that was cherished and cultivated among the Michigan Republican Congressmen in their Thursday morning meetings—had become at the least a political embarrassment as the Watergate crimes emerged and the White House tapes demonstrated Nixon's desire to use Ford and Brown to stop Patman.

Dean, after testifying on the Nixon directions to block the Patman probe, had said: "At some point in time during these investigations, Mr. [Kenneth] Parkinson [attorney for Stans and the re-election committee] was put in touch with Congressman Garry Brown, who was a member of the Banking and Currency Committee.

"To the best of my recollection, this may have resulted from discussions between members of the White House Congressional Relations staff with the Republican members of the Banking and Currency Committee to determine who would be most helpful on the Committee, and Brown indicated his willingness to assist. . . ."

Dean had further testified that on September 8, "Congressman Brown sent a letter to the Attorney General regarding the forthcoming appearance of Secretary Stans and others before the Patman committee . . . which was, in fact, drafted by Parkinson for Congressman Brown."

Dean continued that shortly after the September letter from Garry Brown to Attorney General Kleindienst, "I began receiving increasing pressure from Mitchell, Stans, Parkinson and others to get the Justice Department to respond . . . as a vehicle that Congressman Brown could use in persuading others not to vote in favor of the subpoena. Congressman Brown felt that with this document in hand he would give the Republicans and others something to hang their vote on."

Dean's testimony had enraged yet terrified Garry Brown, for he realized it provided the basis for a charge of "culpable conduct and obstruction of justice." He felt compelled to write a lengthy rebuttal for the record of the Senate Select Watergate Committee.

On July 9, 1973, Representative Brown sent this letter to Chairman Ervin in lieu of a personal appearance, "as my response and rebuttal to the allegations made by Mr. John Dean.

"To say that I was somewhat dumbfounded to learn of the allegation made by Mr. Dean is a gross understatement," Brown said, "since my participation in the bipartisan effort by members of the House Banking and Currency Committee, which resulted in the denial of the granting of subpoena authority to the Chairman of our committee, was in no way connected with the so-called cover-up activities in which Mr. Dean testified he participated."

Admitting he had written letters to the Attorney General questioning the propriety of calling Stans or any other witnesses on the Watergate affair, Brown denied that this was to carry out a White House conspiracy; rather, it was because of his concern that testimony by Maurice Stans "could prejudice the rights of those who might be indicted as a result of the grand jury proceedings that were then in progress."

Representative Brown emphasized the displeasure he had felt with Chairman Patman when he learned in late August 1972 that he had initiated the Watergate investigation "without seeking the concurrence of the committee or even notifying committee members." In a letter to Patman on August 31, Brown had suggested that Patman's staff was "engaging in a frolic of their own."

On September 5, Brown had written a second letter protesting continuation of the investigation on which he had obtained the signatures and concurrence of seven of the Republican members of the Banking and Currency Committee.

In his statement for the Ervin Committee a year later, Representative Brown defended his buzz-saw, activist hindrance of any investigation and his opposition to hearings on "laundered funds" or the significance of Bernard Barker's Miami bank accounts "as being blatantly political in view of the upcoming election."

Brown's statement bore out admission of his continuing actions to block the probe, but reiterated his denial that they were initiated by the Nixon White House or the Nixon re-election committee.

He charged: "It is obvious that Mr. Dean, in his testimony before the Senate Select Committee, either has stated things to be true which he does not know to be true or has engaged in absolute falsehoods."

After apologizing for the length of his statement, Brown said in conclusion, "My purpose in doing so was to establish for the record not only the absence of culpability on my part, but the absence of culpability on the part of the other members of the House Committee on Banking and Currency in opposing the Patman investigation, to the extent that I have knowledge of other members' actions. . . . If opposition to actions proposed by one's colleagues, when that opposition is based on principle and proper political motivation, cannot be voiced without such opposition being interpreted as culpable conduct and obstruction of justice, then we certainly have reached a sorry state of affairs in our political and legislative system."

Garry Brown wrote that letter on July 9, before the White House taping system was revealed, so he could have had no knowledge of any corroboration for Dean's testimony on President Nixon's directions of September 15, 1972, for Haldeman, Ehrlichman and others to put a top priority on a plan "to get Brown and Ford in and work something out . . . no use to let Patman have a free ride here."

The tapes made it perfectly clear that Nixon wanted Brown and Ford to stop Patman, and the record showed that both had worked hard toward that objective and were pleased when it was achieved. Garry Brown was now vigorously denying that he and other House Republicans were motivated by the White House, for that could involve them in a conspiracy to obstruct justice.

Ford did not call attention to himself by making a comparable denial because Dean had not mentioned him by name, saying only that the House Republican leadership was involved in blocking Patman.

The White House used executive privilege to bar the

Senate Committee and Special Watergate Prosecutor Archibald Cox from access to the crucial tapes that could affirm or deny the credibility of Dean's testimony, but this very reluctance to produce the tapes nourished the suspicion that they corroborated Dean.

The only testimony on the contents of the tapes came from Haldeman shortly after Butterfield revealed that essentially all of Nixon's business conferences had been taped since the summer of 1971. Haldeman, whose memory had been refreshed on the September 15, 1972, tape and the March 21, 1973, tape a few weeks earlier, testified in late July on the general content of those tapes.

Although Haldeman disputed Dean on some opinions and conclusions regarding the conversations, the former White House Chief of Staff corroborated Dean on the conversations in general. While his testimony was designed to be a ploy to mislead the news writers and television commentators by stressing in very general terms denial of Nixon's guilty knowledge of the Watergate cover-up, it convinced Committee Counsel Sam Dash, Chairman Ervin and Dean's lawyer, Charles Shaffer, that John Dean was indeed telling the truth.

Much of the press gullibly accepted Haldeman's testimony and concentrated their leads on the differences of opinion it presented on Nixon's guilty knowledge. Dash reduced it to an essential corroboration of a prima-facie case of obstruction of justice against the President. Haldeman provided corroboration on these important points:

1. Conversations did take place in the Oval Office between President Nixon and Dean on September 15, 1972, and on March 21, 1973, and Haldeman was present during some periods when those discussions involved Watergate.

2. The September 15 conversation did congratulate

Dean on his successful handling of Watergate up to that day when the first Watergate indictments were returned against seven men.

3. The September 15 conversation did include the problem posed by the Democratic National Committee's damage suit against the Nixon re-election committee, which was then effectively bottled up by a court order by United States District Judge Charles Richey.

4. The September 15 conversation did involve discussion of the Patman committee investigation and Dean's assessment of the problem it presented.

5. The March 21 conversation did include Dean's warning of a cancer on the presidency and the possible obstruction of justice and covered, as well, Hunt's demands for additional money and assurances of executive clemency.

6. The March 21 conversation included Dean's estimates that it would cost more than a million dollars for payments to the seven Watergate defendants and their attorneys, and President Nixon's comment that it would not be difficult to raise that much money.

The only significant difference between Dean's and Haldeman's testimony involved their conclusion on the President's knowledge of the cover-up. Haldeman denied that Nixon's comments on the million-dollar payoff constituted approval of such a plan; they were only Nixon's way of drawing Dean out on the scheme.

Chairman Ervin, Senator Daniel Inouye and Senator Lowell Weicker agreed that Haldeman's testimony established the general accuracy of Dean's. Sam Dash found it strong enough corroboration to assert that a prima-facie case of obstruction of justice existed against Nixon as he argued for the Senate Committee's need for the tapes as vital in establishing precisely how various comments came into the conversations.

If Gerald Ford, as House Republican Leader, was even casually following the progress of the hearings, he had to understand the overwhelming evidence building the case of obstruction of justice against the President. As a law school graduate, in the top third of his class at Yale, Ford could hardly claim ignorance of such basic criminal law even though he lacked experience in that field.

By now the majority of the public registered an understanding of President Nixon's involvement in the cover-up, and the Gallup poll of August 14, 1973, showed that public approval of Nixon had slipped to 31 percent and that 57 percent disapproved of the way he was handling the presidency. That was the lowest rating any president had received since Harry Truman slipped to the same rating in January 1953 in the midst of the tax scandals that plagued his administration.

In the meantime, public interest mounted in Vice President Agnew's proliferating problems with the United States Attorney's office in Baltimore. The tip of the iceberg of corruption was revealed by Jerry Landauer in a *Wall Street Journal* story in early August; it was augmented to a roaring controversy by early September. Agnew, who a few months earlier had been assuring a wondering public of the innocence of Nixon in Watergate, was now anxiously seeking words of affirmation of his own honesty and political help from his friend Jerry Ford and others.

Ford was one of the few friends in whom Agnew confided his troubles, and the House Republican Leader stood by Agnew to the end. His loyalty extended to taking

the lead in an Agnew-pushed drive to persuade House
Speaker Carl Albert to open impeachment hearings—a
maneuver to block a special grand jury investigation into
Agnew's financial affairs on the grounds that a Vice President could be impeached but could not be subject to a
federal or state criminal indictment while in office.

Accepting Agnew's assertion of innocence in spite of a
serious grand jury investigation under the direction of
a Nixon-appointed attorney general (Elliot Richardson)
and a Nixon-appointed United States Attorney (George
Beall), Ford induced a small group of House Republicans
to join him in requesting of Speaker Albert the favor of
an impeachment hearing for Agnew. However, Albert,
alerted that same day by Attorney General Richardson on
the pending indictment, rejected Ford's request on the
theory that the House should not interfere in a matter
already in the courts.

Ford received his first indication that Spiro would resign in a "Dear Jerry" note hand-delivered on October 10.
On that day Agnew became the second vice president in
the history of the United States to resign the office and
the first to be convicted of federal crime. Agnew entered
a plea of *nolo contendere*—which is, in fact, a conviction—
to a one-count charge of federal income tax evasion.

Under the agreement, Richardson accepted the plea of
no contest to a charge of filing a "false and fraudulent"
income tax return for 1967. This was entered before United
States District Judge Walter E. Hoffman. Other possible
charges involving bribery, conspiracy and other tax-law
violations were dropped in exchange for Agnew's resignation as Vice President, to spare the nation the anguish of
months of indecision. Judge Hoffman sentenced Agnew to

a fine of $10,000 and three years of unsupervised probation and explained that the penalty was influenced by Richardson's plea for leniency.

Agnew's note to Ford was brief and with no knowledge that the House Republican Leader would be his successor:

"Today I have resigned as Vice President of the United States. After an extremely difficult weighing of all the factors, my deep concern for the country required this decision.

"You have been a staunch friend. I shall always count your friendship as a personal treasure. My gratitude and affection will always be yours."

But, Jerry Ford had little time to ponder the "gratitude and affection" of a disgraced political leader, for he and Senate Republican Leader Hugh Scott had been asked by Richard Nixon to canvass Republican leaders on a replacement for Agnew.

Ford knew he was being considered along with former Texas Governor John Connally, Senator Hugh Scott and a half-dozen others, but he did not know and could not have known the devious scheming of the Watergate-plagued Nixon. Would Nixon seek a strong man, a potential leader for the party and a presidential candidate in 1976? Would he choose a genial errand boy who could be confirmed easily but would present no threat to an embattled president?

"Gerald Ford was not Richard Nixon's first choice," Richard Reeves comments in his book, *A Ford Not a Lincoln.* "He was his last choice, in more ways than one."

While it is impossible to know precisely the stratagems of Richard Nixon's mind, Reeves' thesis that Nixon wanted John Connally but was dissuaded by the arguments of Alexander Haig, Melvin Laird and others, can be supported. They argued that Connally was a turncoat, a Democrat, highly controversial, whose extensive financial and business interests might not survive the kind of in-depth FBI investigation for the confirmation hearing required by the 25th Amendment.

Although Ford knew of enthusiastic support in the House and Senate, he says he was unaware he had been selected until he received a call from Nixon as he and his wife, Betty, were dressing to go to the White House for the announcement.

When Richard Nixon, in a media-oriented extravaganza exaggerated almost to the point of burlesque, revealed that Jerry Ford was to receive the nomination for Vice President, there was a spontaneous, warm and strong burst of applause from the assembled Congressmen and Senators. Jerry Ford was one of their own, and Nixon beamed as if the applause were for him rather than the affable, well-liked House minority leader. Nixon deemed it a success because the spontaneous demonstration seemed to erase the Watergate blackboard, seemed to erase the "Spiro who?" and created a euphoric feeling that finally all was well. It was as if the sun would not have to come up on October 13 and newspaper reporters would not return to work to write about the continuing Watergate controversies.

Richard Nixon, once again, had fooled himself, for even a president couldn't wish away the instinctive doubts of the people. While I had heard Nixon, Haldeman and Ehrlichman express a mildly contemptuous attitude toward Jerry Ford privately as a not too astute House puppet and chore boy, Ford's public image was otherwise and made him appear a credible Vice President and an acceptable alternative to Nixon as President, something Agnew had never achieved as far as the public or the Congress was concerned.

Even after Nixon had nominated Ford for Vice President, and after the nomination was confirmed by the Senate and the House, there were leaked stories of Nixon's private efforts to downgrade Ford's ability in snide comments to others. *Newsweek* reported a Nixon comment to Nelson Rockefeller obviously intended to raise doubts. "Can you imagine Jerry Ford as President?" Nixon was said to have asked.

In the House and Senate the hearings were detailed but routine, with only minor impediments to the confirmation. The Senate heard testimony against Ford by Robert N. Winter-Burger, a former Washington lobbyist and author of a 1972 book, *The Washington Payoff*. He alleged Ford had done favors in exchange for campaign contributions, and that Ford had accepted $15,000 in cash from him. Chairman Howard Cannon, a Democrat from Nevada, took Winter-Burger's testimony in a closed session and dismissed it as being without corroboration. It was Ford's word against Winter-Burger's, and in November 1973, in the old-boy atmosphere of Congress, everyone believed Jerry Ford when he said he knew Winter-Burger only casually and had never taken money from him.

The Senate Rules Committee approved the Ford nomination unanimously on November 20, and a week later the full Senate gave approval by a 92 to 3 margin. Voting in opposition were Senator Thomas Eagleton, of Missouri, Senator William Hathaway, of Maine, and Senator Gaylord Nelson, of Wisconsin. Senators Eagleton and Nelson questioned Ford's leadership ability, and Hathaway wished to defer action until President Nixon's role in Watergate was resolved.

In response to Senate Committee questioning, Ford said he did not believe a president had unlimited authority in the area of executive privilege, but declared he did not think the Congress or the public generally have an unlimited right to the personal confidential conversations between a president and his advisers.

Although Ford said he believed Nixon "completely innocent" of any wrongdoing in the Watergate matter, he said that the "public wants the President to prove that [innocence], through documents and so forth." He relied on a Ford gimmick of saying what the public wanted rather than taking a firm stance on his own beliefs. He used the same device when Senator Robert Byrd asked if he believed it would be proper for a vice president to succeed to the presidency and then grant a pardon to the former president. Ford's answer was accepted as a promise not to pardon Nixon.

The House hearings lasted from November 15 through 26, and the committee voted by a 29 to 8 margin to confirm. Chairman Peter Rodino voted against the nomination because of philosophical differences but expressed great respect for Ford's character and integrity. The full House vote on December 6 was 387 to 35, and he was sworn in later that day as the fortieth vice president of the United States.

To those who followed the evidence closely, it was already apparent that Nixon would be impeached or forced to resign. Nixon's firing of Archie Cox as Special Watergate Prosecutor and the resignations of Attorney General Richardson and Deputy Attorney General William Ruckelshaus had brought "a firestorm" of public protest and had given a new impetus to the impeachment inquiry of the House Judiciary Committee. The "Saturday Night Massacre" gave the impeachment inquiry the push of public indignation and outrage the earlier inquiries lacked.

6. Ford: Nixon's Choice

WHEN GERALD R. FORD was sworn in on December 6, 1973, as the fortieth vice president of the United States, it was apparent to those who followed Watergate closely that he would probably become the President of the United States within the year.

At a press conference shortly after he was sworn in, I asked Ford if he accepted the conclusions of Senate Committee Counsel Sam Dash and former Special Watergate Prosecutor Archibald Cox, who had argued in court that a prima-facie case of obstruction of justice had been made against President Nixon. Ford ignored the facts and the basic legal thesis and avoided expressing an opinion by replying that President Nixon had assured him of his innocence of wrongdoing and that he believed in the President. It was a dodge to be expected of any political figure under the same circumstances. President Nixon was his friend of twenty-five years, they had fought together in many Republican Party battles, and only a few weeks earlier Nixon had tapped him for the second highest office in the land—a position he had never hoped to achieve by election. Also, if he voiced criticism, it could be considered a premature effort to push Nixon out, which mutual friends might regard as disloyalty.

From the moment he was sworn in as Vice President, Ford's political sense made him realize, as did everyone else, that for the first time in months the nation had a practical alternative if Richard Nixon were impeached.

Even before Jerry Landauer, of the *Wall Street Journal,* broke the first stories on Vice President Agnew's income tax problem and the likelihood that he had taken large cash payoffs, the former Maryland governor was not considered an acceptable alternative to Nixon. Democratic liberals in the Senate and House felt such personal antagonism toward Agnew that they would have had serious reservations about voting for impeachment of Nixon if it meant installing a Spiro Agnew administration in the White House.

Having a much-disliked and probably dishonest vice president as his likely successor was a decided plus in Nixon's game plan to hold the White House.

Recognizing Jerry Ford as a highly partisan Nixon supporter, I wanted to believe, and I think that most members of the press and Congress wanted to believe, that he would avoid further entanglement in the mire of Watergate. I hoped common sense would convince him that he, and the nation, had everything to lose and nothing to gain from a continuing blind partisan defense of Richard Nixon.

I expressed my fears to Bob Hartmann, a longtime friend who was Ford's major speech writer and general chief of staff, that a thoughtless partisan defense of Nixon by Ford would haunt him for the remainder of his political life.

In my conversation with Hartmann, I defined what I considered the overwhelming evidence that Richard Nixon was involved in the crime of obstruction of justice. I recalled for him that Special Watergate Prosecutor Archibald Cox had made arguments in court that the President was probably involved in crime, and that Sam Dash, the counsel for the Senate Watergate Committee, had declared before United States District Judge John J. Sirica that a "prima-facie case" had been made that Richard Nixon was involved in the crime of obstruction of justice.

The White House counselor avoided any challenge to the facts or arguments of Nixon's involvement in crime, but only stressed technical reasons and the broad "executive privilege" claim to justify resisting efforts to obtain the White House tapes.

I stressed to Hartmann that it was a stronger case of conspiracy and obstruction of justice than had been made against Washington wheeler-dealer Robert G. (Bobby) Baker, Teamster President James R. Hoffa or New York Democratic boss Carmine DeSapio.

Hartmann did not contest my position as I laid out the testimony of White House Counsel John Dean, supported by documents and at least half a dozen other witnesses. I felt that the most important corroborative witness for Dean at that stage was H. R. Haldeman, who had confirmed the essence of the important conversations involving Dean and President Nixon on September 15, 1972, and on March 13 and March 21, 1973.

While most new stories stressed the few points on which Haldeman had differed with Dean, close examination revealed essentially no factual differences. Haldeman corroborated that the meetings between the President and

Dean had taken place, that they had discussed the possibility that convicted Watergate burglar E. Howard Hunt
might talk to the prosecutor or the press, and that a considerable amount of money would be needed to keep Hunt
and other convicted Watergate burglars from talking.
Haldeman even testified that Nixon had indeed made
some comment that it "would be easy" to raise the million dollars Dean suggested would be necessary, but Haldeman concluded that this was Nixon's way of "drawing him
[Dean] out" and not an indication of approval of payment
of hush money to the Watergate burglars.

Hartmann did not agree with my facts, but conceded
that it would be "foolish" for Ford to become involved in
further defense of Nixon at this stage. He said he had made
a similar point with Ford, but added, "All I can do is make
suggestions. You know how Jerry is about his friends."

Bob Hartmann did not use the words "blind partisan
loyalty," but that is what he meant, in addition to a stub-
born quality in Ford that made it difficult to reason with
him.

Hartmann assured me that while he did not completely
accept my view of the seriousness of the case against Nixon,
he did agree that Ford could not stick his neck out at this
stage of the Watergate game without considerable political
danger. He said he had been making that point, would
continue to make that point, but could not state with
assurance that Ford would not make some unwise comment "because there are limitations on what a staff man
can do."

After talking with Hartmann, I mulled the problem
over for several days and decided to try to talk to Ford
personally. We had had a longtime agreeable relationship;
I regarded him as a friend and generally wished him well.

While I was interested in his attitude on the Nixon affair, I was also interested in learning just how closely he was following the details of Watergate and whether he comprehended the seriousness of Nixon's predicament.

It was my hope that in the course of our conversation I might emphasize some aspects of the evidence against Nixon so that Ford, the lawyer, might understand the full meaning of the evidence that Ford, the politician, might have overlooked in conversations with Nixon partisans or his own staff aides who did not have legal training.

I tried to get an appointment, but he was busy with speaking engagements, so I settled for a weekend effort to reach him by telephone. I left my name with the White House switchboard, and a short time later Vice President Ford called back.

Briefly, I recounted my views on the evidence establishing that Nixon was involved in an obstruction of justice, touching on the highlights of Haldeman's corroboration of Dean's testimony. Ford said he had not followed the evidence that closely and thus could not comment or react to the accuracy of my facts and conclusions on Nixon's involvement in crime.

I assured him I did not think it realistic to expect him to make critical comments publicly about Nixon or to lead any charge against the man who had elevated him to the vice presidency. I only wished to urge him to examine the facts closely, to draw his own conclusions and to avoid any sweeping defense of Nixon that could destroy his own credibility.

Vice President Ford said he appreciated my advice, which was similar to comments from his staff and others, but at this point still believed that Richard Nixon was innocent of wrongdoing and had only done what had been

done in many prior administrations. He mentioned the
Bobby Baker case as a Democratic cover-up by the Johnson
Administration, even though Bobby Baker was finally con-
victed.

"Obstruction of justice by the Johnson Administration
does not make it right for the Nixon Administration," I
cautioned, and added that I was certain he would be elevated to the presidency by either the impeachment or
resignation of President Nixon and that therefore it was
important to him and to the nation to avoid loose or irresponsible defenses of Nixon or Watergate.

The Vice President scoffed at my assertion that he would
occupy the White House in a few months and reiterated
earlier comments that he only wanted to serve out the term
as Vice President and retire at the end of 1976. But he did
say he recognized the need for caution in his comments.

But, as House Judiciary Committee Chairman Peter
Rodino assembled a huge staff to consider impeachment,
headed by Counsel John Doar and Minority Counsel
Albert Jenner, a distinguished Republican lawyer from
Chicago, White House pressure increased on Republicans
in the House and Senate to launch a sharp counterattack
against him. Highly partisan Republicans, such as Senator
Hugh Scott, attacked willingly and with gusto, but those
who treasured their integrity avoided the issue of Nixon's
Watergate complicity entirely.

Therefore it was with disappointment on January 15,
1974, that I read Vice President Ford's speech scheduled
for delivery before the 55th Annual Meeting of the American Farm Bureau Federation at Convention Hall in Atlantic City, New Jersey.

After paying brief tribute to the farmers, the Vice President accused "the AFL-CIO, the Americans for Demo-

cratic Action and other powerful pressure organizations" of "waging a massive propaganda campaign against the President of the United States.

"And make no mistake about it—it is an all-out attack," Ford said. "Their aim is total victory for themselves and the total defeat not only of President Nixon but of the policies for which he stands."

Ford characterized the attackers as "a few extreme partisans" who, he said, "seem bent on stretching out the ordeal of Watergate for their own purposes, whatever they might be.

"If they can crush the President and his philosophy, they are convinced that they can dominate the Congress and, through it, the nation," he warned, to alarm the members of this most conservative farm organization.

Ford referred to "the relatively small group of activists who are out to impeach the President." He declared that should they not have the strength to impeach him, "they will do the next most damaging thing. They will stretch out the ordeal, to cripple the President by dragging out the preliminaries to impeachment for as long as they can, and to use the whole affair for maximum political advantage."

In line with White House strategy, Vice President Ford prodded the House Judiciary Committee to "act promptly" when he well knew that the delays were caused to a large degree by White House failure to produce documents and tapes requested by Chairman Rodino.

"Personally, I firmly believe that no valid grounds exist for impeachment of the President," said Ford, who had studiously avoided examination and analysis of the crucial evidence. "I believe that a majority of the committee will reach the same conclusion. But, whatever their feelings, they owe it to all of us to do their job promptly and responsibly."

Ford praised Nixon as the man who "helped lay the groundwork for a lasting peace in the strife-torn Middle East after a generation of hatred and violence.

"None of those things happened by accident," he added. "They happened because a wise and good people were led by a wise and good President."

Then he defended President Nixon with the comment "No one is perfect—no nationality and no executive."

Ford spoke of the "really magnificent achievements" of the Nixon Administration and referred to Watergate as "a tragic but grotesque sideshow."

Obviously, Vice President Ford had not examined the evidence against Nixon, did not intend to examine the evidence against Nixon, and was content to accept Nixon's self-serving claims of innocence. Clearly, Ford did not choose to contaminate his mind by evidence already in the public domain, or he would have had difficulty espousing the personal conclusion that Nixon was not involved in serious crimes.

The effort to avoid the well-documented facts was deliberate self-deception to escape the necessity of criticizing the President, to whom he was indebted, and at the same time to give the impression of backing the President by accepting Nixon's conclusions as to his innocence without question. For the moment, it sidestepped the biased partisan defense of Nixon by Senator Scott, who was engaging in smear attacks on John Dean as a "perjurer" and "embezzler" of the $4,000 in Nixon Committee cash he had "borrowed" for his honeymoon.

On January 20, Hugh Scott said he had seen evidence which could prove the President was innocent of "specific items" in the Watergate affair and establish that Richard Nixon had committed no impeachable offenses. Scott told the press he had urged Nixon to release the information, supposedly a summary of White House tapes of Nixon's conversations with Dean. This evidence would show conclusively, Scott said, that Nixon had no knowledge of the Watergate break-in and cover-up before March 21, 1973, and would prove John Dean had given false testimony.

Vice President Ford's comments were less specific, but he said that Nixon had assured him personally he was innocent in the Watergate affair and had evidence to prove it. To his credit, Ford stayed out of the White House-orchestrated attacks on Dean as "a liar" and "a perjurer," but he continued to press Rodino to finish with the impeachment hearings.

Dean commented to me later, with a sly inflection, that he believed he knew why Ford did not join the pack of Republicans in attacking him as a possible perjurer. The young lawyer was not questioned about contacts with Ford and had spoken only of "the House Republican leadership" role in stopping Patman. He indicated he knew something about Watergate that might be harmful to Ford but, as late as January 1976, when we spoke, said he was not yet ready to disclose it. He was then putting the finishing touches on a book to be published in the summer of 1976.

After Ford's Farm Bureau speech, I called Hartmann to question him on his personal views of Ford's taking the offensive for the White House, and he said he had voiced the same concern to Ford, to no avail, both before the speech and after it.

On February 3, 1974, Vice President Ford modified his all-out defense of Nixon on the CBS television show "Face the Nation," declaring that all relevant tapes and documents should be made available to the House Judiciary Committee. This was his first extensive comment on the White House tapes issue, and it was made after the Grand Rapids (Michigan) press had suggested that Ford should "put some distance between himself and Nixon on Watergate."

Ford's appearance took place the same day Special Prosecutor Leon Jaworski appeared on the ABC television program "Issues and Answers" and sharply contradicted President Nixon's comments in the State of the Union address in which he claimed he had cooperated with the Special Prosecutor. Nixon had said, "I believe I have provided all the material that he needs to conclude his investigation and to proceed to prosecute the guilty and clear the innocent."

Jaworski also contradicted the White House and Senator Scott on the credibility of John Dean. Although Scott had said he had been given documents by Nixon and Haig demonstrating that Dean had perjured himself, Jaworski said he and his staff reviewed all available White House tapes and documents, as well as Dean's testimony, and could find no reason to believe that Dean had lied. Jaworski, who had reviewed all of the still-secret key tapes before the federal grand jury, said he intended to use Dean as a witness in the perjury trial of former White House Appointments Secretary Dwight Chapin.

The Special Prosecutor gave more than a hint of the serious backstage struggle with White House lawyers over "relevant documents" and rejected Nixon's claim of cooperation. "I've had to go after it," Jaworski declared, and added that if more documents were not produced he would go after them with subpoenas.

The dropping popularity of Nixon in the polls and the 410 to 4 margin by which the House voted to give Rodino's committee sweeping subpoena power indicated strongly to Ford that the tide was flowing against Nixon and that he should avoid any more than minor comment.

He remained relatively quiet through the indictment on March 1, 1974, of seven of President Nixon's key White House advisers and political associates, including former Attorney General John N. Mitchell, former White House Chief of Staff H. R. Haldeman, former White House Special Assistant John D. Ehrlichman, former Special Counsel Charles W. Colson, and Gordon C. Strachan, a young lawyer who had served as a key aide to Haldeman.

At the same time, Assistant Special Prosecutor Richard Ben-Veniste handed to Judge John J. Sirica a sealed brown envelope. Much later its contents were revealed: the federal grand jury had named Nixon as an unindicted co-conspirator because they had been advised that a sitting president could not be indicted.

On April 21, Ford conceded that the defeat of Republican James Sparling by Democrat J. Robert Traxler in a special congressional election in Michigan was a result of Watergate. However, in a self-contradictory statement in the same interview, he said that he believed the trip President Nixon made to Michigan on behalf of Sparling had been helpful in narrowing the margin of defeat. He declared that he felt President Nixon could and would be "an asset" to other congressional candidates in "certain selective areas" in the 1974 congressional election.

As pressure increased for release of the White House tapes to the House Judiciary Committee, Nixon stalled until May 3, when he suddenly released a huge edited transcript which he said established his innocence. The strategy did not work, for the distorted editing was obvious and only served to create a mass flight of longtime supporters. Even Senator Scott joined with Senator Jacob K. Javits and other high-ranking Republicans in criticizing the attitudes of the White House as revealed in the more than thirteen hundred pages of transcripts.

Scott, in the sharpest shift of all, called the Watergate conversations "a shabby, disgusting, immoral performance" by all involved. Javits said there was a "shocking lack of discussion of the public interest or what was right or fair. . . ."

House minority leader John Rhodes of Arizona, an unusually forthright political leader, said, "There are areas [in the transcripts] that might possibly be brought up as impeachable offenses having to do with obstruction of justice."

Such stout defenders of Nixon as the *Omaha World-Herald* and the *Chicago Tribune* lashed out at the "low level of political morality in the White House" and painted the portrait of Nixon as "humorless to the point of being inhumane. He is devious. He is vacillating. He is profane."

Although Nixon and some of his aides had altered the truth by the editing, enough of Richard Nixon came through to disillusion his best friends and loyal supporters. Vice President Gerald Ford's comment that he was "a little disappointed" by the transcripts of Nixon's conversations was probably the flabbiest reaction of any political figure who read them.

But later, in a speech before the University of Michigan graduating class at Ann Arbor, Ford spoke only briefly about the "political torment" of the country and defended President Nixon's decision to take his case to the people.

He said, "I cannot imagine any other country in the world where the opposition would seek, and the chief executive would allow, the dissemination of his most private and personal conversations with his staff, which, to be honest, do not exactly confer sainthood on anyone concerned."

And finally: "When all is said and done—and the sooner the better—I firmly hope and fervently pray that our country will be stronger and wiser for its present ordeal."

After zigzagging on Watergate throughout May and June, Vice President Ford on July 6, 1974, told a news conference in Dallas that the odds against impeachment "have fallen considerably" in the last month and that the case against Nixon "has fallen flat."

"I have detected a movement in the House that is favorable to the President," Ford said. "No impeachable offense has been found . . . the case has not been made."

So he continued with his assertions of Nixon's innocence through July, through the weekend of speeches in Mississippi and Louisiana after General Haig told him what was on the June 23, 1972, tape, and even after the tapes were made available through the White House press office on August 5. Ford told a news conference, "I have not listened to the tapes nor have I read the transcripts of the President's conversations with Mr. Haldeman. Without knowing what was said and the content of it, my comment would serve no useful purpose and I shall have none.

"Indeed I have come to the conclusion," he continued, "that the public interest is no longer served by repetition of my previously expressed belief that, on the basis of all the evidence known to me and to the American people, the President is not guilty of an impeachable offense under the constitutional definition of 'treason, bribery or other high crimes and misdemeanors,' Inasmuch as additional evidence is about to be forthcoming from the President which he says may be damaging, I intend to respectfully decline to discuss impeachment matters in public or in response to questions until the facts are more fully available."

Even after the House Judiciary Committee approved a third article of impeachment against Nixon on July 30, 1974, Ford continued to assert that he was innocent. He had not yet been told of the damaging evidence that Special Counsel Fred Buzhardt had come across a few days earlier in reviewing an Oval Office conversation of June 23, 1972, between Nixon and H. R. Haldeman.

Buzhardt told White House Chief of Staff Al Haig, and shortly before noon on August 1 Haig requested a meeting with Vice President Ford. He characterized the tape as "devastating, even catastrophic" for Nixon and asked Ford if he was prepared to assume the presidency "within a very short time."

Ford has related that he was "shocked and stunned" by the revelation, and nonresponsive when Haig asked for his recommendation on the timing of the resignation and the handling of the transition. Together they discussed eight options advanced by various White House staff people, but Ford, keeping in character, declined to make a recommendation. The options included Nixon pardoning himself; Nixon pardoning the Watergate defendants and then himself and then resigning; and Ford pardoning Nixon after Nixon resigned.

Although Ford made inquiry about a president's pardoning power before any criminal action is instituted, he made no commitment, and asked Haig to give him "time to think" and to talk to his wife and White House Counsel James St. Clair.

There were other conversations the next day, Friday, August 2, in which St. Clair reiterated the seriousness of the new evidence, but Ford repeated that he did not wish to make any recommendation.

With the knowledge that evidence existed that Haig, St. Clair and Buzhardt believed proved Nixon's implication in the obstruction of justice, Ford left Washington on Saturday to keep scheduled weekend engagements in Mississippi and Louisiana. In speeches and press conferences on Saturday, August 3, Sunday, August 4, and Monday, August 5, Vice President Ford continued to state he believed President Nixon had committed no crime and should not be impeached.

On Monday morning, August 5, Robert P. Griffin, assistant Senate minority leader and a Republican from Michigan, declared that Nixon should resign. "We've arrived at the point where both the national interest and his own interest would be served by resigning," Griffin said. "It is not just his enemies but many of his best friends—and I number myself among them—who believe resignation would be the most appropriate course."

Late Monday, President Nixon released the transcript of the three conversations with Haldeman on June 23, 1972, and within a matter of hours his last-ditch defenders on the House Judiciary Committee switched their votes in favor of impeachment.

At the Cabinet meeting on August 6, Vice President Ford reiterated his position that he was "making no recommendation to the President as to what he should do in the light of the new evidence." In the next forty-eight hours it was left to others in the Republican Party to convince Nixon he should resign, and that resignation was announced on August 8 and became effective the next morning. Gerald R. Ford became the first president of the United States to assume the office under the 25th Amendment, through the provisions of which Richard Nixon had nominated him for vice president. It could be said without fear of contradiction that Gerald Ford was elevated to the presidency by one man—Richard Nixon.

7. A Short Honeymoon

As A NEW president, Gerald R. Ford touched the heart of America when he pledged "a little straight talk" to end "our long national nightmare." The nation wanted sincerity and integrity after the two years of fabrication and deception by Richard M. Nixon in the Watergate cover-up. Though President Ford did not express direct disapproval of his predecessor's crimes and dishonesty, his affirmative comments were replete with phrases assuring honest government and the importance of truth from government officials.

"In all my public and private acts as your President, I expect to follow my instincts of openness and candor with full confidence that honesty is always the best policy in the end," President Ford said as he took office as the thirty-eighth president of the United States on August 9, 1974. A welcome thought, it was applauded by Democrats and Republicans alike as a sincere reaction to the corruptive secrecy of the Nixon era.

As I listened, I wanted to believe it. I pushed to the back

of my mind the picture of Gerald Ford, longtime friend and admirer of Richard Nixon, his stout defender to the very end and the man who killed Representative Wright Patman's plan to conduct Watergate hearings before the 1972 election.

I wanted to forget that House Republican Leader Ford had schemed with the Republican members of the House Banking and Currency Committee to block Chairman Patman's efforts to subpoena John Dean, John Mitchell, Maurice Stans, Jeb Magruder and more than a dozen other key witnesses to testify in public hearings on the Watergate burglary.

I wanted to forget Ford's ringing defenses of Nixon on Watergate, defenses that represented either blind partisan loyalty or ignorance of criminal law in the face of massive public evidence of a criminal obstruction of justice.

In those days immediately after Nixon's resignation, I forced myself to be optimistic about a Ford administration and about the honesty and integrity of its leader. As a member of the House, Ford had been a consistent critic of executive secrecy in Democratic administrations, and as President he should be able to see and understand the corruptive influence of abused discretion and secret decisions. Everything in that August 9 speech seemed to say he was aware of his extremely partisan role as a Republican member of the House, but that as President of the United States he would rise above it.

The new President said he was "acutely aware that you have not elected me as your President" and acknowledged his enormous responsibility to the Congress and the American people. He repeated the essence of his testimony in the Senate confirmation hearing when he declared, "I believe that the truth is the glue that holds government together, not only our government but civilization itself. . . . That bond, though strained, is unbroken at home and abroad."

President Ford then drew from a phrase in Nixon's resignation speech on the need for "healing the wounds of this nation" and the necessity to "bind up the internal wounds of Watergate, more painful and more poisonous than those of foreign wars."

Ford compassionately requested "your prayers for Richard Nixon and for his family." In the spirit of that moment it was a charitable expression of sympathy for members of the Nixon family, who, like himself, had been the victims of the falsehoods and deceptions of the former president.

This tall, blond man with the open face and frank speech came across as the antithesis of the dark visage and deceptive rhetoric that characterized Nixon. The pipe-smoking amiability of the University of Michigan football star contrasted sharply with the striving of the up-tight man who failed to make the varsity at little Whittier College. Likewise, the easy grace of Betty Ford and the handsome Ford children made them the joy of photographers and editors throughout the month of August.

It was an intoxicating period for President Ford, his family and those in his political entourage, as the public opinion polls shot upward to register a startling 71 percent approval of his handling of the presidency even though he faced no critical decisions.

"Our Constitution works," the new President assured a nation that had developed serious doubts as Nixon clung to the presidency in the face of massive evidence of serious crime. "Our great Republic is a government of laws and not of men."

In foreign affairs, the new President announced that

Secretary of State Henry A. Kissinger would stay on. While Kissinger had many critics in Republican and Democratic ranks, his remaining was assurance that a man of some experience and popularity would be at the helm to help Ford as he assumed his new command.

As Ford met with congressional leaders of both parties and with his economic advisers, he declared that control of inflation was the "high and first priority" of his administration. Although he outlined no specific program, Congress and the nation were willing to wait, relieved to have a Chief of State giving top attention to the nation's problems and not to a cover-up of his participation in a crime.

There were decided disadvantages to Ford's swift and unprecedented ascent to the presidency, but there were also clear advantages. His elevation from House Republican Leader to President was in the wake of the two greatest scandals in American political history. He had not campaigned for the job, nor was he bound by any public promises in attaining the vice presidency, because he was the personal selection of President Nixon in the wake of the forced resignation of Spiro T. Agnew.

The prevailing trend at that time was to believe the best of Gerald Ford and to stress his strong points with optimism for what those strengths could mean to a Ford administration in Washington, to the nation and to the world. His life and political career demonstrated much that was admirable and suggested that as President he could rise above the highly partisan Republicanism and political loyalties expected of the Republican House Leader.

The press and the nation, looking for a hero image to contrast with Watergate, found Gerald Ford's clumsy sincerity a welcome relief from the slick deceptiveness of the sanctimonious Richard Nixon, who often appeared a glib shyster even when telling the truth.

That August, I easily rationalized Ford's long defense of Nixon as a requirement of his job as Republican House Leader and as Nixon's Vice President. I overlooked some of Ford's past actions with a hopeful projection of what straight talk and good open administration or government might accomplish.

In one conversation with Representative H. R. Gross, the conservative Iowa Republican, I was extolling Ford's record in a manner that glossed over or excused a few controversial points. "Come down off that cloud," the crusty Iowa Republican verbally slapped me on the cheek. "Ford will probably be better than Nixon, and that's only because Nixon made such a mess of it, but I have seen Jerry Ford operate for twenty-five years. Jerry Ford will deal on anything, and don't forget it."

Gross reminded me that Ford constantly talked Republican frugality but was always in the front ranks of those going along with pay boosts and fringe benefits for members of Congress. He commented that Ford "bought the Nixon line" on the Family Assistance Plan without consulting Republican House members, and "jammed it down our throat."

"He double-crossed me on the Adam Clayton Powell case," Gross said, "and put [Representative] Clark Mac-Gregor up to put through his compromise with the Democrats that permitted Powell to use his congressional pay to pay back what he had stolen."

That conversation took place on August 13, a full week before President Ford unsettled some of his conservative former colleagues by telling an audience of veterans in Chicago he favored "leniency" for Vietnam war draft evaders and deserters and wanted them "to work their way back" into the American system.

Why was Ford on August 19 voluntarily championing "leniency" for draft evaders and deserters at a veterans' convention? It was already apparent that the VFW convention resolutions would include a declaration of "total opposition to both general and selective amnesty for draft dodgers and military deserters." Most observers rejected suggestions that a Ford initiative on amnesty could be used to set the stage for a pardon for Nixon and other Watergate defendants, by stealing a plank from the liberal Democrats' platform.

The uneasiness of conservative Republicans increased the next day when President Ford announced his intention to nominate Nelson A. Rockefeller for Vice President. The sixty-six-year-old former New York Governor was detested by a large number of conservative Republicans who resented his refusal to work for Republican presidential candidates in 1964 and 1968.

Despite demonstrating spectacular success in New York State politics by winning four successive terms as Governor, Rockefeller had botched efforts to win the Republican nomination for President in 1960, 1964, and 1968. Senator Barry Goldwater, the 1964 Republican standard-bearer, accused Rockefeller of having "ducked out on at least two presidential races," and said he doubted whether Rockefeller would be acceptable to rank-and-file Republicans in 1976.

Though Goldwater indicated support for the nomination, he and Representative Gross, along with others, surmised that the vice-presidential nomination was the first move to boost Rockefeller to the Republican presidential nomination in 1976. Gross recalled that when

nominated for Vice President, Ford had said he would
not be a candidate for the Republican nomination in
1976 because he had "told Betty" he would retire from
political life at the end of that year.

At a press conference in October just after his vice-
presidential nomination, Ford told reporters he had given
up his longtime goal to be Speaker of the House because
he saw no possibility in the foreseeable future for the
Republicans to control the United States House of Representatives. He said that he had decided against running
for re-election to Congress in 1976, would take his congressional pension geared to the minority leader salary and
retire to Grand Rapids.

Now, August 20, 1974, in the flurry of questions raised
about Rockefeller gaining a leg up on the 1976 Republican presidential nomination, Ford said he would probably seek the 1976 Republican nomination for himself.

Then, on August 22, the House Judiciary Committee
issued its final report, giving details of the "clear and
convincing evidence" that Richard Nixon had been involved in a criminal obstruction of justice, had abused his
presidential power and had defied congressional subpoenas. The basic American goal of "equal justice under
law" made it extremely difficult for Nixon's friends and
political associates to argue logically against his being
ringleader of the White House Watergate gang. Even
Representative Charles Wiggins, California Republican
and Nixon's most articulate defender in the Watergate
hearings, concluded that, distasteful as it might be to send
a former president to jail, it might be necessary "if we
are truly to have 'equal justice under the law.'" Most
other Republicans avoided suggesting any favored treat-
ment for the president whose deceptions and lies had

embarrassed them personally, damaged the Republican Party and minimized the chances of any Republican election gains in either the House or Senate.

However, Senator Hugh Scott, the Republican Senate Leader, was apparently unconcerned that the Nixon White House had made him appear foolish in his unjustified attacks on John Dean and in his equally absurd defenses of Nixon. In the third week in August he referred to suggestions that Nixon was indictable, but argued that the former President could not get a fair trial because of the publicity surrounding the Watergate scandals and his resignation.

In a public appeal for sympathy for Nixon, Scott declared with emotion, "The man has been punished. For God's sake, enough is enough."

And when Chesterfield Smith, president of the American Bar Association, declared that "no man is above the law" and that "judgments should be made on the merits of Mr. Nixon's case, just like anyone else," Scott declared that any "prosecution [of Nixon] would be persecution."

"He's been hung," he said, "and it doesn't seem to me [that] in addition he should be drawn and quartered."

A few days later Nelson Rockefeller, the newly designated vice-presidential nominee, offered his opinion that Nixon should not be prosecuted, which was defended to me by a Rockefeller aide as "simply political posturing" in his bid for support for his nomination from Nixon's few remaining friends in the Senate and House.

Political observers assessed Ford's comments on amnesty and the Scott and Rockefeller comments on Nixon as setting the stage for pardoning Nixon and cooling liberal criticism of Ford's "compassionate act" of immunity to draft evaders and deserters.

On August 27 I learned that a presidential press conference would be held the next day, and late in the afternoon I called my friend Bob Hartmann, who, in addition to being Ford's major speech writer, was a political confidant and counselor to the President. I questioned him about Ford's position on a pardon for Nixon and on the large number of stories and columns that saw his comments on amnesty as a ploy to soften the liberal Democrats for a pardon. Hartmann said it just wasn't so, and that President Ford was being misinterpreted, so I countered with the suggestion that the August 28 press conference was an excellent opportunity for Ford to state there would be no pardon for Nixon or other Watergate defendants in the foreseeable future. Hartmann said he agreed with me and would try to get him to clarify the issue, but he added, "You know Jerry."

The next day at the press conference, Helen Thomas, of United Press International, piped out the first question:

"Mr. President, aside from the Special Prosecutor's role, do you agree with the Bar Association that the law applies equally to all men, or do you agree with Governor Rockefeller that former President Nixon should have immunity from prosecution? And, specifically, would you use your pardon authority, if necessary?"

It was a question broad enough to permit President Ford to set out precisely what his views were. Instead, he started his answer by recalling that in the swearing-in ceremony "I had hoped that our former President, who brought peace to millions, would find it for himself."

Avoiding any position on the ABA president's comments about equal justice under law, President Ford leaped to support, and in many ways to adopt, the Rockefeller position:

"Now, the expression made by Governor Rockefeller, I think, coincides with the general view and the point of view of the American people. I subscribe to that point of view, but let me add, in the last ten days or two weeks I have asked for prayers for guidance on this very important point."

Then he added pointedly, "In this situation, I am the final authority. There have been no charges made, there has been no action by the courts, there has been no action by any jury. And until any legal process has been undertaken, I think it is unwise and untimely for me to make any commitment."

Had we been assessing a statement by Richard Nixon, I would have weighed his words carefully for deceptions, but Ford seemed to be saying that until there was some court action or jury action involving Nixon, he would take no action, and that to take any immediate action would be "unwise and untimely."

The question was raised of political grumbling from Ford's conservative allies and their suggestion that he was "moving too far to the left."

"I don't think I have deviated from my basic philosophy, nor have I deviated from what I think is the right action," Ford responded. "I have selected an outstanding person to be Vice President. I have made a decision concerning amnesty which I think is right and proper—no amnesty, no revenge, and that individuals who have violated either the draft laws or have evaded selective service or deserted can earn their way or work their way back. I don't think these are views that fall in the political spectrum right or left."

Several other questions touched on the possibility of a Nixon pardon, and none of his answers jarred my belief that the President had made no final decision but, although he was "not ruling it out," was keeping his options open.

"Mr. President, you have emphasized here your option of granting a pardon to the former President," a questioner said, and President Ford replied, "I intend to."

"You intend to have that option," the questioner repeated. "If an indictment is brought, would you grant a pardon before any trial took place?"

"I said at the outset," Ford replied, "that until the matter reaches me, I am not going to make any comment during the process of whatever charges are made," and his reply seemed to solidify assurances that he would make no early decision on a Nixon pardon.

Ford was also asked, "Do you feel the Special Prosecutor can in good conscience pursue cases against former top Nixon aides as long as there is the possibility that the former President may not also be pursued in the courts?"

"I think the Special Prosecutor, Mr. Jaworski, has an obligation to take whatever actions he sees fit in conformity with his oath of office, and that should include any and all individuals," President Ford replied in what seemed a conviction to apply the same standards for presidents, cabinet officers and lesser government officials.

On the general question of what he intended to do to avoid future Watergates, Ford commented:

"Well, I indicated that, one, we would have an open Administration. I will be as candid and as forthright as I possibly can. I will expect any individual in my Administration to be exactly the same. There will be no tightly controlled operation of the White House staff. I have a policy of seeking advice from a number of top members of my staff. There will be no one person, nor any limited number of individuals, who make decisions. I will make the decisions and take the blame for them or whatever benefit might be the case."

On the question of whether he planned "to set up a code of ethics for the executive branch," Ford replied with the confidence gained by three weeks in the Oval Office: "The code of ethics that will be followed will be the example that I set."

The press conference had reassured the press and the public that the question of a Nixon pardon appeared to be largely academic until some action was taken by the Special Prosecutor.

The Gallup poll, published on September 1, 1974, disclosed that in the first national check on his popularity Ford received a heady rating of 71 percent, with a bare 3 percent registering disapproval and 26 percent undecided. The Gallup Poll noted "a high measure of bipartisan support" for Ford, with 68 percent of the Democrats and 77 percent of the Republicans indicating approval. The typical reaction of those polled regarding Ford's performance was acclaim for "his open approach to the nation's problems." Eight to one approval for Ford was found among some traditionally Democratic groups that never gave President Nixon majority approval, according to the Gallup poll.

President Ford's high popularity with the public and the era of good feeling with the Congress were shattered on Sunday morning, September 8. Without notice to the public, and with only slight notice to the White House press secretary, Jerald F. terHorst, President Ford announced a full and unconditional pardon for Nixon, covering all possible crimes the former President might have committed between January 21, 1969, and his resig-

nation on August 9, 1974. President Ford had not consulted the Justice Department or the Special Watergate
Prosecutor on the impact of the pardon on the pending
prosecution of the major Watergate cover-up case. Most
of the advice from White House Counsel Philip Buchen,
his old law partner from Grand Rapids, was obtained
from Nixon's lawyer, Herbert J. (Jack) Miller.

Miller, a former Assistant Attorney General in charge
of the criminal division, was a highly competent and experienced Washington lawyer, but he could hardly be
expected to give objective legal advice when he was serving as an advocate for Richard Nixon. Little noticed in
the first day of shock at the pardon was an agreement to
give Nixon title to all of the White House tapes and
papers, under joint control with President Ford.

The instant reaction of much of the disillusioned public was that it was "a Ford political deal" to pardon Nixon
within one month of assuming the office of President,
but no one questioned President Ford's candor or credibility when he said he had greatly underestimated public
and congressional reaction.

I recalled the perceptive comment by Representative
Gross that "Jerry Ford will deal on anything, and don't
forget it."

8. The Pardon Shock

By GRANTING HIS longtime friend and political benefactor Richard Nixon a full and unconditional pardon, President Ford dynamited his own credibility, his reputation for sincerity and the hopes of the Republican Party in the 1974 congressional elections. His stated intention was to "firmly shut and seal" the Watergate book. However, Ford's unprecedented action to assure that Nixon would not be indicted, tried and convicted for the serious crimes he committed created a new furor and raised more doubts about the trustworthiness of those elected to high government office.

A nation and a Congress willing to accept his word as basic truth, and his actions as being honorably motivated, now raised questions about anything President Ford said. In talking to Senators and Congressmen—Democrats and Republicans—I found bitterness because Ford had deceived them, and anger with themselves for having been taken in by the Grand Rapids equivalent of the shyster "country lawyer." I felt, as they felt, a personal letdown because of my deep hope that Gerald Ford would give the country the "simple honesty" which he promised and the nation craved.

Mary McGrory, the Pulitzer Prize winning columnist for the *Washington Star-News,* caught the mood best in the days immediately following the pardon. "And what made him [Ford] think he could get away with it?" McGrory asked, then answered:

"Here the press must step forward with bowed head. Reading his notices for the first month in office, Ford learned that he was irresistible, invulnerable and invincible. The Washington press corps lost its head over Gerald Ford. A thousand reporters turned overnight into flacks for Jerry Ford. They raved about his decency, his smile, his English muffins, his peachy dancing.

"Richard Nixon was part of the reason but not all of it. Reporters were battered by two years of open warfare in the press room. . . . Contrary to the rhetoric of the Nixon-Agnew years, about acid-throwing elitists, reporters are just like Peorians or the machinist's wife in Dayton. They would like to 'support the President.' They want to see the system work. . . .

"In their lust for decent leadership, they went all out, promising themselves and their readers a rose garden. They joyfully chronicled the overtures to the Vietnam exiles, the blacks, the women. They babbled about fresh winds and total change. They forgot everything they knew about Gerald Ford. . . . They dwelt on his accessibility to the press and his good humor as he careened around the country, one day protesting the innocence of Richard Nixon, one day cavilling at White House tactics. . . . Nothing suggests that he understood that Watergate was anything but a party headache. During the great constitutional drama, he was only a heckler."

Mary McGrory concluded that column with a comment that becomes more perceptive with each passing month: "He perhaps did us all a favor by slapping us all awake that Sunday morning."

One of those who benefited most from this rude slap was veteran *Detroit News* Washington correspondent Jerald F. terHorst, who served for just one month as the White House press secretary. He resigned in protest, saying it was unfair to pardon a former president while his subordinates remained in jail or went on trial for serious crimes. Also Jerry terHorst was not informed about the pardon and was embarrassed because he consequently gave erroneous information to a former newspaper colleague.

The day after terHorst resigned, September 10, John W. Hushen, deputy press secretary who had previously been a spokesman for Attorney General John Mitchell, declared that President Ford was studying a plan to pardon all of the Watergate criminals. This announcement touched off an even more furious protest from Republicans and Democrats alike. Assistant Senate Democratic Leader Robert Byrd commented, "I hope this will get no further than a study." Representative William Scherle, an outspoken Iowa Republican, called the pardon "his stupid mistake" which would be compounded by "letting all of the Watergate crooks off the hook."

In polling the Iowa congressional delegation on their reactions to the suggestion that all Watergate defendants be pardoned, I found unanimity of opposition. Representative H. R. Gross, a conservative Republican, had precisely the same response as Senator Dick Clark, a liberal Iowa Democrat: "Two wrongs do not make a right." Gross added that "pardoning Nixon at this juncture did not make sense, and obviously had not been thought through from the standpoint of its impact on other Watergate cases and on our whole system of criminal justice. It would be a further outrage if all of the Watergate defendants are pardoned and will destroy any respect that is left for our laws."

John Hushen reported that, within forty-eight hours of the pardon, over 17,000 telegrams and mailgrams were received and that these were running "about 6 to 1" against Ford's action. He said only that "thousands" of telephone calls were coming into the White House and estimated that they were running "about 60 to 40" for President Ford; but he conceded that these were only estimates and that all of the calls were not getting through because of the jammed White House switchboard.

The Nixon pardon was a *fait accompli* and probably could not be reversed, but Congress immediately took steps to warn President Ford that any further pardons would be regarded as irresponsible and a criminal abuse of the pardoning power.

In the face of the escalating furor, the White House retreated, saying President Ford was not considering pardons for other Watergate defendants and trying to give the impression that Hushen's original announcement had not been authorized by the President. Most of the press corps recognized that Hushen was the fall guy for a blunder the President had made.

The Senate and House, disregarding assurances from the White House that no others would be pardoned, moved forward with a resolution of "disapproval" of any presidential action to pardon defendants "until the judicial process has run its full course with respect to such matters." The "sense of the Senate resolution" passed by an overwhelming 55 to 24 margin, with even minority leader Hugh Scott and assistant minority leader Robert Griffin voting with Senator Robert Byrd, the West Virginia Democrat. Although it made no mention of the Nixon pardon, the lopsided support was indicative of the strong feeling against the pardon expressed in letters to Congress.

Angry over the Nixon pardon but unable to rescind it, Congress took every other possible step to indicate its displeasure with the President Ford they had been lavishly praising only weeks earlier. The frustrated Senators and Congressmen acted to block Ford's agreement to give Nixon the White House tapes, and cut deeply into Ford's request for a huge $850,000 appropriation for Nixon's transition expenses. The fund was slashed to $200,000, and many legislators believed even that was too generous for the man who had shamefully abused the power of the presidency and then engaged in criminal acts to conceal it from Congress and the public.

The President's explanation of his reasons for pardoning Nixon did not satisfy the public, the Congress or the press, for it smacked of the same kind of clever rhetoric and logic Nixon had used in explaining that by refusing to produce the subpoenaed White House tapes he was not covering his own crimes but, rather, "preserving the power of the presidency."

Ford had said he "dare not depend upon my personal sympathy [for Nixon] as a longtime friend," but then had made compassion and sympathy the cornerstone of his explanation of the ultimate use of a discretionary power to pardon.

Stories had begun to seep out of the White House in August indicating discussions between White House Chief of Staff Alexander Haig and Ford concerning a pardon for Nixon and the other Watergate defendants. Some were reported to have taken place just prior to Nixon's resignation which cleared the way for Ford to become President. Other discussions were reported to have taken place just prior to the August 28 press conference. All of this led to speculation that a "deal" had been made between Ford and Nixon, engineered by Nixon staff people who had remained in the Ford White House.

President Ford faced blunt questions in his next press conference on September 16.

"There was no understanding, no deal between me and the former President, no deal between my staff and the staff of the President," Ford told a dubious press.

It was called to President Ford's attention that during his confirmation hearings "you said that you did not think that the country would stand for a president to pardon his predecessor. Has your mind been changed about such public opinion?"

The man of candor quibbled over whether he had given a misleading answer under oath. "I was asked a hypothetical question. In answer to the hypothetical question I responded by saying that I did not think the American people would stand for such action." Then he rationalized further: "I think if you will reread what I said in answer to that hypothetical question, I did not say I wouldn't. I simply said that under the way the question was phrased, the American people would object." Despite his pettifogging there was no question that Senator Robert Byrd and most other members of the Senate Rules Committee believed that Ford had assured the Congress he would not pardon Nixon.

Another reporter queried, "In view of the public reaction, do you think the Nixon pardon really served to bind up the nation's wounds?"

"I must say that the decision has created more antagonism than I anticipated," Ford replied. "But as I look over the long haul with a trial or several trials of a former president, criminal trials, the possibility of a former president being in the dock, so to speak, and the division that would have existed . . . I am still convinced, despite the public reaction so far, that the decision I made was the right one."

President Ford finally, reluctantly, recognized me for a question. Many loose ends were hanging, but I asked the question I believed went to the heart of his thinking on ethical standards in government generally and the tone of his administration.

"Mr. President, at the last press conference you said, 'The code of ethics that will be followed will be the example that I set.' Do you find any conflict of interest in the decision to grant a sweeping pardon to your lifelong friend and your financial benefactor with no consultation for advice and judgment on the legal fallout?"

President Ford winced at the words "friend" and "financial benefactor," but his answer indicated that he understood what I meant. "The decision to grant a pardon to Mr. Nixon was made primarily, as I have expressed, for the purpose of trying to heal the wounds throughout the country between Americans on one side of the issue or the other. Mr. Nixon nominated me for the office of

Vice President. I was confirmed overwhelmingly in the House as well as in the Senate. Every action I have taken, Mr. Mollenhoff, is predicated on my conscience without any concern or consideration as to favor as far as I am concerned."

Examined closely, Mr. Ford's answer was as craftily evasive as any Nixon reply. He recognized, I was sure, that the head of a federal regulatory agency would have been vulnerable to conflict of interest charges and would have had to disqualify himself if a case had came before him involving a longtime personal or political friend, particularly if that person had been of any assistance to him in getting the appointment.

By any normal standard of conflict of interests President Ford should have barred himself from making any decision that would benefit Richard Nixon. He conceded the longtime personal and political friendship, but he also had received a promotion from a $49,500-a-year post as the House minority leader to the $62,500-a-year salary of Vice President, with all increased congressional pension rights. But, greater than the pension boost was the additional $60,000-a-year-plus lifetime pension he would receive as a former president unless impeached.

The pension benefits Richard Nixon had bestowed upon Gerald Ford, in addition to his $200,000-a-year salary as President, couldn't have been bought for a million dollars—and many Washington decisions have been sold for less. Only Gerald Ford knew how much these factors weighed in his decision, for he had confided in no one that these obvious ethical questions gave him concern.

The least Ford should have done before granting the pardon would have been to seek advice from some of his old and trusted friends, such as Senator Robert Griffin, of Michigan, former Defense Secretary Melvin R. Laird or Ford's successor as House minority leader, John Rhodes, of Arizona. But he consulted none of them before making the decision that was to leave the Republican Party in tatters.

If this represented the ethical standards of the Ford Administration, we were back in business at the same old conflict of interest stand, for lesser favoritism had precipitated hundreds of critical investigations in my twenty-four years in Washington.

In my "Watch on Washington" column for October 5, 1974, I wrote, "The American people can hope Cabinet officers and agency heads do not take too literally President Ford's statement that the code of ethics of his administration will be the example he sets."

We had applauded his assertion that he wished to set an example, but I added that in the light of the Nixon pardon "there is much reason to wish that he will establish a code of ethics that is a more certain guideline than his example."

The immediate political losers on the Nixon pardon were the Republicans running for Senate and House seats, particularly those who had hoped to get a boost from Gerald Ford after putting their necks on the line for Richard Nixon almost until the end. One of those was Representative Wiley Mayne, a Republican member of the House Judiciary Committee who had voted against all of the impeachment resolutions until the disclosure of the contents of the crucial June 23, 1972, White House tape. While cautiously critical of Nixon on several aspects of the Watergate affair, Mayne had loyally voted with the pro-Nixon block in the Judiciary Committee on almost all procedural as well as substantive matters, and had himself been hurt in the process.

With President Ford's stock soaring in August, Mayne hoped the popularity of the new President would enhance his own chances for re-election against Democrat Berkley Bedell, an aggressive millionaire businessman. In August, Mayne enthusiastically anticipated a visit to his northwest Iowa district by President Ford, which he hoped would give him enough of a boost for victory. The September pardon and the aftermath were a sledgehammer blow to his re-election chances, forcing him to be critical of the timing of the Nixon pardon, though he sought to avoid a split with Gerald Ford.

Mayne satisfied no one when he said that his "first impression is that it [the pardon] is premature and might well have been deferred" until Special Prosecutor Leon Jaworski indicated what action he would take against Nixon. Mayne, as many other Republicans, had made requests of the White House for Ford to visit his congressional district, and now they were placed in the awkward position of trying to determine whether the man who pardoned Nixon would be helpful or harmful. Mayne simply stated perfunctorily, "The President of the United States is always welcome in my district," and indicated that a visit to Sioux City "would be good for the Republican organization."

Representative Scherle, an enthusiastic supporter of Ford for the vice-presidential spot, said bluntly of the Nixon pardon: "It destroys any chance of getting effective cooperation on the energy problem and inflation, drags Watergate back into the campaign and smashes his credibility." And privately he moaned, "Why did he do it now?"

"It is also going to put a hell of a crimp in his chances of nomination and re-election in 1976," Scherle said, then raised the question of whether President Ford really wanted to run for re-election or was planning to bow out in favor of Nelson Rockefeller.

Assistant Democratic Leader Robert Byrd, one of the shrewdest and most objective political analysts in Congress, declared that "there was nothing Ford could have done that would hurt him as much with Congress."

"His high popularity and the image of credibility were his greatest assets in dealing with Congress," Byrd said. "He has brought Watergate back as an issue when he didn't have to do it." The West Virginia Democrat added that the pardon "demonstrates that someone is above the law" and revives "the lack of faith in government."

"Could it be that he didn't realize the political risk involved, or is there some reason he felt he had to do it without regard for the political risk?" Byrd raised the question that was on everybody's mind.

Others more bluntly suggested "a Ford-Nixon deal" that could only be uncovered through a congressional inquiry. Representative Bella S. Abzug, a New York Democrat, and Representative John Conyers, a Michigan Democrat, were among the first to introduce resolutions of inquiry into the circumstances surrounding the pardon.

Ford's critics stressed the contradictory nature of his tesimony before the Congress in connection with his nomination for Vice President and his comments at press conferences. Representative Elizabeth Holtzman, a New York Democrat, declared that production of White House tapes of the conversation between Nixon and Ford was vital to establishing what Ford knew about the Watergate cover-up.

The shock following the Nixon pardon caused members of the Congress and the press to reflect back on the Ford-Nixon relationship throughout the entire Watergate affair in search for further clues to why Ford felt compelled to take such an extreme political risk for his political mentor. It had not put Watergate behind the nation but had brought it back into the full spotlight. It seemed unlikely that President Ford's compassion for Nixon was the only factor involved.

9. Search for the Motive

CONGRESS WAS WEARY of Watergate-related investigations in September 1974, and this was particularly true of the Judiciary Committee and its chairman, Peter Rodino, of New Jersey. The committee had handled, successively, the Ford vice-presidential nomination hearings, the Nixon impeachment investigation and hearing and, currently, the complicated investigation into Nelson A. Rockefeller's finances in preparation for hearings on his nomination for Vice President.

However, public uproar over the pardon and the Nixon-Ford White House tape agreement resulted in nineteen bills and resolutions being introduced in the House requiring further inquiry. Seventy House members, both Democrats and Republicans, demanded investigations and legislation to preserve the public's right to know the full story of Watergate as well as the full story of President Ford's pardoning of Nixon.

When William Hungate, Chairman of the House Judiciary Subcommittee on Criminal Justice, called his committee to order on September 24, he remarked that "recent events caused many responsible citizens and members of Congress serious concern that the complete story of Watergate may never be recorded.

"The pardoning of former President Nixon," he declared, "has certainly jeopardized the opportunity for full public disclosure of information gathered by the Office of Special Prosecutor bearing on former President Nixon's role in the Watergate affair. Moreover, the agreement entered into between the former President and the General Services Administration has caused many to fear that additional information relevant to Watergate will be forever withheld from public scrutiny.

"The Congress has dealt responsibly with Watergate, but Watergate will not be behind us until the record of Watergate is complete."

Representative Gilbert Gude, a Maryland Republican, was the first witness to comment critically on President Ford's misleading press conference statement prior to the Nixon pardon. Gude said, "At his first news conference after assuming office, President Ford indicated that while he thought that former President Nixon has suffered enough, the legal proceedings in the Watergate affair should be allowed to run their course before any consideration of a presidential pardon." Gude declared he had supported this procedure for three reasons:

"First, it reaffirmed the people's commitment to equal justice under the law regardless of power or position.

"Second, it insured the right of the former President Nixon and the country to have a judgment by the courts of Mr. Nixon's involvement, if any, in any offenses against the United States.

"Third, it preserved the President's option if Mr.

Nixon by fair and due processes had been found guilty of any crime."

The Maryland Republican declared that, as a result of President Ford's decision to pardon Nixon, "the courts now will not be able to make a judgment in this matter, and the people will not have the normal judicial resolution of this matter as is appropriate to the American way." Gude continued that it appeared there was "a substantial body of evidence that was not available to the committee during the course of the impeachment proceedings," and he made specific reference to the still-undisclosed White House tapes of Nixon's conversation that might be relevant. He said there was confusion about the authority of Special Watergate Prosecutor Leon Jaworski to make a full report and that he wanted to "clarify any ambiguities and insure that Mr. Jaworski has the authority to issue a report on former President Nixon's involvement in Watergate."

Representative Elizabeth Holtzman asked, "Do you have the same sense of flexibility · about allowing the Special Prosecutor to make a report with regard to materials that are not presently in his possession—tapes, for example—but that are in the possession of the White House at this time?" She pinpointed the tapes as the best evidence to unwind the whole Watergate story.

"Certainly any additional evidence that came to hand during the period in which he was compiling the report should be part of the report," Gude replied, with neither of them making reference to possible Ford conversations with Nixon.

Representative Bella Abzug, however, zeroed directly in on President Ford by challenging the legality of the pardon and the arrangement under which Ford was to turn the tapes over to Nixon for eventual destruction. She called it an "abuse of presidential power" that left "festering suspicions of White House deals [and] deceptions."

"Most wounding of all," she added, "is what Mr. Ford's action has done to our concept of equal justice for all and the belief that the President is accountable for his actions and not above the law. This is the very concept that was supposed to have been reaffirmed by this committee in its impeachment proceedings and vindicated in Mr. Nixon's forced resignation."

She listed a dozen witnesses required to clarify the question of the pardon, including President Ford, Attorney General William Saxbe, White House Chief of Staff Alexander Haig and Richard Nixon. "What promises were made or conditions set for a pardon, if any?" she asked, and added that relevant tapes or transcripts should be obtained by subpoena.

"There are suspicions that Richard Nixon may have made a deal on the pardon with Gerald Ford before nominating him to the vice presidency," Representative Abzug said. "If Richard Nixon made Ford's elevation to Vice President conditional upon the promise of a pardon, or even if Mr. Nixon conditioned his own resignation on a promise of receiving a pardon, then conceivably Mr. Ford could be charged with accepting a bribe, which is an impeachable offense. Grim as this possibility may be, it is nonetheless the duty of this committee to investigate the facts and make a determination," she continued.

Abzug declared aloud what many were whispering when she voiced the "suspicions that General Haig, who reportedly was instrumental in convincing Mr. Nixon to resign, may have held out to him the promise of a pardon. . . . There are suspicions arising from the belief that in the negotiations for the pardon, the roles appear to have been switched, with Mr. Ford acting as supplicant and Mr. Nixon dictating the terms of the pardon, the so-called statement of contrition and the agreement on the tapes," Representative Abzug charged relative to the grave questions before the committee and the nation. "In the wake of the pardon, Gerald Ford has created an enormous credibility problem for himself and the presidency. He is in a particularly vulnerable position because he is the first nonelected president in the history of our nation and because he was named to the vice presidency by a discredited and impeachable president."

The New York Democrat capsuled the Judiciary Committee's responsibility: "The committee . . . which recommended confirmation and the Congress which confirmed his [Ford's] nomination also have the responsibility to the American people to investigate and report to them on the conduct of President Ford in connection with the pardon and the agreement on the tapes."

A dozen more Democrats and Republicans testified on the necessity for full disclosure on Watergate, the pardon and the Ford-Nixon agreement on the tapes, which would eventually result in their destruction. Significantly, among those testifying was Representative Margaret Heckler, the Massachusetts Republican who now realized she had been misled and used by Ford and the White House in the vote to block the House Banking and Currency Committee investigation pushed by Chairman Wright Patman.

"To forget [Watergate] would invite a repeat of the tragedy," Representative Heckler testified. "This bill assures the American public of a complete and factual record.

"There are scattered admissions of guilt and reams of testimony," the lawyer-legislator said. "But much of the record has been supplied by secondhand sources and those espousing certain interpretation of the facts. The American people deserve better."

She added that "the most touching illustration of the need for this type of legislation" was a conversation she had had with a history teacher in her district. "The dilemma she faces in the classroom is no doubt repeated in thousands of schools and colleges across the country," she said. "Today's young people are losing confidence in their system of government after months on end of the Watergate trauma. These students still have questions for which their civics books do not have an answer.

"To some, inaction by the Congress would be complicity in its last act of cover-up," Mrs. Heckler told the committee. "Watergate must not be allowed to whimper into the history books without a complete accounting of the facts. The record must be available so that a future Watergate is prevented."

With those words ringing in his ears, Chairman Hungate made his request of the Ford White House for information, documents and tapes relevant to the pardoning of Nixon. Despite the official nature of the inquiry from a properly authorized committee of Congress, the Ford White House sent Hungate only copies of press conferences and White House legal briefings prepared by White House Counsel Philip Buchen. Some members of the committee considered this insulting, but Hungate kept his patience. This was as frustrating as dealing with the Nixon White House during the impeachment inquiry, and Hungate had hoped it would be different. A reasonably quick answer, questioning a few key witnesses, would mean he and the committee could button up the pardon inquiry and get back to other work.

When several committee members charged President Ford with "stonewalling" in the same manner as the Nixon White House, the President surprised the Judiciary Subcommittee and the Congress by announcing he would break precedent to appear in person to answer questions. Members were so eager to participate in this historic and unprecedented appearance of a president for questioning by a congressional committee that they accepted rules and a time frame totally unsatisfactory to anyone who was serious about obtaining the full truth.

Although Chairman Hungate set a properly serious tone in discussing the pardon, he did not require President Ford to testify under oath, which his past contradictory statement indicated should have been a minimum condition.

Hungate noted that the Paris newspaper *Le Monde* had commented: "No European republic invests its president with the right of pardon sweeping and irrevocable as that which Gerald Ford exercised in favor of Richard Nixon. In a sense, the royal pardon takes over from the executive privilege behind which the former President took refuge so long as a way of preventing Congress and the law courts from investigating his conduct."

But Hungate recalled the "personal friendship" existing between President Ford and his former colleagues in Congress, and applauded his "voluntary appearance."

"I am convinced that the issue of the pardon will not be behind us until the record of the pardon is complete," Hungate said to the full Judiciary Committee just prior to a mawkishly sentimental welcome to "our distinguished visitor" by Chairman Peter Rodino, an ex-officio member of every subcommittee.

The special rules adopted for the appearance of President Ford limited each committee member to five minutes, with no advance questioning of other White House witnesses in order to lay the groundwork for proper inquiry.

President Ford used the televised hearing as his forum for reiterating the reasons for the pardon, expanding only slightly on his conversations with General Alexander Haig on August 1 and August 2. But he did admit that, after being told of the existence of the incriminating June 23, 1972, White House tape, he had continued to assert that Richard Nixon was innocent.

"My travel schedule called for me to make appearances in Mississippi and Louisiana over Saturday, Sunday and part of Monday, August 3, 4 and 5," President Ford said. "In the previous eight months, I had repeatedly stated my opinion that the President would not be found guilty of any impeachable offense. Any change from my stated views, or even refusal to comment further, I feared, would lead in the press to conclusions that I now wanted to see the President resign to avoid an impeachment vote in the House and probably conviction in the Senate.

"For that reason, I remained firm in my answer to press questions during my trip and repeated my belief in the President's innocence of an impeachable offense," President Ford said to explain his political deceptions. "Not until I returned to Washington [on Monday, August 5] did I learn that President Nixon was to release the new evidence [White House tapes] late on Monday."

At the Cabinet meeting on Tuesday, August 6, Ford

said, he had "announced that I was making no recommendation to the President as to what he should do in the light of the new evidence. And I made no recommendation at the meeting or at any time after that.

"In summary, Mr. Chairman, I assure you that there never was at any time any agreement whatsoever concerning a pardon to Nixon if he were to resign and I were to become President," Ford said firmly, undoubtedly recognizing that many no longer believed him.

In that October 17, 1974, testimony President Ford minimized compassion for Nixon and the Nixon family, stressing that "the purpose was to change our national focus.

"I wanted to do all I could to shift our attention from the pursuit of a fallen president to the pursuit of the urgent needs of a rising nation," Ford declared, even though he had said at his press conference one month earlier that "the decision [pardon] has created more antagonism than I anticipated."

He was ignoring the opinions of Congressmen and Senators who believed the Nixon pardon was the most divisive action he could have taken.

Gerald Ford basked in the limelight in the hearing room of the Rayburn Building as he appeared before old friends and acquaintances in the royal role of President of the United States. He skillfully evaded direct answers to several Congressmen who asked about "equal justice under the law," and filibustered to consume as much of the minutes allowed each member as possible.

Only Congresswoman Elizabeth Holtzman pelted him directly with the devastatingly serious questions on many minds. Aware of Ford's ability to exhaust the time without giving direct answers, Holtzman fired a staccato series of the unanswered crucial questions on the pardon and assailed him with the "very dark suspicions that have been created in the public's mind."

"We must all confront the reality of these suspicions and the suspicions that were created by the circumstances of the pardon which you issued—the secrecy with which it was issued, and the reason for which it was issued which made people question whether or not, in fact, it was a deal."

"May I comment there?" President Ford interrupted. "I want to assure you, the members of the subcommittee, the members of Congress, and the American people, there was no deal, period, under no circumstances."

The self-serving denial did not carry the weight it would have carried two months earlier, and Holtzman ignored it as she rolled off a series of questions which she said should be answered if there was time.

"I think, from the mail I have received from all over the country as well as my own district, that the people want to understand how you can explain having pardoned Richard Nixon without specifying any of the crimes for which he was pardoned, and how you can explain having pardoned Richard Nixon without obtaining any acknowledgement of guilt from him.

"How do you explain your failure to consult the Attorney General of the United States with respect to the issuance of the pardon, even though in your confirmation hearings you had indicated that the Attorney General's opinion would be critical in any decision to pardon the former President?

"How can the extraordinary haste in which the pardon was decided on and the secrecy with which it was carried out be explained? How can you explain the fact that the pardon of Richard Nixon was accompanied by an agreement with respect to the tapes which in essence, in the public mind, hampered the Special Prosecutor's access to these materials and was done, also in the public's mind, in disregard of the public's right to know the full story about Richard Nixon's misconduct in office?

"In addition, the public, I think, wants an explanation of why Benton Becker [a Washington lawyer friend of Ford's] was used to represent the interests of the United States in negotiating a tapes agreement when, at that very time, he was under investigation by the United States for possible criminal charges.

"How, also, can you explain not having consulted Leon Jaworski, the Special Prosecutor, before approving the tapes agreement? I think, Mr. President, that these are only a few of the questions that have existed in the public's mind and unfortunately still remain unsolved."

She concluded that "suspicions have been raised that the reason for the pardon and the simultaneous tapes agreement was to insure that the tape recordings between yourself and Richard Nixon never came out in public. To alleviate this suspicion once and for all," she asked, "would you be willing to turn over to this subcommittee all tape recordings of conversations between yourself and Richard Nixon?"

"Those tapes, under an opinion of the Attorney General . . . belong to President Nixon," President Ford answered, evading the issue of whether he would be willing to turn them over to the subcommittee. "Those tapes will not be delivered to anybody until a satisfactory agreement is reached with the Special Prosecutor's office. We have held them because his office did request that, and as long as we have them held in our possession for the Special

Prosecutor's benefit, I see no way whatever that they can be destroyed."

Time ran out before Holtzman could press President Ford for a direct answer or explain that it was not likely that the House Judiciary Subcommittee would destroy any White House tapes.

Representative Lawrence J. Hogan, a Maryland Republican who had been extremely critical of Richard Nixon, seemed more anxious to win approval from the new President than to obtain information. He chided Representative Holtzman as "the gentlelady from New York" and said he was "frankly amazed at . . . her accusatory opening statement because . . . it is the usual, ordinary and routine procedure of this subcommittee, and the committee, to operate under the five-minute rule."

The Maryland Republican did not bother to inform the television audience that under normal circumstances the committee members have as many five-minute periods as they feel are necessary to get answers. He explained away her complaint that there was no questioning of other White House witnesses as preparation for President Ford's appearance with the comment that the idea of calling other witnesses was "rejected by the members of the subcommittee" because it was felt to be "totally inappropriate" since "the resolution of inquiry is directed to the President of the United States."

Neither Hogan nor any other members offered a logical explanation as to why the committee should not obtain as many documents and as much testimony as possible before questioning such a key witness as President Ford on a matter as grave as a charge of "a pardon deal."

Hogan fawned on President Ford, disregarding his inconsistent and deceitful statements at press conferences on the pardon, and praised him for his "openness and candor," before beginning a superficial questioning on the obvious artifice of using his five minutes.

"Now, Mr. President, I know that you followed very carefully the deliberations of this committees during the impeachment inquiry," Hogan started, with an assumption completely at odds with Ford's continued avowals of Nixon's innocence, "and I know you are also aware that this committee unanimously concluded that the President was guilty of an impeachable offense growing out of the obstruction of justice."

This opened the way for President Ford to use the House Judiciary Committee's judgment on Nixon's guilt while adroitly avoiding a personal judgment on Nixon. He answered, "The unanimous vote of the House Committee on the Judiciary, all thirty-eight members, certainly is very, very substantial evidence that the former President was guilty of an impeachable offense. There is no doubt in my mind that that recommendation of this full committee would have carried in the House, which would have been even more formidable as an indication of criminal activity, or, certainly, to be more specific, an impeachable offense."

On the subject of the criticism of Ford for not requiring a specific admission of guilt from Nixon before issuing the pardon, Hogan asked, "Do you not feel that the very acceptance of the pardon by the former President is tantamount to an admission of guilt on his part?"

"I do, sir," President Ford answered.

"So again, those who say that they would have preferred the former President admit his culpability before a pardon was issued are overlooking that fact?" Hogan phrased the leading question in another fashion, and Ford answered,

"The acceptance of a pardon, according to the legal authorities, and we have checked them out very carefully, does indicate that by the acceptance, the person who accepted it does, in effect, admit guilt."

Hogan ended his questions by thanking President Ford for "your candor and your openness and your cooperation with this coequal branch of government." Not a question was asked about the production of White House tapes of a Ford-Nixon conversation in the Oval Office or the Executive Office Building, or of telephone conversations that were assumed without question to be included in the tapes and in the custody of the General Services Administration.

Hogan's questioning was no worse than that of the other Republican members of Hungate's committee. Most of the Democrats were unwilling or unable to break his dodging the issue of the potentially embarrassing Ford-Nixon tapes. He did not deny their existence; he only raised legal questions to avoid the issue.

But neither Hogan nor anyone else followed up Holtzman's questions to insist on a direct answer from the President on whether he would make the recordings of all Nixon-Ford talks available to the subcommittee. But the questions would not fade, any more than Watergate burglary and bugging questions had faded in the two-year period between the break-in and the House Judiciary Committee votes to impeach Nixon.

Only Richard Nixon and Gerald Ford knew what might have been preserved on tape in the fall of 1972, when the Nixon White House enlisted the services of House Republican Leader Ford to block the hearings by Wright Patman's Banking and Currency Committee. From the vantage point of 1976, it is now obvious why President

Nixon knew the hearings must be stopped in order to keep the full Watergate story under wraps until after the 1972 election.

Possibly other insiders—H. R. Haldeman, John Ehrlichman or even John Dean—had intimate knowledge of Ford's full role. From the White House tapes already published, we know that Nixon directed Haldeman to assign Ehrlichman the task of involving Ford actively in killing Patman's investigation. Dean, as a coordinator of the Watergate cover-up in the White House, might have information or documents relative to Ford's handling of Patman.

From records now in the public domain, it is obvious that John Dean has a great deal more information about Ford's role than he has been questioned about in appearances before Senate and House committees and in federal court. Dean was not asked about any conversations he or others had with Gerald Ford on the aborting of the Patman committee hearings, because the emphasis was on Richard Nixon's activities in 1973 and 1974. An in-depth probe of Ford's role would only have delayed action on Nixon's crime.

Available White House transcripts indicate that the crucial period for Ford-Nixon conversations, or other Oval Office conversations relative to Ford's activity, occurred between September 15 and election day, November 7, 1972. Congressional anger over the Nixon pardon resulted in special legislation to assure preservation of the Nixon tapes, and it is likely that the information contained in them will be accessible to future historians, if not to contemporary newsmen and authors.

Without the special legislation, the Ford Administration would have complied with the agreement to give the tapes to Nixon, and he would have been free to destroy them after September 1, 1979. The arrangement between Nixon and Arthur F. Sampson of the General Services Administration was made public by President Ford in the announcement of the Nixon pardon. Sampson, with the approval of the Ford White House and the Justice Department, had agreed that the tapes and related papers were the property of Richard Nixon, and as such would be transferred to a government storage facility about ten miles from San Clemente, Nixon's California residence. There Nixon would have control over access but would agree not to withdraw the original papers or tapes unless they were subpoenaed, although he could copy any of the papers he wished until September 1, 1979.

On September 1, 1979, the tapes would become government property, but Sampson had agreed that he, or his successor, would then destroy any tape which Nixon wished destroyed. Nixon would continue to have access to any existing tapes for an additional five years, or until September 1, 1984. On that date, or earlier, should Nixon die, all remaining tapes would be destroyed.

Such explicit authority for a former president to destroy records of his administration was highly unusual. In his letter of agreement Nixon said he would order destruction if necessary "to guard against the tapes being used to injure, embarrass or harass any person."

The information on the White House tapes bestowed great power on the person with control, which could be used to blackmail anyone in public life who could be embarrassed by the contents of those tapes. Congress decided wisely not to entrust a man with Mr. Nixon's track record with that control, and a three-man United States Appeals

Court panel rejected Nixon's contention that it was an unconstitutional seizure of his property.

In upholding the order of United States District Judge Charles R. Richey to dismiss Nixon's complaint as being "without merit," the special three-judge panel said there was justification for the Congress to take special action with regard to the Nixon papers and tapes.

"The court finds nothing in the separation of powers doctrine to support [Nixon's] contention that the legislature may not pass a statute in any way touching upon the prerogatives of the executive," the 105-page decision ruling said.

The ruling, written by Appeals Court Judge Carl McGowan, further stated: "The court finds . . . that Congress has ample reason to mandate screening by government archivists rather than control by Mr. Nixon, who lacks their expertise and disinterestedness."

The panel, including Appeals Court Judge Edward A. Tamm and United States District Judge Aubrey E. Robinson, Jr., declared that the Congress could legitimately consider Nixon to be less likely than his immediate predecessors or successors to dispose of the material responsibly.

While any former president wants his administration to be viewed in the best light, there is understandably a normal risk in the selection of materials to accomplish this. The court said this risk "might rationally be thought by Congress to be considerably magnified by reference to the circumstances surrounding Mr. Nixon's departure from office.

"The temptation to distort or destroy the historical record might be thought by Congress to be less resistible in the event that the material provided some foundation for allegation that misconduct took place," the Court of Appeals noted in words which could apply to President Ford or anyone who might conceivably be embarrassed by conversations preserved on the Nixon White House tapes.

That Court of Appeals decision, handed down on January 7, 1976, gave some assurance that eventually all or most of the politically relevant White House tapes will become public. However, Nixon's lawyer, Herbert J. Miller, said he would take an appeal to the United States Supreme Court, which will delay further revelations until months after the 1976 presidential election. Unless more information comes into the public domain through court depositions from White House lawyers, the mystery will remain intact with regard to Ford's full role in stopping the Patman probe, which Nixon believed so vital to the Watergate cover-up.

10. Fronting for Flanigan

THE NIXON heritage continued to plague the White House as President Ford's nomination of Peter M. Flanigan in mid-September 1974 as United States Ambassador to Spain touched off a bitter battle with Senator Thomas Eagleton and did additional damage to Ford's already-eroded image for rectitude. It was difficult to determine whether the Ford Administration battled for the Flanigan nomination for weeks because of President Ford's personal desire to send the New York millionaire fund raiser to Madrid or because Donald Rumsfeld wanted to accommodate Flanigan, who had been a colleague in the Nixon White House.

Flanigan, as Special Assistant to President Nixon, had been involved in a large number of controversial actions in Watergate-related matters. Some testimony by Herbert Kalmbach, Nixon's personal lawyer and a major Nixon fund raiser, implicated Flanigan in an attempt to "sell" an ambassadorship to Dr. Ruth Farkas, a wealthy New Hampshire contributor to the 1972 Nixon re-election campaign.

Flanigan had also been subjected to sharp congressional charges of Treasury Department favoritism in the licensing of an oil tanker Flanigan owned to be used on lucrative runs between Alaska and the West Coast. In addition, he had been under fire in the heavy controversy over alleged White House involvement in the ITT antitrust suits.

Many Republicans were surprised and shocked when President Ford nominated Flanigan, because the requirements for Senate confirmation would give the Democrats an open opportunity to comb over aspects of Watergate scandals in the middle of the 1974 congressional campaigns. Ford was courting additional trouble while the Nixon pardon issue still flamed.

Why did Flanigan, a multimillionaire New York investment banker, want the nomination? And, if Flanigan did want it, why would Jerry Ford take such a controversial step during an election campaign?

Almost immediately, Senator Eagleton requested that President Ford withdraw the nomination and "exorcise the Nixonian influence from his administration.

"If President Ford wants to divorce his administration from Watergate and all its nefarious manifestations, he will immediately withdraw Mr. Flanigan's nomination," Senator Eagleton told the Senate on September 25, 1974.

Eagleton declared that the nomination of Nixon's "Mr. Fixit" was "an insult to the Senate and an affront to the American people," recalling Kalmbach's testimony implicating Flanigan in the attempt to "sell" the ambassadorship to Dr. Farkas.

Senator Eagleton reminded the Senate that Ford had "sounded a call for integrity and openness in government."

"It was a refreshing change after five years of corruption and secrecy," Eagleton said. "But rhetoric alone will not suffice to divorce President Ford from the mentality and attitude of the Nixon White House. The President can make a clean break with the Watergate albatross only by matching his words with his deeds."

He recalled "the President's unfortunate and premature pardon of Mr. Nixon" and added that the "negative influence is best exemplified by the blanket endorsement of nominations made by President Nixon and the appointment of a number of former Nixon aides to important government posts.

"Nowhere is this insensitivity to the nation's post-Watergate temperament more apparent" than in the nomination of Flanigan as Ambassador, he continued.

"The President could perpetrate no more cruel hoax, whether intentional or not, than to nominate a man as American Ambassador who has been accused under oath of participating on behalf of Richard Nixon in the illegal sale of an ambassadorial position," Senator Eagleton told the Senate.

He then explained the seriousness of Kalmbach's testimony before the House Judiciary Committee during its impeachment inquiry, in which Kalmbach had said he was told by Flanigan to contact Dr. Farkas concerning an ambassadorial assignment to Costa Rica.

"According to Kalmbach, Flanigan told him, 'She is interested in giving $250,000 for Costa Rica.' "

Then Eagleton quoted further from Kalmbach's testimony:

"It is clear in my understanding of that conversation [with Flanigan] . . . that she would contribute $250,000 to the President's campaign, and in return for that $250,000 she would be appointed Ambassador to Costa Rica."

Eagleton declared that "Mr. Kalmbach acted on that

understanding, and in August 1971 he offered Dr. Farkas Costa Rica for $250,000."

Senator Eagleton cited other evidentiary documents presented to the House Judiciary Committee confirming the seamy practice of selling ambassadorships. He cited a memorandum from Gordon Strachan, an assistant to White House Chief of Staff H. R. Haldeman, that "discussed the necessity to inform two other purchasers that commitment to give them European posts could not be met."

"The Senate Watergate Committee was pointing to the illegality of such commitment, and Mr. Haldeman had decided that their donations would have to be returned," Eagleton said, but quoted from Strachan's memorandum to Haldeman:

"The only commitment that Kalmbach is aware of at this time is Farcas [sic] for Costa Rica."

Senator Eagleton said that those documents made it seem "clear that Mr. Kalmbach made that illegal commitment to sell an ambassadorship on the authority of Mr. Flanigan."

He noted that Kalmbach had entered a plea of guilty to a charge of illegally offering an ambassadorship to Mr. J. Fife Symington in exchange for a campaign contribution and was serving a federal prison term.

"Mr. Peter Flanigan, on the other hand, has now been nominated by President Ford as Ambassador to Spain," Senator Eagleton told the Senate, and, to point up the contrast, asked the rhetorical question: "I wonder what Mr. Kalmbach thinks of that."

Senator Eagleton said the charges against Flanigan were so grave that it would be "inappropriate" for the Senate Foreign Relations Committee even to consider his nomination at this time.

"I think it is far more appropriate that the Justice Department investigate whether he was guilty of participating in illegal activity," Senator Eagleton said, and added that Flanigan's role in the Dr. Farkas nomination "is not an isolated case."

"He established a track record of highly questionable behavior during his years as a Nixon aide," Eagleton declared.

Eagleton also detailed Flanigan's "highly questionable" behavior in the ITT affair, in which he admitted having hired Richard Ramsden, a friend and former employee of his former firm of Dillon, Read & Co., to "advise" the head of the Antitrust Division, Assistant Attorney General Richard McLaren, in the ITT merger case.

The Missouri Senator told the Senate that the Justice Department, in deciding to abandon the prosecution of ITT, had acted on Ramsden's advice and that the decision had taken place in the same time frame that ITT offered $400,000 to subsidize the Republican National Convention.

"Mr. Flanigan had no statutory authority to involve himself in the ITT suit, but, as was his custom, when big business was involved, he did intervene to the advantage of his client, ITT," Senator Eagleton declared.

He then cited certain additional serious allegations against Flanigan that he said the Senate Foreign Relations Committee should investigate thoroughly and then question Flanigan about under oath. Among them were the following:

"First. Forcing the resignation of CAB board member Robert Murphy, after Murphy ruled against American Airlines, which company had illegally given $55,000 to President Nixon's re-election campaign.

"Second. Interfering with the independence of the Corporation for Public Broadcasting by attempting to influence a crucial vote by the board.

"Third. Protecting businesses against adverse antipollution rulings by the Environmental Protection Agency.

"Fourth. Influencing the Postal Service to sell $250 million in bonds to Wall Street underwriters rather than to the United States Treasury. One of the underwriters involved, I hasten to add, was Dillon, Read & Co., Mr. Flanigan's former employer.

"Fifth. Protecting the oil industry by stopping a Cabinet-level task force report recommending that oil import quotas be scrapped.

"Sixth. Using his position to obtain a Treasury Department exemption so that a foreign tanker owned by one Peter Flanigan could engage in domestic shipping. This exemption would have increased the value of Flanigan's company by $6 million."

Flanigan had issued denials of improper intervention in all of these cases, but in each instance testimony or documents, or both, existed which contradicted Flanigan to some degree.

Concerning the sale of the ambassadorship to Dr. Farkas, Flanigan's denial was directly at odds with Kalmbach's detailed testimony under oath before the House Judiciary Committee as well as with White House memorandums.

On October 2, Senator Eagleton reiterated his charges before Chairman J. William Fulbright and the members of the Senate Foreign Relations Committee. This time he went into further detail, added several new counts, and declared that questions of whether Flanigan was involved in impropriety could not be answered until the committee had conducted a full investigation, which would include questioning of Kalmbach, Stans, Haldeman, Ehrlichman and Mitchell.

Since Haldeman, Ehrlichman and Mitchell were then on trial before United States District Judge John J. Sirica in the Watergate cover-up case, Eagleton said that action on the Flanigan nomination would have to be postponed until that trial was concluded.

He declared that to approve the Flanigan nomination without such an exhaustive investigation "would be to ignore the existence and lessons of Watergate.

"To do such would demean the post of United States Ambassador. To do such would demean the Senate of the United States. To do such would demean the citizens of the United States."

Flanigan sat silently in the rear of the hearing room as Eagleton spelled out the indictment against him and of the Ford Administration for having nominated him.

When called to testify, Flanigan acknowledged that he had singled out Dr. Farkas as a wealthy New Hampshire businesswoman who would be "a good prospect for solicitation" for political funds by Herbert Kalmbach.

But the well-poised Flanigan cooly denied he had ever bartered ambassadorships for contributions during his five-year tenure as a Special Assistant to President Nixon.

He denied specifically having a conversation with Kalmbach in which he purportedly had said, "Herb, we would like to have you contact a Dr. Ruth Farkas in New York. She is interested in giving $250,000 for Costa Rica."

Kalmbach had testified that he met Dr. Farkas in New York by ararngement with New Hampshire Congressman Louis C. Wyman and that he had discussed the appointment with her. According to Kalmbach, Dr. Farkas objected with these words: "I am interested in Europe, I think, and isn't $250,000 an awful lot of money for Costa Rica?"

A few months later Dr. Farkas increased her contribution to $300,000 and eventually was appointed Ambassador to Luxembourg.

Flanigan told the Senate Foreign Relations Committee he was instrumental in rejecting large financial contributions from J. Fife Symington and Vincent de Rouet, which had been offered in exchange for promises of European ambassadorial posts.

Eagleton said that the instructions for Kalmbach to return the money to Symington and de Rouet took place when the Special Watergate Prosecutor and the Senate Watergate Committee started pointing out the illegality of selling ambassadorships.

"It's Kalmbach versus Flanigan," he explained, pinpointing the issue. "It's Kalmbach who is in the penitentiary for selling ambassadorships. It's Flanigan who is going to the posh coast of Spain. This is not equal justice under the law."

Flanigan explained his involvement in obtaining Richard Ramsden for expert advice on the ITT matter. He said he entered the picture after President Nixon called Attorney General Richard Kleindienst and ordered him to drop the ITT antitrust appeal. Flanigan declared that he contacted Ramsden only because "McLaren didn't know where to find him."

"I submit that I see nothing wrong with one member of the executive asking another to help get a job done," Flanigan said.

Flanigan insisted he had not intervened at the Treasury Department to obtain the waiver of the Jones Act to permit the Liberian ship *Sansinena* to transport oil from

Alaska to the West Coast. He explained that he had trans-ferred his stock in the tanker corporation to his father, and his father had sold the stock a few days prior to the date when the Treasury Department issued the waivers that would have meant more than $5 million in windfall profits because of the lucrative domestic commerce.

He declared he was "in no way involved" in a Postal Service decision to sell the $250 million bond issue through private underwriters, including his former firm, Dillon, Read & Company.

Both Eagleton and Flanigan cited letters from Special Prosecutor Leon Jaworski for the purpose of making op-posite points. Flanigan and the White House quoted the part of a Jaworski letter that said the Special Prosecutor had advised the White House "that based on the evidence now in this office, no charge was contemplated against Mr. Flanigan."

Jaworski's letter to Eagleton had also said, "We did point out that the appropriate person with the White House may wish to consider the testimony concerning Mr. Flanigan by Mr. Herbert Kalmbach . . . relating to the ambassadorial appointment of Mrs. Ruth Farkas."

Flanigan cited the Jaworski letter to the White House as evidence that he had been cleared of any connection with the then ongoing investigation of White House am-bassadorial and financial dealings with Dr. Farkas.

Senate Republican Leader Hugh Scott, a member of the committee, supported Flanigan by relating that he had talked with Jaworski on the Flanigan nomination and was told, "We know the whole story. He is not under in-vestigation. He [Flanigan] is not a target."

Senator Eagleton cited the same response as indicating that the Dr. Farkas investigation was not completed, and that Jaworski was pointing out the testimony as indicative of a problem area even though no criminal case could be made against Flanigan.

Eagleton countered Scott's attempted gloss of the problem when he returned to the witness table for concluding arguments after Flanigan's testimony.

"And I am sorry that Senator Scott has departed," he said, "because I will be more specific. In response to his allegation that no investigation is now going forward before Leon Jaworski with respect to any other higher-ups, Senator Scott, I am sorry, Senator Scott, but you are absolutely wrong, because there is an investigation pending before Mr. Jaworski with respect to Maurice Stans, and records have been subpoenaed. And Mr. Maurice Stans tried to avoid the production of these records, until recently he was compelled to produce a whole series of records on which Mr. Stans pleaded executive privilege. And [there] still is outstanding before Federal Judge Hart a subpoena for further records pertaining to Stans, how he raised his money, what promises were given in return for that money, and who did his bidding.

"So, I say to you, Mr. Chairman, this case is very, very much alive. There is nothing that is dormant about this from the Special Prosecutor's office insofar as the fund-raising activities of 1971 and 1972 and the payoffs that were promised, whether for favoritism in terms of who might be appointed as Ambassador, whether it was a banana Republic if the price was right, or if the price was better your [sic] get Luxembourg.

"So, I have sat here, Mr. Chairman, with dismay and concern listening to the testimony of Mr. Flanigan. And I am no more convinced as to his nonparticipation in these affairs than I was when the day started."

A day after the Flanigan-Eagleton confrontation, Ron Nessen, White House press secretary, said that President Ford "stands by" his recommendation of Flanigan as Ambassador to Spain.

On October 8, Senator Robert Byrd announced his intention to let the Flanigan nomination remain standing during the thirty-three-day recess for the 1974 elections. Nominations pending during any recess of more than thirty days, under Senate rules, expire unless an exception is made by unanimous consent.

Senator Byrd, a member of the Senate Judiciary Committee and a primary inquisitor of Flanigan on the ITT matter, had commented that Flanigan's involvement in that matter "leads me to the inescapable conclusion that Mr. Flanigan is not a suitable man . . . to represent the United States as an Ambassador."

He declared that the intervention by Flanigan "was essential in the changing of the Justice Department's position on the ITT case; that position was allegedly changed due to ITT's offer of $400,000 to the Republican National Committee site in 1972. . . ."

On October 9, the Senate Foreign Relations Committee agreed unanimously to postpone action on the Flanigan nomination until after further testimony and investigation. With Assistant Democratic Leader Byrd poised to oppose unanimous consent to the nomination standing for more than thirty days, it was headed for a procedural graveyard.

While Ford could revive the Flanigan nomination, the New York investment banker, despite his denials, was in deep trouble on the case made against him. No one expected President Ford to resubmit the nomination after the election recess.

On November 16, 1974, President Ford and Flanigan agreed that both of them were losing in the battle in the Senate Foreign Relations Committee and that a fight with the tenacious Senator Eagleton, supported by an even more tenacious Senator Byrd, was futile. Senate Republican Leader Scott could finagle many a canny swap with his political horse trading, but neither Eagleton nor Byrd was in a trading mood.

In his letter asking President Ford not to resubmit his name as the nominee for Ambassador to Spain, Flanigan stated the long delay was not "in the best interest of your relations with the Congress nor the country's relations with Spain."

The Republican millionaire investment broker blamed his troubles on "the distortions" of the record of his involvement in the selling of ambassadorships. He said that the problem of delays persisted "though the false charges and insinuations have already been answered.

"It had been my belief that five years as Assistant to the President and Director of the Council on International Economic Policy provided a record which would command prompt Senate support," he said, ignoring the blemishes the ITT affair and the Watergate investigations had left on that record.

"I will never forget the continued strong support given to me by you and Secretary Kissinger," Flanigan wrote. "My purpose in coming to Washington has been to serve the President—not to burden him. Given the current political climate, I can best do this by asking that you not resubmit my nomination."

In his response, President Ford lent his name to approval of Flanigan's record by stating his "reluctance and deep regret" in agreeing not to resubmit the Flanigan nomination and create another political brawl with the Democrats. "In doing so, I want to assure you once again of my confidence in you and my admiration for your abilities," the President wrote.

President Ford said that in his opinion Flanigan had served the nation "with the highest distinction. . . . You can be justly proud of the critical role you played to sharpen our country's vital trade and economic policies under the most challenging circumstances.

"You deserve the heartfelt thanks of your fellow citizens, and I want to take this opportunity to express my own lasting gratitude," was President Ford's lavish praise to the man whose name was synonymous with the White House tampering on the ITT affair, and the high pressure and high level financing of Richard Nixon's campaigns.

And Ford further lauded Flanigan's offer to continue in public service and pledged that he would not hesitate to take advantage of his talent at some future time. He acclaimed Flanigan's "selfless reasons" for asking that his name be withdrawn, allowing the impression to remain that Leon Jaworski had given him a clean bill of health on the sale of the ambassadorship.

In fact, Jaworski had simply said that there were no plans to prosecute Flanigan at the time in connection with the sale of ambassadorships. The Special Prosecutor's letter fell far short of absolving Flanigan in its statement that "the White House may wish to consider the testimony concerning Mr. Flanigan by Mr. Kalmbach," on the Ruth Farkas matter.

President Ford again demonstrated a lack of ethical sensitivity in not realizing the inherent problems in the

Flanigan nomination, and a lack of political sensitivity in making ITT and Watergate live issues for his administration and the Republican congressional candidates in 1974 and for himself in 1976.

11. Finessing the Farm Vote

As House Republican Leader, Gerald R. Ford had followed the lead of the White House on farm issues in the Eisenhower and Nixon administrations and supported three unpopular Republican Secretaries of Agriculture—Ezra Taft Benson, Clifford Hardin and Earl Butz. It was partisan Republican politics, and had never created problems in his own Michigan congressional district dominated by the manufacturing city of Grand Rapids. From 1955 on, Ford had consistently voted against farm-support legislation.

Had he not granted Richard Nixon a pardon, President Ford would have had fewer difficulties with specific domestic issues. Midwestern farmers, like other voting blocks, were so relieved to have an honest president in the White House that they would have sacrificed to a certain extent their own economic self-interest, for a while, at least. But, after the Nixon pardon, proving himself on farm issues was the only way Ford could be helpful in congressional races in the farm belt.

When Ford took office, Congressmen representing farming states knew American agriculture was in trouble. Spiraling inflation and serious drought conditions forced feed costs up, but farmer and rancher producers of meat, eggs and dairy products were receiving less than the cost of production.

Democratic Senator Herman E. Talmadge, of Georgia, Chairman of the Senate Agriculture Committee, declared that "serious shortfalls in corn and other feed grains could have a severe impact on the ability of meat, egg and dairy producers to stay in business."

Representative William Scherle, a Republican farmer-Congressman, signaled the White House that President Ford had to assure farmers he would support programs guaranteeing at least the cost of production.

August corn-production figures released by the Agriculture Department predicted a drop of 12 percent from 1973, indicating that inflation production costs faced by the livestock industry in 1974 could be even worse in 1975.

As the protests against low beef prices increased, President Ford scheduled a speaking trip across the Midwest to assure the farmers and ranchers the federal government would help despite past Ford votes against farm programs. The trip was also to promote Republican candidates for the Senate and House in Missouri, Kansas, Nebraska, Iowa and South Dakota.

On October 15, President Ford was speaking in Kansas City, Missouri, at the national convention of the Future Farmers of America on the need for citizen mobilization to fight inflation. President Ford promised "every farmer the fuel and fertilizer he needs to do the job, plus a fair return for his crop." The President received wild applause, although he failed to spell out what he meant by the "fair return" guarantee.

The next day in Lincoln, Nebraska, Sioux Falls, South Dakota, and Indianapolis, Indiana, he pledged the farm communities "an adequate return and a fair profit for their time, land, investment and labor" if they would increase production of grain and meat products in the fight against inflation. Again he neglected to spell out details, and inquiry during the next few days at the White House and the Agriculture Department revealed that no farm plan had yet been completed but that President Ford had just inserted the phrases in his speech because farm-state Republicans had demanded some assurance that farmers would receive "cost of production" if they were to try to attain maximum production to comply with Ford's request to fight inflation.

President Ford deplored the "wasteful protest" of members of the National Farmers Organization who had slaughtered and buried calves in Wisconsin the previous day to dramatize the impossibility of coping with high feed costs and low beef prices.

In both Lincoln and Sioux Falls, the President expressed deep concern for the "tremendous cost-price squeeze in which America's dairymen find themselves." He told the farm communities that the previous Friday he had met with representatives of the dairy farmers and was "very sympathetic with their problem."

Because of that concern, he promised on October 16 that "no action will be taken to change the present system of dairy import quotas without a thorough review of market conditions and a full opportunity for our dairy producers to be heard at that time." This was indeed good news for the dairy producers who had been told that a decision had been made to increase the dairy import quotas.

President Ford praised the productivity of the American farmer and said he was "convinced that over the long haul the American farmers can compete against any farm producers in the world.

"If all aspects of our economy functioned with the efficiency and almost miraculous output of the American farmer, I am convinced that inflation would be a problem of much smaller proportions," Ford told the cheering crowds.

In Des Moines, Iowa, on October 25, President Ford again engaged in vague rhetoric to convince the farmers, whose corn and soybean crops were stunted by drought and destroyed by early frosts, that he shared their concern.

He declared that urbanization of America had downplayed the role of the farmer, "but recent problems have refocused national attention on the farmer as one of our greatest assets, an asset we are all proud of."

"This is the time we should be expanding farming in America," the President declared. "Let us encourage our young people to remain on the farms and others to return to them. Americans can no longer expect the farmer to sacrifice so that others can live well," he said in his best frank, open manner, to an audience anxious to hear what he was telling them.

"All Americans now realize that we are all in this problem together," he said, and the farmers in the audience had no difficulty accepting that thesis. "The farmer should not be called upon to make an extra sacrifice. It must be shared by all.

"The American farmer, we know, can be relied upon

for the strength of the community. The American farmer can outplant, outgrow and outmarket any farmer—I don't care what nation he's from," the President said, and his audience applauded and nodded agreement. "If the farmer gets a fair shake, the American farmer can feed not only the people of the United States but human beings from all over the world. In the immediate years ahead, American agriculture will be our greatest asset in the world trade market."

President Ford completed his major farm speech without ever telling, even vaguely, what farm programs he would propose. He left the heads of the four principal farm organizations puzzling over what he had in mind.

All four leaders doubted he had a farm program and described Ford's speech as "just campaign rhetoric." Officials of three of the organizations—the National Farmers Union (NFU), the National Grange and the National Farmers Organization (NFO)—said that Ford probably would not remember his promises after the election, although they hoped he would suggest legislation to guarantee cost of production for farmers.

But William J. Kuhfuss, President of the American Farm Bureau Federation, said he was afraid President Ford might really mean what he was saying and embroil the government in tampering with the free play of the farm markets and the free enterprise system.

The Farm Bureau opposed the "target price" farm-support legislation on the books in the fall of 1974 and very strenuously opposed the increases in those target prices proposed by Senator Hubert Humphrey, the Minnesota Democrat, and others.

Representatives of the other three major farm organizations—the NFU, Grange and NFO—favored increases in the "outrageously low" target price then pegged at $1.38 a bushel for corn, $2.05 a bushel for wheat and 38 cents a pound for cotton because of sharp increases in fuel, fertilizer and labor costs.

The legislation Humphrey had introduced in May 1974 to give farmers cost of production assurances pegged corn at $2 a bushel, wheat at $3 a bushel and cotton at 50 cents a pound.

Representatives of the NFU, NFO and Grange said that Humphrey legislation to increase "target prices" would essentially provide cost of production prices for three basic agricultural products, although it would leave soybeans and other feed grains largely uncovered.

Roger G. Lewis, National Secretary of the National Farmers Union, said he believed Ford would "have a hard time backing away from his promises," though this would entail administration support of measures comparable to the Humphrey legislation.

"I don't see how anyone who has made those statements in a prepared speech can back away from support of the higher target prices in the Humphrey bill or can refuse to go along with making the escalation clause [on increased costs] applicable to the 1975 crop year," Lewis said.

However, after the election, when the Democratic Congress had passed milk-price-support legislation requiring supports at not less than 85 percent of parity, Gerald Ford vetoed the bill on the advice of Agriculture Secretary Earl Butz. He declared the bill would require "an immediate increase of $1.12 per hundredweight in support price for milk, to a record high of $7.69." He stated that the initial step would increase fluid milk prices to consumers by about 6 cents per half gallon.

"These significantly higher prices would be inconsistent

with the Administration's continued and concerted efforts to combat inflation and its serious effects on the nation's economy," Ford said. "Moreover, such prices would ultimately be damaging to the dairy industry and milk producers.

"A dairy farmer cannot be well served by government action that prices his product out of the market," Ford said. "It also would be detrimental, since the government would be required to buy the large surpluses of manufactured dairy products which this legislation would generate. This would cost taxpayers more than $400 million during the life of the bill. It is clearly in the best interest of producers, consumers, taxpayers and the government that this legislation not be signed into law."

As far as the dairy farmers were concerned, Ford's veto of the milk legislation did not square with his campaign promise of "an adequate return and a fair profit on their time, land, investment and labor." But, for the man who had been able to exonerate Nixon, it was no strain to declare in this case that he had promised no more than to take another look at the problems of the dairy farmer.

On April 22, Congress cleared for President Ford's signature an emergency farm bill to provide a one-year increase in farm price supports and income guarantees. The Ford Administration, then the President personally, had asked for all-out farm production as an essential step in the battle against inflation, and the farm legislators wanted laws enacted that would assure the cost of production on cotton, wheat, corn and other feed grains by increases in the target prices.

The legislation set the target price on cotton at 45 cents per pound—6 cents above the figures in the Humphrey bill. The bill cleared for Ford's signature boosted the target price on corn to $2.25 a bushel—20 cents above the Humphrey bill. And wheat was to be pegged at a target of $3.10 per bushel—10 cents above the Humphrey bill. It also included a mandatory government loan program for soybeans for the first time, which was estimated at about $3.94 per bushel.

The bill included another try at forcing Secretary Butz to boost milk price supports to not less than 80 percent of parity, softening by 5 percent the bill Ford had vetoed in January.

On April 17, 1975, the Senate passed the Emergency Farm Bill by a voice vote, and five days later the House passed the same measure in the face of Butz' threat of a presidential veto. The House vote was 248 to 166, which was 28 votes short of the two-thirds majority needed if President Ford followed the advice of his Secretary of Agriculture.

The Senate-House conference on the emergency farm-support legislation had pared it down from a three-year to a one-year program in the hopes President Ford might accept it, and they had reduced all of the higher support levels in the Senate version.

In seeking to contradict the Administration's contentions that the bill would result in increased costs to the consumer, Chairman Talmadge commented:

"We have done everything within our power to trim the potential cost of the bill and to avoid a presidential veto. The idea that this legislation will be a burden for consumers ignores what the cost will be if we do not have adequate production. . . . If the market functions efficiently, we would deliver more products in 1975 at less cost to consumers than with current prices."

He accused the Agriculture Department of using "scare

tactics in estimating costs." "They start with a claim that the cost could exceed $19 billion, compared to $210 million by the committee," Talmadge said.

Representative Thomas S. Foley (Democrat, Washington), Chairman of the House Agriculture Committee, also challenged the exaggerated cost figures. He observed that the Administration first estimated that the dairy-support provisions would cost consumers 6 cents a gallon on milk, but later dropped it to an increase of 1 cent a gallon. And Phil Burton (Democrat, California), Chairman of the Democratic Caucus, predicted that if the bill were not enacted, prices to consumers in the cities "are going to go up, rather than down."

While Ford didn't keep his 1974 campaign promises to give farmers "an adequate return and a fair profit on their time, land, investment and labor," he kept his promise to Agriculture Secretary Butz to veto the farm-support bill. Ford's whole record in the House indicated he would have voted against the farm program, so the veto was not out of character.

On May 1, President Ford declared that "although the aim of this [farm] bill is laudable, its result would be costly not only to consumers and taxpayers but to American farmers in the long run." He declared that in his view the bill "would damage our international market position, which is so essential to American agriculture's long-term interests."

Ford's rationale for abandoning his October campaign promises was that approval "would not be in the public interest," because it included unspecified provisions that surpassed the line against "excesses" he had drawn in a March 29, 1975, speech. "I promised all Americans that, except where national security interests, energy requirements or urgent humanitarian needs were involved, I would act to hold our fiscal year 1976 deficit to no more than $60 billion," Ford said.

The President warned that new spending programs the Congress was considering could easily raise the Federal deficit "to an intolerable level of $100 billion."

"This must not happen," Ford said, and he specified the farm target-price boosts as "an example of increased nonessential spending" that could add an estimated $1.8 billion to the Federal deficit. "Approval of this bill would undermine the successful market-oriented farm policy adopted by this Administration and the Congress," Ford said.

"Prospects for farmers, it is true, are not as bright this year as in the recent past," the President added, acknowledging the economic squeeze that farmers were complaining about. "Farm production costs have been pushed upward by the same inflationary pressures that affect other industries. Demand for certain farm products has simultaneously slackened because of the recession. Prices paid by farmers are currently 11 percent above year-ago levels. In contrast, the index of prices received by farmers is now 7 percent below levels of a year ago.

"The Administration recognizes that some farmers have experienced financial difficulties due to this cost-price squeeze," President Ford continued, and conceded that a "number of positive steps to assist farmers" fell far short of the pledges in his 1974 farm speeches.

It was true, Ford hadn't promised any specific level, but he had recognized the cost-price squeeze and had vowed to help them get "a fair profit."

Then the President praised the "American farmers [who]," he said, "have responded magnificently during the past several years to produce food and fiber for this nation and the world."

"This has made agriculture our leading source of foreign exchange," he added. "This year, despite very trying circumstances, most farmers are again seeking full production.

"They have my support for a vigorous export policy for their products," the President said, extending his promises. "I recognize that agricultural exports have been restrained [by export controls] twice in the past two years. We have now eliminated all restrictions on exports, and we are determined to do everything possible to avoid imposing them again. Our farm products must have unfettered access to world markets."

This assertion not to impose export controls in the foreseeable future, endorsed by a firm resolve not to interfere with international grain sales, assuaged a doubting Congress. "This Administration is determined to act in support of the American farmer and his best interests," Ford said. "It will not act to distort his market."

Trusting his affirmation not to impose export controls, the 94th Congress sustained Ford's veto. The vote was 245 to 182—40 short of the two-thirds majority needed to override—and the first time the 94th Congress had failed in an attempt to override one of Ford's vetoes. The Administration was jubilant over its great victory in restricting the size of the federal deficit. But it defeated farm-belt legislators' attempts to raise price supports for the 1975 crops of wheat, cotton, corn and other feed grain and to provide for quarterly adjustments in dairy price supports.

Supporters of the legislation protested that President Ford and Butz had misrepresented the federal deficit, but Ford ignored the substantial gap between his figures and

those of the Agriculture Committee. He commended the
House for acting "in the best interests of the economy, of
the consumer and of the farmers themselves." He admon-
ished the backers of the bill that it would have refired inflation and "set back the recent progress made in freeing
farmers from federal controls."

That seemed to reiterate his pledge of avoiding export
controls, and he had promised in his veto message to review the farm price situation and raise loan rates for wheat,
corn and soybeans under the authority of the 1973 farm
act should there be further deterioration.

But President Ford found it impossible to adhere to his
oft-stated pledge to keep international grain trading free of
governmental interference. In July, rumors of impending
Soviet grain sales caused commodity prices to jump, but
the high hopes of farmers were dashed when Secretary
Butz—responding to White House pressure—established on
August 3 a "hold" on further sales to the Soviet Union.
Consumer groups and labor union groups feared mount-
ing farm prices would send food prices skyrocketing.

The initial restraints, which resulted from poor corn
conditions in the area west of the Mississippi, were meant
to be temporary. Butz announced that all grain companies
had been asked, and had voluntarily agreed, to report any
potentially large export sales before negotiations began.
Originally, this informal embargo was to be lifted after
the August 11 crop report was announced by the Department of Agriculture.

However, it was extended on a week-to-week basis because of a fear that continuing drought would further cut
the corn crop, and on August 18 the embargo became
entangled in a labor dispute. Longshoremen in Houston,
Texas, refused to load grain destined for the Soviet Union,

the boycott being supported by AFL-CIO President George Meany. The powerful labor leader declared that shipments would be halted "indefinitely" to "protect the American consumer and the American shipping industry" until the Ford Administration formulated acceptable grain policies toward the Soviet Union.

While Meany nobly claimed that his interest lay in saving the consumer from price boosts, his critics, including Senator George McGovern, alleged that the prime motivation was the intention of the maritime union to negotiate a more favorable freight-rate agreement with the Soviets so that greater amounts of grain would be carried in American ships. McGovern accused Meany of blackmailing the Administration, and wheat exporters and some farm groups charged that shipping more grain in American bottoms would increase consumer prices, since the American taxpayers subsidized U.S. shipping.

Ford announced on September 9 that he would negotiate a new long-term grain agreement with the Soviet Union after Meany agreed that the maritime union would suspend its boycott for one month. It meant the embargo would continue until at least mid-October, and all of the farm organizations viewed it as appeasement of labor at their expense.

The American Farm Bureau Federation—the organization always most closely attuned to Republican administrations—accused Ford of "capitulation to political blackmail." A spokesman for the Agriculture Council of America said, "We're telling Mr. Meany to get the hell out of farmers' business." And the wrath of the farming community escalated when the September 11, 1975, crop report predicted a record corn crop in spite of the bad weather in the area west of the Mississippi.

Representative Neal Smith, Democrat of Iowa, declared that "Ford doesn't know what a promise means, or he simply doesn't understand that an embargo on international sales is in fact the most stringent control the government can impose upon farmers."

The long-range agreement with the Soviet Union, announced by Ford in late October when the embargo was lifted, did not satisfy the farm organizations or the critics, who believed that the embargo of more than two months had wrecked farm markets beyond repair.

Although the "farm vote" had lost much of its direct political punch in the years since the 1920's and 1930's, it was still substantial enough to mean the difference between winning and losing elections in the farm belt. The drop in farm population since 1920 had been drastic. At that time the U.S. farm population of 32 million was approximately 30 percent of the total, but by 1972 it had dropped to 9.6 million, or only about 4.6 percent of the total.

Loss of the farm states meant defeat for Senator Hubert Humphrey, the Democratic standard-bearer, against Richard Nixon in 1968. Winning the farm vote gave President Harry Truman his surprise victory over New York Governor Thomas E. Dewey.

Republican as well as Democratic farmers were angry at President Ford. They considered his professed admiration and sympathy for them but concluded that he had permitted their interests to become the pawns manipulated by Secretary of State Henry Kissinger in the international games he played. They felt they had been sold out to appease Big Labor.

Gerald Ford was running true to form, trying to please everybody with political rhetoric and with no serious commitment to following through with what he said he would do. Ford, as a minority leader in the House, had found a certain strength in being able to plead ignorance of facts in breaking seeming commitments. It permitted bending to the last wind of compromise on almost any issue, and it was easy to rationalize that he really hadn't promised the farmers anything except "fair prices"—a term that could be subject to a thousand different interpretations when it came time to writing or endorsing farm programs.

Settling down to think about a specific farm program was the least of his worries in the fall of 1974, as new and unexpected problems developed in connection with the nomination of Nelson Rockefeller as Vice President. It was an embarrassment of Rockefeller riches secretly given in large amounts to people in public life that Ford had to consider in his next test on ethical standards.

12. Rockefeller's Gifts

NELSON A. ROCKEFELLER had stepped on a lot of conservative toes in his quest of the Republican presidential candidacy, so the nomination of the sixty-six-year-old former New York Governor for Vice President was certain to be controversial.

But, when Ford announced his choice, no one would have forecast that Rockefeller's wealth would be an embarrassment to the President.

President Ford made a pitch for a quick approval and a superficial investigation of Rockefeller's finances by suggesting to the Congress that it was important to get the nomination confirmed as soon as possible. But Senator Robert C. Byrd, the Assistant Democratic Leader, declared, "The important consideration is to make sure there is no conflict of interest."

Many members of the Senate and House committees would want to know all about Rockefeller's holdings in oil and banking, and in virtually every other area, to assure themselves on this score.

Rockefeller, always secretive about his net worth, which had been estimated to be between $100 million and $600 million, said he would comply with "whatever the law says" regarding disclosure of his wealth and pledged to cooperate with Congress to that end.

While President Ford was defending his own credibility in the Nixon pardon uproar, another problem was burgeoning in the FBI's quiet investigation into Nelson Rockefeller's finances and campaign tactics. No doubts were raised that the multimillionaire had enriched himself at public expense or from payoffs from those who dealt with New York State when he was Governor.

Rockefeller's money problems arose when the FBI and Senate and House investigators, in combing his finances, uncovered an unusual pattern of "gift-giving" to others in political life. The recipients of those "gifts" included Secretary of State Henry Kissinger, $50,000; former New York State Republican Chairman L. Judson Morhouse, $86,000; and William D. Ronan, Chairman of the Port Authority of New York and New Jersey, $550,000.

The favor to Kissinger took place in early 1969, between his leaving Rockefeller's staff and joining the Nixon Administration as Special Assistant to the President for National Security Affairs. The gift was disclosed by the Gannett newspaper chain and was confirmed by a spokesman for the Secretary of State on October 4, 1974. The explanation was that Rockefeller wanted to make him a gift "at the close of their some fifteen years of association."

But, Senator Byrd, who was a member of the Senate Rules Committee, pointed out that it was also the start of Kissinger's work as a public official in the Nixon Administration, where his decisions might be useful to Rockefeller's own political interests or the Rockefeller family's

banking and oil interests. The same basic point was made
by Representative Donald Edwards and Representative
Edward Mezvinsky, both members of the Senate Judiciary
Committee, which would pass on the Rockefeller nomination.

Reports on the Morhouse gift surfaced at about the
same time and were confirmed by a Rockefeller spokesman.
Morhouse, a former member of the New York State Thru-
way Authority, had been sentenced to two 3-year state
prison terms in 1966 on bribery and unlawful fee charges
arising from a state liquor authority scandal in New York.
The conviction was upheld by the New York Court of
Appeals, but Rockefeller, as Governor of New York, had
commuted his sentence in 1970. Hugh Morrow, Rockefeller's press spokesman, said the Morhouse gift of $86,000
was to help solve the former New York Republican Chairman's "overwhelming financial problems." Morrow's explanation was that Rockefeller loaned Morhouse $100,000
in 1969, when Morhouse was New York Republican Chairman, then an unsalaried post. Because of Morhouse's financial distress and serious illness, Rockefeller had canceled
the $86,000 outstanding balance in 1973 and paid federal
and state gift taxes of about $48,000.

Performing such financial favors for a former political
chairman was certainly outside the purview of most political figures.

The whopping $550,000 to William Ronan was justified
as "the Governor's desire to help keep a good man in government." The "gift" to Ronan, Morrow said, was also
in the form of a debt cancellation, made after Ronan
resigned in April 1973 as Chairman of the New York State
Metropolitan Transportation Authority, which carried a
salary of $75,000 a year.

The debt had accumulated from a series of loans over the years, Morrow explained, and Rockefeller had canceled the entire obligation in the spring of 1973 before Ronan became Chairman of the Port Authority of New York and New Jersey. It was important that the "gift" be effective on a date when Ronan was neither on the New York State Metropolitan Transportation Authority payroll or on the Port Authority payroll, for laws and regulations barred acceptance of gifts while in those jobs.

Morrow compared the Ronan "gift" to "the year-end bonus given to executives of large corporations." The gift taxes on the debt cancellation totaled $330,000, and Rockefeller said his lawyers had assured him it was all quite proper. At the time of the Rockefeller nomination hearings, Ronan was a paid financial adviser to the Rockefeller family and also received $12,500 a year as a trustee of the New York State Power Authority.

Members of the Senate Rules Committee and the House Judiciary Committee, then studying the Rockefeller nomination, scheduled further testimony. They were particularly sensitive because their own salaries were pegged at $42,500 a year, and they faced a justifiably constant stream of criticism for any unusual favors, entertainment or "gifts" of even a few thousand dollars.

Representative Edward Mezvinsky, an Iowa Democrat who was a member of the House Judicary Committee, voiced the concern of many Democrats and some Republicans: "Just because it is a small amount of money to Rockefeller does not mean that the recipients of these gifts do not feel greatly obligated."

A Republican member of the House Judiciary Committee, Representative Wiley Mayne, said he was particularly "troubled by the lack of judgment" Nelson Rockefeller displayed in the huge gift to Ronan. A dependable supporter of the Nixon and Ford administrations, the "giftgiving" left Mayne undecided about approving the confirmation of Rockefeller as Vice President.

"It is going to depend upon how Nelson Rockefeller answers the question on the gifts to Dr. Ronan, and [on] a number of other things that trouble me," Mayne said after he had questioned Ronan on the possibility of a conflict of interest if Ronan were to be appointed to high public office in a Rockefeller administration.

Under questioning by Mayne, Ronan, then a $100,000-a-year employee of the Rockefeller family, said he had no intention of coming to Washington if Nelson Rockefeller was confirmed as Vice President, but that he could see no problem of conflict of interest if he did decide to take such an appointment.

Mayne said that although he did not consider Ronan's responses "completely satisfactory . . . there is apparently nothing illegal about it [the gift].

"Rockefeller has admitted by hindsight [that] the decision to make the gifts was poor judgment, but Dr. Ronan was without remorse and what troubled me is that he still does not understand the serious questions of conflicts of interest it could raise," Mayne said. "Gifts of this magnitude boggle my imagination, and I'm sure that it boggles the imagination of all of my constituents, who are also accustomed to thinking in much more modest terms when it comes to gifts."

President Ford said he could find no impropriety in Rockefeller's giving such large gifts, and he saw nothing particularly wrong with his Secretary of State accepting $50,000.

"I have looked into the one that involved Dr. Kissinger,"

President Ford said, and observed, "I think to put this in proper perspective you have to recognize that Governor Rockefeller is a very, very wealthy man and that he has been extremely generous with many, many charities over a good many years, and he obviously sought to compensate former employees or friends for whatever services they performed."

The beacon of a single high standard of ethics for every person in the Ford Administration flickered more than a little in putting the facts in the perspective of Rockefeller's being "a very, very wealthy man," and Ford's additional comments dropped the standards of propriety to whatever was within the law.

"In the case of Dr. Kissinger, I have been assured that every tax that could be applied has been paid and that all legal problems involving that particular case were solved satisfactorily," President Ford said. "Under those circumstances, I do not think there was any impropriety in the relationship between Dr. Kissinger and former Governor Rockefeller."

The President said he hadn't looked into the Morhouse and Ronan gifts "as deeply because Mr. Morhouse and Mr. Ronan are or were state employees. But I assume in those two cases, as I found out in the Dr. Kissinger case, that the law had been adhered to and that there was no impropriety."

While President Ford defended Rockefeller's pattern of generous gifts, a new controversy erupted involving Rockefeller's financing of a derogatory biography of former United States Supreme Court Justice Arthur J. Goldberg. *Arthur J. Goldberg, The Old and The New*, written by Victor Lasky and published in 1970 during Rockefeller's campaign against Goldberg for Governor of New York, was financed by Nelson Rockefeller's brother Laurance with an investment of $60,000.

In response to newspaper reports that congressional probers were looking into the financing of the Goldberg book, Rockefeller issued a statement saying he was unaware of the manner in which the book was financed in 1970 and had only recently learned of the $60,000 investment by Laurance.

"Had he told me about it at the time," Rockefeller explained, aware of the criticism of Nixon's political committee for covertly financing circulation of derogatory material about opponents, "I would have been totally opposed to it and would have strongly advised against his participation in any form."

Rockefeller said he learned of Laurance's investment through the Federal Bureau of Investigation during a background check made in connection with the vice-presidential nomination. He said he told the FBI agents he had heard of the Goldberg book at the time "but knew nothing about its preparation or financing . . . really didn't pay any attention because I never felt that such books coming out during campaigns cut much ice one way or another. I never heard any more about it until the book was out and someone showed me a copy, which I never even opened."

But, while Goldberg was expressing shock that the Rockefellers "would participate in such a dirty campaign trick," it was revealed that the Rockefeller campaign organization had received 100,000 copies of the book in 1970.

Rockefeller called Goldberg by telephone to apologize for the "derogatory" book, and added, "I take full responsibility for the whole regrettable episode."

The book incident dominated the hearings, and the

"gift-giving" took on secondary importance as House Judiciary Committee members were informed in late October that Nelson Rockefeller and his political associates had engaged in "a cover-up" of the former Governor's role in financing the book. In a closed session of a House Judiciary subcommittee, members were told that misleading statements were made by Rockefeller and others associated with the plans for the Goldberg book.

Representative Don Edwards, chairman of the subcommittee, made a written report to Judiciary Committee Chairman Peter Rodino listing what appeared to be "outright lies" and "planned falsehoods" by some of Rockefeller's associates. It charged that Nelson Rockefeller himself had made misleading statements on relevant points.

Committee members said that "some of Rockefeller's relatives and political associates may be guilty of crimes for the false statements to the FBI agents."

"When the picture is viewed as a whole there can be no doubt in anyone's mind that it was a willful cover-up to protect [Nelson] Rockefeller from any responsibility for the Goldberg book," one committee member said. Chairman Rodino revealed to reporters that something in the 2,300-page FBI report was likely be embarrassing to Governor Rockefeller, but he would not explain it at the time.

The second phase of the Rockefeller confirmation hearings opened in the Senate Rules Committee on November 13, with Rockefeller in a totally apologetic posture on the Goldberg book. He called it a "hasty, ill-considered decision in the middle of a hectic campaign."

"Let's face it, I made a mistake," Rockefeller said, and he immediately took steps to admit that his statements to the FBI and his initial report to the Congress had not been accurate. He admitted that he, not Laurance, had

initiated the financing of the Goldberg book. He stressed
that his previous "incorrect" version was the result of a
faulty memory, and that he was "delinquent in not clearing this up sooner."

Some committee members said they could see little difference between the misstatements to the FBI by Rockefeller and his associates and the misstatements of some of
Nixon's aides on Watergate that had resulted in federal
indictments and convictions.

Rockefeller stoutly defended the propriety of his substantial money gifts to Kissinger, Ronan, Morhouse and
others, though he recognized that such largesse to public
officials and political figures by a man with political aspira-
tions might be subject to some unflattering interpretations.
But he said that, on "humanitarian" grounds, he was
"hesitant" to make a pledge to agree to make no more
gifts while serving as Vice President.

"There might be a case where I would feel in humanity
that I ought to do something," Rockefeller declared, as
he was pressed by Senator Claiborne Pell and others.

Criticism and disapproval of the financing of the Goldberg book was softened by the public sympathy generated
for both families when tragic ailments struck the wife of
President Ford and the wife of Nelson Rockefeller in
September and October.

On September 28, the White House announced that
Betty Ford successfully underwent a radical mastectomy.
No clinical evidence could be detected that the cancer had
spread to other areas, but there was an outpouring of
sympathy for the fifty-six-year-old woman and for the
family.

Rockefeller announced only two weeks later that his
wife, Margaretta (Happy), had undergone surgery for re-

moval of her left breast. The forty-eight-year-old woman was given a 90 percent chance of full recovery and released from the hospital on October 24. However, she underwent a second mastectomy on November 25—the same day the Rockefeller confirmation was opposed by the conservative Liberty Lobby, the National Right to Life Committee, the liberal National Lawyers Guild and the American Conservative Union.

On November 13—between her mastectomy operations —Happy Rockefeller appeared with her husband at the Senate Rules Committee hearing, in which he explained "the conflict between what I said first and what I said later" relative to the Goldberg book.

"I have already apologized to Mr. Justice Goldberg, publicly and privately, and I want to take this opportunity to publicly apologize to my brother Laurance for having gotten him involved in an undertaking which is out of character for the family."

Then he gave his revised version of the Goldberg book incident: "Jack Wells [a New York lawyer] dropped into my office to tell me of a project he was promoting on behalf of a client of his, Victor Lasky, to write and publish a book on Mr. Justice Goldberg. This was in July of the campaign. He was looking for financial backers of a corporation he was setting up for this purpose.

"I referred Jack Wells to my counsel, Donald O'Brien, and sent a message to my brother Laurance asking if he could help Jack Wells find some investors. That was the extent of my involvement in this project. Total time, about fifteen or twenty minutes. Later I saw a copy of the book, but I never really looked at it.

"My brother, who wanted to be helpful, did not have time to find other investors and therefore simply authorized his people, when he got the message, to underwrite the project while other investors were being sought—and that is the only connection my brother Laurance had with the project. . . . No other investors were forthcoming. Therefore, the office staff authorized payment based on my brother's underwriting.

"My mistake was that I should have killed this project in the beginning when Jack Wells originally brought it to me," Rockefeller added. He said that his "confusion" when he talked to the FBI was because he had spent so little time on the book and because the interview was hurried two days after he was nominated.

"It [the interview] . . . covered more than thirty years of public and private activities—and my memory of the book [and] its origins was extremely sketchy," Rockefeller said. "There was no attempt whatsoever to cover up the facts. . . . The tragedy was, and this is where I made my second mistake, that I responded to a press inquiry before I had obtained the full story of what actually happened— and as a result, I was extremely unfair to my brother by what I said."

Rockefeller told the committee that when he had referred to the Goldberg book as "derogatory" he had not read it, but that Goldberg had characterized it as "pornographic."

"I have now read the book. Pornographic it is not," he said. "Scurrilous it is not. It is not anything that by any stretch of the imagination goes beyond the limit of the kind of political comment to which all of us in public life are subject from time to time, and to which I have been subjected in full measure from other authors over a long period of time."

While President Ford gave tacit approval to the propriety of Rockefeller's gift giving, and was uncritical of either the financing of the Goldberg book or the "conflicting" accounts Rockefeller had given, the White House put pressure on the committee for quick approval of the nomination.

"The national interest is not well served by a continued vacancy in the vice presidency, and I remain firmly convinced that Governor Rockefeller is eminently qualified for this office," Ford wrote Chairman Cannon of the Senate Rules Committee while putting similar pressure on Chairman Rodino of the House Judiciary Committee.

In defense, Chairman Cannon reviewed the multiplicity of problems that had arisen because of the size of the Rockefeller fortune, the Goldberg book financing and "those several million dollars' worth of loans and/or gifts made by the nominee [Rockefeller] to friends, aides, political associates and others.

"Certainly, one hard question is whether such loans or gift giving by one of this country's wealthiest and most philanthropic men and his family to governmentally involved persons establishes a bond of allegiance which does not measure up to the proper standard of rectitude established for American political life in 1974 and beyond," Cannon said.

He declared that "the Rockefeller wealth itself, massive as it is . . . is singularly and properly not an issue. . . . At issue is the use of such wealth in governmentally associated areas."

Cannon noted the "unassailable advice of one political observer" who had said, "There is a sign on the political wall that reads 'No Tipping Allowed.'"

The Senate Committee Chairman also declared that "the potential wedding of this economic and political power requires a comparable scrutiny of those of us charged with such scrutiny."

But the efforts of Senator Robert Byrd and some other Democrats were met by scoffing charges of "politics" by Senator Hugh Scott, the Senate Republican Leader and a senior member of the Rules Committee.

Such full disclosures of Rockefeller's finances became confusing to the public rather than enlightening. Rockefeller's net worth was estimated by the Congressional Joint Committee on Internal Revenue Taxation at $73 million, higher than Rockefeller's own latest estimate of $62 million. He had made a total of $3,265,374 in political contributions over a period of eighteen years, and many of the contributions had gone to members of the Senate and House who would be voting on his nomination. A total of $1,031,637 had been put into his own presidential campaigns, and the political contributions of the Rockefeller family had exceeded $20 million.

In testifying, Rockefeller conceded that his generosity could be "misinterpreted" and offered to "cut it out" as far as political figures were concerned. He volunteered to pledge in writing to forego gifts or loans to federal employees and, if confirmed, to limit "nominal gifts" to birthdays, weddings or events of severe medical hardship.

This public relations coup drowned out questions of propriety and credibility, and the Senate Rules Committee on November 22 voted 9 to 0 to recommend confirmation, and the Senate confirmed the nomination by a vote of 90 to 7 on December 10. The opposition votes were cast by Republicans Barry Goldwater, Jesse Helms, of North Carolina, and William Scott, of Virginia. Democratic opposition was registered by James Abourezk, of

South Dakota, Birch Bayh, of Indiana, Howard Metzen-baum, of Ohio, and Gaylord Nelson, of Wisconsin.

The House Judiciary Committee continued its hearings until December 12, when confirmation was recommeded by a committee vote of 26 to 12. The opposition votes were cast by twelve Democrats. On December 19, the House voted 287 to 128 to approve the nomination, after six hours of debate in which an unusual coalition of liberal Democrats and conservative Republicans expressed dis-approval. The Iowa House delegation was split three to three. Representative Mayne had dropped his concern over the "gift giving" and was joined by Representative William Scherle and Representative John Culver.

Representative Edward Mezvinsky remained opposed, as he had in the Judiciary Committee votes, and was joined by Representative Neal Smith, a moderately liberal Demo-crat, and Representative H. R. Gross, an independent-minded, conservative Republican.

Rockefeller's swearing-in ceremony at the Capitol with President Ford in attendance was the first live television coverage of a function in the United States Senate. It was also the first time in the history of the United States that neither the President nor the Vice President had been elected by the people. They had been nominated and confirmed by the Congress under the 25th Amendment to the Constitution.

The conservative Republican opposition to Rockefeller was based in part on the belief that there was a Ford-Rockefeller "deal" for Ford to drop out of contention in 1976, so that the vice presidency would merely be a step-ping stone to the presidency. Others decried President Ford's defense of Rockefeller's gift giving and the Golberg book matter as having done even more damage to his already severely battered credibility.

Representative Gross spoke for many of the Rockefeller opponents when he declared that "in the wake of Watergate, with all its evils and corruption—largely spawned by the misuse of vast sums of money—we need not even a hint of additional tarnish.

"I hold no brief for Arthur Goldberg's ill-fated journey into the New York political arena," Gross said, "but I cannot accept the Rockefeller denial of knowledge of the issuance of a $60,000 undermining campaign document and then the admission that he did. Neither can I accept the explanation of loans, all too often converted to gifts, to political associations."

President Ford had managed to push the Rockefeller nomination through the Congress, but it had taken its toll on what was left of his reputation for candor and high governmental ethical standards.

13. The Nixon Legacies

THE NOMINATIONS OF Nelson Rockefeller to be Vice President and Peter Flanigan to be United States Ambassador to Spain were not isolated instances of Ford selections that hurt his credibility as a man of candor and strict ethical standards. Other such selections were the naming of Andrew E. Gibson to head the Federal Energy Administration (FEA), Alexander M. Haig as Supreme Commander of the North Atlantic Treaty Organization (NATO), and Robert C. Seamans, Jr., as head of the Energy Research and Development Administration (ERDA). All three had served in the Nixon Administration, and all had scars that made it apparent that the appointments would be controversial.

Probably the most questionable was the nomination of Gibson, a man with ties to the oil industry, to head the energy agency. Gibson, fifty-two years old, had served as Maritime Administrator in the Nixon Administration from March 25, 1969, to July 1972, and for several months more as Assistant Secretary of Commerce for Maritime Affairs.

In January 1973, Gibson accepted a post as President of the Interstate Oil Transport Company of Philadelphia and remained with that firm for sixteen months prior to his resignation in May 1974. His severance arrangement with Interstate Oil Transport called for payment of approximately $88,000 a year for ten years, in settlement of the $1 million contract he had with the firm.

It was an excellent arrangement for Gibson, but his critics thought the benefits conferred by a firm dealing with the oil industry much too profitable for a federal energy czar.

Because the Interstate Oil Transport Company had been the beneficiary of a number of Maritime Administration decisions when Gibson headed that agency and afterwards, the Senate Interior Committee staff launched an inquiry into possible conflicts of interest shortly after the nomination was announced on October 29, 1974.

On November 6, the *Wall Street Journal* carried a news story that the Gibson nomination "may face rough sailing" and called attention to the former Maritime Administrator's ties to shipping and the oil industry. It noted that Interstate Oil Transport, formerly a small Philadelphia tug and barge operation, was starting to come into the big time "thanks mainly to subsidies and loan guarantees from the Maritime Administration."

The *Journal* story, by staff reporters Les Gapay and Albert R. Karr, noted that what made Gibson's lucrative settlement "especially touchy" was that Interstate Oil received essentially all of its revenues from oil and utility industries by transporting petroleum along the East Coast and the Gulf of Mexico.

Further complicating Gibson's problem was the fact that Interstate Oil Transport was owned by the I.O.T.

Corporation, which also owned International Ocean Transport Company, a major tanker operation. Cities Service Company, identified by the *Journal* as the fifteenth-largest oil company in the United States, owned 50 percent of I.O.T.

The fine detail of the *Wall Street Journal* story should have served notice of serious trouble on the Ford White House, for it was obvious that the Federal Energy Administration would administer price controls on petroleum products and was one of the agencies involved in trying to step up domestic energy development. This would place Gibson, as FEA Administrator, with governmental jurisdiction over the oil business and shipping.

In addition to pointing out possible conflicts of interests in the future, the *Wall Street Journal* called the Senate Interior Committee investigators' attention to approval by the Maritime Administration of $4.5 million in mortgage insurance for Interstate Oil on March 16, 1972, when Gibson headed that agency. The actual clearance of the mortgage insurance so vital to Interstate's development was signed by another Maritime official while Gibson was out of the city, but the routine signing by someone else did not change his general responsibility.

Probably of more importance to Interstate Oil Transport was the Maritime Administration's clearance on June 27, 1972, of a $90.6 million subsidy. It involved construction of three supertankers, at a total cost of $210.2 million, under terms providing for Interstate to operate the tankers. Gibson told the *Journal* that he didn't participate in the negotiations on the subsidy because he had left his Maritime post to become Assistant Secretary of Commerce for Maritime Affairs.

Although Gibson didn't officially assume the Com-

merce Department title until July 7, 1972, he said he
physically left the Maritime Administration in early June.

The morning the *Wall Street Journal* article appeared,
White House press secretary Ronald Nessen told reporters
that President Ford knew all about Gibson's background.
However, a short time later he corrected his statement to
the White House press corps and said that "because of
the urgency of naming a replacement for [the ousted]
John Sawhill, the usual background checks were waived."

"Before the nomination is sent to the Senate, these
checks will be completed," Nessen assured the press on
November 8. The name of each prospective nominee is
referred to the Federal Bureau of Investigation for a
routine investigation of business affiliations and activities
and background studies of any unusual employment. Even
persons who have had a full-field FBI investigation, such
as Gibson had, are usually subjected to an "update"
probe before a new appointment.

Gibson, who had helped form a shipping industry-
labor committee to work for the Nixon-Agnew ticket in
1972, said he had expected to be nominated by the White
House to be Deputy Director of the International Labor
Organization in Geneva. He was as surprised as anyone
when the decision was made to name him Federal Energy
Administrator following the sudden dismissal of Sawhill.

Although Gibson insisted there was no possibility of a
conflict of interest because of the "ironclad contract" for
severance from Interstate Oil Transport, the threat of a
full investigation and hearings before the Senate Interior
Committee panicked the White House. Chairman Henry
M. Jackson, a presidential aspirant, would have a field
day exploring the plush ten-year severance agreement.

The New York Times reported a likelihood of congressional scrutiny of Gibson's role as a top Nixon Administration negotiator in the talks that preceded the controversial sale of American wheat to the Soviet Union in 1972. Gibson had also been a participant in later talks resulting in the United States-Soviet trade agreement that same year, which was equally controversial.

After initially saying he would "stand behind" the nomination, President Ford on November 12 withdrew Gibson's name to avoid a lengthy confirmation hearing that he said would not be in "the best interests of the nation."

Gibson had requested that his name "not be transmitted to the Senate," although he defended the propriety of his activities as Maritime Administrator and declared that the $88,000-a-year severance contract with Interstate Oil would not interfere with his objectivity as a federal energy administrator.

He called his severance contract "specific and unconditional" and declared it would not inhibit him "in discharge of my official responsibilities as Federal Energy Administrator." But, he said that the nation's energy problems required immediate attention, and, since it was apparent the confirmation process could be lengthy, "in the best interests of the nation" it was better for Ford to name someone else.

President Ford accepted his request with "deepest regret" and expressed his confidence in Gibson's integrity and ability. He said he hoped to appoint him to another government post "when appropriate" and after an FBI investigation.

"We sought you out because of your proven record as a superior government manager," President Ford said. "We need people in public service of your ability and your experience." Ron Nessen said that White House Chief of Staff Donald Rumsfeld, in overall charge of personnel, took full responsibility for the decision to nominate Gibson. He also said that neither Rumsfeld nor President Ford knew of Gibson's severance contract with Interstate Oil Transport. Others in the White House knew of the contract but not the details, Nessen added.

"The matter was handled imperfectly in the White House and the matter is now resolved," Nessen said, understating the Gibson problem and hoping that this would end the Senate investigation. Other controversies were brewing for Ford nominees, including the fuss over the selection of General Haig, Nixon's last White House Chief of Staff, for a position as Commander of the NATO forces.

Opposition flared when the North Atlantic Treaty Organization, following a request from President Ford, announced on September 16 that Haig would succeed General Andrew J. Goodpaster at NATO's Brussels headquarters effective December 15. Two days later the *New York Times* reported that Haig had been instrumental in persuading Ford to grant a pardon to Nixon, pleading the possibility of Nixon's physical and mental collapse. Both Haig and Ford denied any discussion of the mental or physical condition of Nixon prior to the decision, but other questions were raised about Haig's role as White House Chief of Staff after H. R. Haldeman left on May 1, 1973.

General Haig's defense of Nixon was enthusiastic and down to the last wire, and he played an important role in the distribution of distorted versions of the White House tape transcripts that resulted in Senator Hugh Scott's calling John Dean a liar and a perjurer.

Neither the Senate Watergate Committee, the House Judiciary Committee nor the courts had ever questioned Haig and others in order to get a satisfactory explanation of the responsibility for the distorted editing of "the blue book" of White House tapes released by Nixon on April 30, 1974.

The bulky transcripts were so misleading with regard to some of the conversations between Nixon, Haldeman and Dean that the editing had to be a deliberate effort to hide Nixon's involvement in the criminal obstruction of justice. Since the blue-book transcripts were made available to the public, the court and committees of the Senate and House as a part of a carefully planned deception, distribution of the book was itself an act of obstruction of justice by those who knew it was a distorted version of the conversations and that relevant conversations were eliminated with the notation: "material unrelated to presidential actions."

General Haig performed other questionable duties when he was Henry Kissinger's chief deputy on the National Security Council. He served as courier for Kissinger in delivering to J. Edgar Hoover the list of names of newsmen and NCS subordinates who were to be wiretapped to stop leaks of information.

Within a few days after Haig's appointment to NATO was announced, pressure started to build for immediate Senate hearings. A group of Democratic Senators led by William Proxmire, of Wisconsin, and Harold Hughes, of Iowa, wrote to Armed Services Committee Chairman John Stennis, a Democrat from Mississippi, to demand hearings. Other critics of the Haig appointment included Senator Dick Clark, of Iowa, Senator Stuart Symington, of Missouri, and Senator Robert Byrd, of West Virginia.

Significantly, Senators Symington and Hughes were themselves members of the Senate Armed Services Committee, and Senator Robert Byrd was the assistant majority leader of the Senate.

The Ford White House position was that the appointment did not require Senate confirmation and that, therefore, Haig would not appear. Proxmire called on Haig to waive the legal arguments and appear voluntarily so that the Senate could "clear the air about his role in the Nixon Administration."

But the White House ignored the demands of Senator Proxmire and other Haig critics who contended that Commander of the NATO forces was a "position of importance and responsibility" that required Senate hearings and confirmation. President Ford did not wish to permit General Haig to be questioned about the transition period and the pardon, and General Haig did not wish to testify. They had an able ally in Senator Stennis, who was one of the last-ditch supporters of Nixon and who, in April of 1973, had advised him to "tough it out."

Chairman Stennis simply turned a deaf ear to the pleas of Proxmire and others for hearings, which were to include exploring the FBI wiretaps on newsmen and NSC employees, Haig's role in the Watergate transcript dispute, and his role in persuading Ford that Nixon should be granted a full and unconditional pardon. "He is a political general," Senator Hughes said, and recalled Haig's meteoric rise from colonel to general while serving in the Nixon White House. "Then he retired as a military man to take a sensitive political position in the Nixon Administration," the Iowa Democrat said. "It is my understanding that he does not have much of a track record in military commands."

Senator Clark questioned "the wisdom and propriety" of the appointment. "This country has maintained a long and steadfast tradition of strictly separating the military establishment from the civilian government," he said. "General Haig's easy passage from one to the other and back again is inconsistent with that tradition and sets a disturbing precedent." The Iowa Democrat declared that it will "certainly give a strong incentive for other officers to attempt to advance their own careers by allying themselves with political causes and political officials."

But the stonewalling by General Haig and President Ford was buttressed by Chairman Stennis, with the result that on November 1, Haig went to Stuttgart, West Germany, to replace General Goodpaster as Commander of the United States Forces in Europe; and on December 15, in Brussels, he became Supreme Commander of NATO forces. General Haig had successfully bypassed the discomfiture of answering the probing questions about his service in the Nixon White House and his conversations with President Ford on the Nixon pardon.

President Ford was equally successful in overriding Senator Proxmire's objection to the naming of former Air Force Secretary Seamans as head of the Energy Research and Development Administration. However, in the Seamans case he received the bipartisan endorsement of Senator Edward Brooke and Senator Edward Kennedy, both of whom seemed unaware of Seamans' role in the wrongful firing of A. Ernest Fitzgerald, an Air Force cost analyst, a few years earlier.

Shortly after the Seamans nomination was announced, Senator Proxmire attacked the rewarding of "incompetency and inefficiency" in connection with the handling of the multibillion-dollar contract with Lockheed Aircraft

Corporation for the C-5A jet transport plane. Fitzgerald, a cost analyst on the C-5A project, had testified before Proxmire's Joint Economic Committee on the nearly $2 billion in cost overruns, and had thereby displeased his Air Force superiors.

Later Fitzgerald was fired in what Seamans and an Air Force coterie tried to pass off as a legitimate reduction-in-force discharge. In addition, both the Air Force and Secretary Seamans tried to bar Fitzgerald from an open hearing before the Civil Service Commission. Fitzgerald and his lawyers were in litigation for six years before he was able to win a Civil Service decision that he had been "wrongfully" discharged and should be reinstated with back pay.

The record of Fitzgerald's case in the Civil Service Commission and in the federal court left a very black mark on Seamans' career. It proved that he and his top aides had distributed false information to the effect that Fitzgerald was "a security risk" and had a "conflict of interest," long after the Air Force Office of Inspection had cleared Fitzgerald of those charges.

When United States District Judge William Bryant ordered an open Civil Service hearing as essential to give Fitzgerald simple due process of law, Seamans refused to testify about conversations he had had with the Nixon White House on the Fitzgerald case in the period prior to the discharge. Seamans also permitted high-ranking officers and civilians to refuse to give testimony that Fitzgerald and his lawyers argued was essential to pin down the responsibility for the malicious smear campaign against him.

Proxmire, in opposing Seamans to head the Energy Research and Development Administration, said that his appointment by President Ford "conveys the worst kind of message to the bureaucracy.

"Had Seamans paid more attention to his job and less to the petty vendettas of the contractor bail-out crowd, the taxpayers might have been saved hundreds of millions of dollars," Proxmire declared.

White House Chief of Staff Donald Rumsfeld acknowledged to me that the White House was aware of Seamans' role in the Fitzgerald matter, but the White House press office said there had been no public protest over his nomination. With the Congress tied up in the wild flurry of business at the close of 1974, with the Rockefeller nomination occupying the interest of the country and with the major debates on the stalled energy and tax programs commanding attention, Senator Proxmire could stir little concern among the Democrats.

One special hindrance to arousing effective Democratic opposition was the knowledge that Senator Kennedy, political glamour boy of the Senate, intended to endorse the Seamans nomination. Senator Proxmire, busy with hearings on the economic conditions, prepared a list of questions for Chairman Henry Jackson to ask when Seamans appeared before the Interior Committee.

After hearing the fulsome praise of Seamans from Senator Kennedy and Senator Brooke, Chairman Jackson asked Proxmire's questions in a totally desultory fashion. Seamans, despite the ruling by the Civil Service Commission, continued to insist that Fitzgerald's discharge was a bona fide abolition of the position.

Jackson did not vigorously follow through on Proxmire's questions or on a number of those that defined the former Air Force Secretary's accountability. Also, Jackson compliantly agreed to Seamans' suggestion that he be

permitted to submit written answers later. Senator Proxmire, whose serious objections had been submitted in
writing, said he assumed that Seamans would be put under
oath to respond to them. But Jackson negligently failed
to put Seamans under oath.

Senator Proxmire's statement for the record read: "I
conclude from the record and from personal experience
with the former Secretary when he testified before the
Joint Economic Committee that he did not competently
manage the Air Force, that he exercised poor judgment
on a number of occasions and that he intentionally misled
the Joint Economic Committee and Congress.

"I am concerned that some of the worst aspects of Air
Force procurement practices may be carried over to
ERDA," Proxmire said, but no one in Congress cared
to hear the litany of Seamans' malfeasance and misfeas-
ance in public office, for there was a rush to adjourn.

The Ford White House had more important things to
worry about than charges that Seamans had misled Congress, for Secretary of State Kissinger's probity was mired
in the quicksand of his role in wiretapping newsmen and
subordinates and his approval of dubious covert activities
by the Central Intelligence Agency in Chile.

14. Cover-up for Kissinger

GERALD FORD INHERITED Dr. Henry A. Kissinger, the rotund Secretary of State and devotee of jet diplomacy who was constantly smiling himself on and off airplanes.

His frantic pace from one trouble spot to another kept many people convinced that peace might really be at hand if Kissinger could just locate cloud nine.

As Richard Nixon struggled to keep from going under the flood of Watergate, Henry Kissinger loomed larger as the maker and executor of American foreign policy.

In the confusion and desperation of the foreign affairs mess, the average citizen, uncomprehending the incomprehensible, simply felt compelled to "let Henry do it."

And the wily Dr. Kissinger didn't try to clarify it—maybe he couldn't have—but he recognized that knowledge is power and so shared his secrets on a "need to know" basis. As far as he was concerned, neither the State Department bureaucracy nor the President had the "need to know" the whole picture, but he built the ego of the insecure Nixon by constantly praising him as the "decision maker." While Kissinger insisted he was "only the instrumentality" of the President, his constant smile convinced us that the Special Assistant to the President for National Security Affairs was a power unto himself.

His public declarations cleared him of responsibility if his free-wheeling operations backfired, but he retained enough credit for himself by carefully leaking select bits of information to select columnists, reporters, congressional leaders and diplomats, who would whisper of his glorious triumphs but never reveal the source of the information as Kissinger.

Thus Dr. Kissinger, instead of President Nixon, was awarded the 1973 Nobel Peace Prize for negotiating an end to the Vietnamese war. He shared the accolade with North Vietnam's Le Duc Tho, a high-ranking member of North Vietnam's Politburo. This most controversial selection in the history of the Nobel award prompted the resignation of two members of the committee—Helge Rognlien, Chairman of Norway's Liberal Party, and Einar Hovdhaugen, a former member of the Center Party. Never before had a member of the Nobel Peace Prize Committee resigned, and bitter criticism of the committee erupted from all parts of the world.

Though he won the peace prize but lost the war, Dr. Kissinger was forced to claim "the press of other business" in order to avoid personal embarrassment after Tho refused to accept his share of the prize because "peace has not really been established in South Vietnam." Arrangements were made for United States Ambassador to Norway Thomas Byrne to accept the medal as proxy for Kissinger. Byrne entered the auditorium by a rear entrance to avoid anti-American demonstrators.

The Watergate-embattled Nixon was forced to take a

back seat to Dr. Kissinger and praise him repeatedly as "our great Secretary of State." The controversy over the Nobel prize evaporated as the Vietnam settlement deteriorated to little more than a strategic retreat by the Nixon Administration, a retreat littered by shattered promises and shattered South Vietnamese leaders trusting Kissinger and Nixon to back them.

Nonetheless, the ever-busy Dr. Kissinger headed the list of most admired people in 1973, and his ratings in the Gallup Poll were rising when Nixon sent his brief resignation note to him on August 9, 1974. Although Secretary of State Kissinger had lost considerable credibility already with Washington reporters and with both parties, his star shone brightly enough with the public that President Ford dared not replace him but was compelled to assure Americans that he would keep "our great Secretary of State."

In the midst of the turmoil of Nixon's last days in the White House, the Senate Foreign Relations Committee, under the guidance of Dr. Kissinger's good friend, Chairman William Fulbright, issued a report which it hoped would put an end to the allegations that Dr. Kissinger had lied to the committee about his role in the wiretapping of newsmen and his National Security Council colleagues.

During his confirmation hearing as Secretary of State before the Senate Foreign Relations Committee, Dr. Kissinger had denied he had initiated the taps on his subordinates and the newsmen, leaving the distinct impression that the decision was arrived at by Nixon and J. Edgar Hoover, Director of the FBI.

Records and testimony received in the Nixon impeachment hearing before the House Judiciary Committee indicated that Dr. Kissinger's role in placing the wiretaps between May 1969 and February 1971 had been much more significant. Committee members questioned whether Dr. Kissinger had given false testimony in his confirmation hearing. They released FBI documents relating to his conversations with J. Edgar Hoover and noted that Alexander Haig, then Kissinger's deputy at the NSC, had handcarried a list of names from Dr. Kissinger to the FBI to identify those whose telephones should be tapped in trying to trace leaks of "national security" information.

The charges of Kissinger's requesting wiretaps began in May of 1974 and reached a crescendo in June in a fiery news conference when he flatly refused time after time to answer reporters on the specific question of his denials that he had initiated the wiretaps. A few days later, on June 11, in Salzburg, Austria, Dr. Kissinger threatened to resign if his name were not cleared.

On June 10, Kissinger had written to the Foreign Relations Committee admitting considerably more facts about his participation but still maintaining that the wiretaps had been initiated by President Nixon. He claimed he had only supplied the names of possible sources of the leaks. In his letter to Chairman Fulbright, Kissinger demanded a review of the wiretapping testimony because the accusation that he had misled the committee jeopardized his ability to conduct the foreign policy of the United States.

Fulbright explored the delicate matter of the credibility of the Secretary of State in six closed sessions, receiving testimony from Attorney General William Saxbe, FBI Director Clarence Kelley, former Secretary of State Dean Rusk, General Alexander Haig, then White House Chief of Staff, and Bernard Wells, a retired FBI agent. In addition to reviewing Justice Department files, the committee also received written answers to questions from President Nixon, former Attorney General John Mitchell and a former FBI official, William C. Sullivan.

Although the committee reported it was "unable to settle to its satisfaction some questions about the initiation and termination" of the wiretaps, it concluded that, from the information available at the time of his confirmation hearing, Kissinger's role "did not constitute grounds to bar his confirmation as Secretary of State."

"Probably it will never be possible to determine exactly what took place . . . time has taken its toll in life, memory, health and records," the committee reported. "But it [the committee] did establish to its satisfaction that Secretary Kissinger's role in the program was essentially as he described it in testimony last year. . . . If the committee knew then what it knows now, it would have nonetheless reported [Kissinger's] nomination favorable to the Senate," the committee report said.

This was the public expression of confidence Dr. Kissinger had demanded as his price of continuing, and a State Department spokesman reported that the peripatetic Henry was "gratified" by the committee action and "no longer sees any reason for resignation."

The unsatisfactory report, with the conclusion written before the investigation was started, lifted the cloud of controversy from Kissinger at a time Ford needed him most, but it did not dispel the doubts of many of his critics. The wiretapping issue was to be raised again later, as well as were questions about the execution of his detente policy and Dr. Kissinger's role in approving questionable CIA activities in Chile and other parts of the world.

Doubts about Kissinger's detente policy began to surface a few weeks after Ford became President. While there was strong approval for a U.S. policy of seeking better relations with the Soviet Union, many believed that Kissinger's implementation of detente turned it into a one-way street, with the bulk of the concessions being made by the United States and the major economic and military advantages accruing to the Russians.

Senator Fulbright, one of Dr. Kissinger's stoutest allies in Congress, scheduled hearings in August 1974 to take testimony supportive of Kissinger and detente. Chairman Fulbright's opening statement on August 15 set the tone of those hearings when he declared, "The heart and core of the policy of detente . . . is the lessening of the danger of nuclear war. . . . There is no rational alternative."

Initially, Secretary of State Kissinger was to be heard first so that he could detail the Administration's position, to be followed by Senator Henry Jackson, a leading critic of some of the specific arms agreements, proposals and trade agreements being pushed and defended by Kissinger. The Nixon resignation upset the order of the schedule, and it now became the Nixon-Ford policy, but with the phenomenal Kissinger still as the dominant force.

The first witness on behalf of the Kissinger trade-reform bill, which would give the Soviet Union most-favored-nation status, was more effective than Secretary Kissinger might have been at that juncture.

W. Averell Harriman, former Ambassador to Russia, former high State Department official and former United States representative to the Paris peace talks, declared that "failure to grant most-favored-nation status has become in the Soviet mind a hostile position by the United States."

The aging Democratic diplomat, who had dealt with the Soviet Union for fifty years, declared that Leonid Brezhnev, the Communist Party leader, had publicly committed himself to detente and would be "politically embarrassed if it ran into a dead end" because of action by the United States Congress. He was critical of belligerent comments by U.S. officials on military needs and said it strengthened the Soviet military hard-liners.

But George F. Kennan, also a former Ambassador to the Soviet Union, declared a few days later that, while he welcomed limited improvements made in relations with the Soviet Union, "detente" was really nothing new because the United States had consistently sought to take all reasonable steps to improve relations. Although he urged cautious steps forward in the field of trade, he warned against overoptimism about the results.

Others urged expanded trade as having a favorable impact on the businessman and farmer and being helpful to the U.S. balance of payments, but there were many who stressed that the short-term gains to the Soviet Union were clear but that "what the United States stands to gain is debatable."

Adam B. Ulam, Director of the Russian Research Center at Harvard University, supported continuing efforts to improve relations, but warned that any improvement would come from "hard bargaining rather than magic incantations and sonorous declarations."

United States officials should be "uncompromising and persistent in demanding that the Soviet Union observe its international obligations and not pursue policies hostile to those of the United States," Ulam said. He declared that realism and prudence are needed, not summit meetings and one-sided concessions.

Senator Jackson, already an obvious aspirant to the 1976 Democratic presidential nomination, said he did not believe it was a question of "whether we should or should not have detente."

"Everyone wants peace," Jackson told the *New York Times* editors. "The question is what kind of detente. You can have a good detente; you can have a bad detente."

The criticism by Jackson and others was aimed at the large grain sales to the Soviet Union in 1972, which were unnecessarily subsidized by the American taxpayers, unsettled American commodity markets and proved to be a tragedy for the American economy. Kissinger had been the major pilot on the grain deals and the supporter of low-interest loans and credits to the Soviet Union through the Export-Import Bank, the export of goods and high-technology items, the granting of favorable trade status, and the cutbacks in U.S. arms spending.

Jackson declared that Kissinger's concessions to the Soviet Union in many cases contributed little or nothing to improved relations, but that the United States was so eager to have the relationship continue that it had become an easy mark for the Soviet Union.

"I think first we should engage in hard bargaining with the Soviet, just as the Soviet do on every transaction," he said, and he complained about the United States offering "only programs that it knew in advance the Soviet would accept."

Additional disapproval came from George Meany, President of the AFL-CIO, who said, "The answer is not this so-called business that has been presented in the last year or so as detente. The answer is . . . cooperation between the two superpowers in the interest of world peace and trade deals with the United States on the basis of give-and-take, and not unilateral, one-way concessions."

During this public debate in the first month of the Ford Administration, probably before Kissinger had thoroughly briefed the new President on his foreign policy, additional problems arose for the ubiquitous Secretary of State, who also served as Special Assistant to the President for National Security Affairs.

As Special Assistant, Dr. Kissinger wore many hats. He headed interdepartmental committees on intelligence and, most importantly, was Chairman of the so-called Forty Committee, an ultrasecret, top-level intelligence panel with the authority to examine and approve all CIA covert activities.

In the first week of September, while Ford was in the last throes of making the Nixon pardon decision, Representative Michael J. Harrington, a liberal Massachusetts Democrat and a member of the House Armed Services Subcommittee on Intelligence, wrote to Representative Thomas E. Morgan, a Democrat from Pennsylvania and Chairman of the House Foreign Affairs Committee.

The letter, which discussed secret testimony given by CIA Director William E. Colby in April, was leaked to the *Washington Post*. It contained the essence of Colby's testimony that the CIA had been authorized to spend more than $8 million from 1970 to 1973 to create conditions in Chile that would make it impossible for Marxist President Salvador Allende Gossens to govern. Allende was killed in a military coup that upset his government on September 11, 1973.

The news reports on Colby's secret testimony immediately raised questions about whether Kissinger and other

State Department officials had misled committees of Congress in testimony a few months earlier.

President Ford, undoubtedly coached by his Special Assistant for National Security Affairs, rushed to defend the CIA's activities in Chile as well as Kissinger's honesty and integrity in his testimony. In an unusual admission at a press conference, President Ford acknowledged the CIA's spending of millions of dollars, but he said the funds had been used only for purposes of strengthening the political parties and newspapers that Allende had been trying to destroy. These actions were "in the best interests of the people of Chile and certainly in our best interest," President Ford said at his September 16, 1974, news conference, and he backed Kissinger's statements that the United States had "no involvement in any way whatsoever" in the coup that overthrew Allende and resulted in his death.

CIA Director Colby gave testimony corroborating the lack of direct CIA involvement in the coup and defended covert activities by the nation's top intelligence organization.

"I think it would be a mistake," he said, "to deprive our nation of the possibility of some moderate covert-action response to a foreign problem and leave us nothing between a diplomatic protest and sending in the Marines." But Colby declined to go into detail on any CIA activities.

While public debate roared over the controversial actions by the CIA in Chile and the contention that the agency had been a rogue elephant charging around with no specific authority, Colby defended the CIA's operation against Allende as having been approved by The Forty Committee, which Kissinger headed and dominated. This placed Kissinger in the position of direct responsibility for whatever had been wrong or questionable, and it was somewhat at variance with testimony he and other State Department officials had given Congress.

Kissinger made no personal comment on Representative Harrington's charge that "The Forty Committee is Kissinger," but a State Department spokesman countered that all members of the committee must approve any decision. President Ford replied that the proper committees of Congress for CIA oversight had been kept informed on all panel decisions. But this ran contrary to a statement by Senator Stuart Symington, the veteran Missouri Democrat and member of the Senate congressional oversight committee, that it had been a surprise to him to learn of the CIA's involvement in Chile.

The tempo of disagreement increased with accusations that State Department officials, in mid-1973, had misled the Senate Foreign Relations Subcommittee on Multinational Corporations, headed by Senator Frank Church, an Idaho Democrat.

Jerome Levinson, counsel for the Multinational Subcommittee, charged that two State Department officials had deceived the subcommittee as to the involvement of the International Telephone and Telegraph Corporation (ITT) in the 1970 election in Chile. Levinson identified the two as Charles A. Meyer, former Assistant Secretary of State for Inter-American Affairs, and Edward M. Korry, Ambassador to Chile from 1967 to 1971. Both had told the subcommittee that the United States had stuck to a noninterventionist policy after Allende's election.

The State Department, with approval of Secretary of State Kissinger, declared that it would stand behind the honesty of the statements of its officials, but it failed to dissuade Senator Church from authorizing a staff review of the 1973 testimony for possible perjury.

The staff report recommended further investigation into the possibility of perjury by Meyer and Korry, as well as an investigation of testimony by former CIA Director Richard Helms and William Broe, former head of CIA's Latin American division.

The report also accused Dr. Kissinger of deceiving the Senate Foreign Relations Committee about CIA activities in Cuba at the time of his confirmation hearing. It questioned secret testimony Kissinger had given that "we have absolutely stayed away from any coups" since 1970. It characterized Kissinger's testimony as "disingenuous" because, as head of The Forty Committee at the time, he had authorized spending for the purpose of creating an atmosphere of political instability in which the coup against Allende did take place.

With the question of Kissinger's credibility at stake, the President who made candor his hallmark pulled down the secrecy curtain of "national security" in the first stages of a long tug-of-war with the Congress on releasing information about the role of the United States in coups and the legality of actions taken in connection with those coups. Members of the House and Senate Intelligence committees, and others, questioned whether Dr. Kissinger was not using his role as Secretary of State and national security adviser to President Ford to conceal his responsibility for controversial actions, as well as evidence involving the question of his own credibility.

President Ford resisted demands that Kissinger be stripped of his position as Special Assistant for National Security Affairs. He also got out a hurried denial of pub-

lished reports that his four-man transition team had recommended that the Secretary of State be removed.

Although political controversy and confusion over Representative Harrington's "leaks" of the Colby testimony
caused delays in the House Intelligence Committee investigations of the intelligence activities, the Senate Committee headed by Senator Frank Church moved quickly.
These investigations provided a constant headache for
Kissinger and placed President Ford in a position of permitting "executive privilege" to be used as the ultimate
cover-up apparatus. Ford gave Kissinger full support and
a free hand in the strategy of blocking the committees
from obtaining the facts.

Senator Church's committee, in its report on the involvement of the United States government and the CIA
in plots to assassinate five foreign leaders, was extremely
critical of the Nixon White House and Dr. Kissinger with
regard to events leading up to the slaying of Chilean Army
commander General Rene Schneider on October 22, 1970.

The death of General Schneider took place at the hands
of a Chilean group that attempted to kidnap him. Although the report absolves President Nixon and Dr. Kissinger of responsibility for the slaying, it establishes that
the United States had instructed the CIA to play a direct
role in organizing a military coup in Chile to block
Allende from taking office, with the knowledge that such
a coup could result in the death of General Schneider and
others as well.

Secretary of State Kissinger and General Alexander
Haig, then his Deputy Assistant at the White House,
concede that the White House approved CIA actions
between September 15 and October 15, 1970, but they
contend they were not informed of later actions that

culminated in the kidnapping and slaying of General Schneider on October 22. On that important point, they are contradicted by the testimony of CIA officials who state that "activities in Chile after October 15 were known [by the White House] and thus authorized by the White House," according to the Senate Intelligence Committee.

In the maze of CIA cover-up techniques, Kissinger and Haig had "plausible deniability," and the Church committee permitted the contradictions to stand unresolved.

But on the House side, Chairman Otis Pike and his Intelligence Committee stated in their report that Kissinger and Ford tried to bottle up the facts on major intelligence blunders in Chile, Cyprus, Vietnam and the Middle East in which Dr. Kissinger had major responsibility.

Both President Ford and Kissinger promised cooperation and then engaged in stalling, time-wasting delays, delivery of meaningless or misleading edited documents, and absolute cut-offs of access to classified documents while silencing key witnesses and engaging in sneak attacks on the committee.

Some members of Pike's committee compared these tactics to Nixon's use of executive privilege to hide the White House tapes, which were the conclusive evidence in establishing responsibility for the Watergate cover-up.

Then President Ford and Kissinger tried to suppress, on "national security" grounds, the Pike committee report on the manner in which they and the CIA had obstructed the investigation. CBS Correspondent Daniel Shorr obtained that report and delivered it to the *Village Voice* in New York, which published two special supplements in February 1976 on details of the Pike committee's experience with the cover-up for Kissinger.

Careful study of the material published by the *Village Voice* indicates no real "national security" secrets, and the only damage to U.S. foreign policy is the revelation of Kissinger's responsibility for intelligence failures and the underhanded, sneaky tactics that were used to cover his blunders.

In attempting to suppress the House Intelligence Committee report, the Ford White House sought to give the public the impression that a report of a White House commission that had been headed by former Ambassador Robert Murphy was a frank, tough critique of the State Department and the CIA and that it went about as far as any government should in disclosing its past intelligence failures.

But Murphy's 278-page report, developed and written under the strong influence of Vice President Rockefeller, was distinguished more by its evasion of controversy than by its depth or forthrightness. Majority leader Mike Mansfield, usually a mild-mannered and uncritical man, lashed out at "its timidity and its paucity of substance."

"A surfeit of words masks the absence of clarity," Senator Mansfield said, and characterized the report as "thin gruel being served in a very thick bowl." Mansfield and Republican Senator James Pearson, of Kansas, both members of the twelve-member commission, questioned whether the report was worth the two years' time and the $2 million it had cost the taxpayers.

At the press-conference unveiling of the report, Ambassador Murphy said he had made no effort to explore the reason for the much-publicized resignation of Assistant Secretary of State Dixy Lee Ray as Secretary of State Kissinger's chief science adviser.

Dr. Ray, former Chairman of the Atomic Energy Com-

mission, resigned in June 1975, complaining that in the
five months since she had taken office on January 19, Dr.
Kissinger had never consulted her on any problems of
science and technology. In fact, as an Assistant Secretary
of State she had been unable to arrange an appointment
with Dr. Kissinger to discuss the high cost of and leaks
of technology in some of the international agreements
he was making and announcing without the consultation
required by law.

Ambassador Murphy was surprised to learn in the press
conference that his commission staff had interviewed Dr.
Ray several weeks earlier. Murphy acknowledged that he
and other commission members were not informed by
the staff of Ray's complaints about Dr. Kissinger's method
of operation, although he did have some awareness of
"general talk" of Kissinger's lack of consultation with his
subordinates.

While no effort was made by Murphy to pin down complaints that Kissinger was running "a one-man show" with
no consultation in areas in which he had no personal
competence, the report was filled with praise for Dr.
Kissinger's special abilities.

It also included a tribute to Dr. Kissinger by Rockefeller that was the ultimate in praise for his longtime
friend and associate as "an extraordinarily skillful Secretary of State to whom America owes a great debt."

Ambassador Murphy's report was devoid of any criticism of Kissinger and declared its agreement with Rockefeller's conclusion, and it was no surprise that he was
President Ford's selection to head a new three-member
Intelligence Oversight Board to police the Central Intelligence Agency.

With the eighty-two-year-old Ambassador Murphy as

Chairman and two equally establishment figures—Leo Cherne, founder of Democrats for Nixon, and Stephen Ailes—serving on the oversight group, neither President Ford nor Dr. Kissinger would have to worry about any boat-rocking exposure of questionable conduct at the CIA. If Murphy came across illegalities or improprieties, Ford could count on his committee to whisper it in his ear but to avoid unseemly and politically unwise public discussion even if the national security was not involved.

President Ford resisted the idea of any effective oversight from Congress permitting even a small Joint Intelligence Committee access to everything the CIA was doing. Representative Pike, frustrated and unjustly maligned by both direct and sneak attacks, asked, "Have we really learned anything from Watergate? Jerry Ford asks us to trust him without any consideration for what would have happened if we had trusted Richard Nixon to police himself."

It was difficult to determine how much of Ford's actions and attitudes were cunning power grabs and how much unthinking giving in to the schemes of those in his administration bent on continuing control and cover-up. But there were examples in departments other than state.

15. Comeback for Executive Privilege

TWENTY-FIVE YEARS in the House were believed to have given Gerald Ford the understanding and respect for the role Congress must play in the administration and enforcement of law.

Democrats and Republicans resented and opposed the Nixon Administration's arrogant refusal to be accountable to Congress, and Gerald Ford had protested sharply against the corrupting influence of excessive secrecy in earlier Democratic administrations.

Likewise, one would have thought that four-plus terms as a Representative from Maryland would have developed in Secretary of Commerce Rogers Morton a high regard for the role of Congress as a monitor on the executive branch.

The genial six-foot-six-inch bear of a man, admired and respected by his colleagues on both sides of the aisle, would have been judged most unlikely to bring embarrassment to his friend in the Oval Office or to place his reputation in jeopardy by a confrontation with Congress.

But in August 1975—shortly after his confirmation as Secretary of Commerce—Rogers Morton was locked in a determined political struggle with Representative John Moss, a California Democrat, on the politically explosive question of accountability to Congress.

Moss, a bulldog of tenacity on government information policy issues, personally liked Rog Morton. But he refused to let personal friendship interfere with principle. He had not allowed politics to interfere with criticism of Johnson or Kennedy administration officials when the Secretary of Defense, Robert S. McNamara, was espousing unusually restrictive secrecy policies totally unrelated to national defense.

Moss, now the new Chairman of the House Commerce Oversight Subcommittee, sought access to reports made to the Commerce Department by American business firms on the impact of the Arab boycott against companies dealing with Israel or which were owned or controlled by Jewish interests.

"Free trade and freedom from religious discrimination are fundamental to the spirit of America," Moss declared on September 22, 1975, as his subcommittee headed into a showdown with the Ford Administration. "Today's hearing also deals with the right of Congress to obtain the truth from the executive branch.

"Without access to information," Moss continued, "Congress cannot carry out its mandate under Article I of the U.S. Constitution to enact the laws of the land, and it most certainly cannot carry out its mandate of legislative oversight to determine whether existing law is being properly administered."

With regard to the Arab boycott, he said, "We seek to learn to what extent this boycott has impacted on domestic commerce," and explained the broad language of the Arab action:

"By the terms of this boycott American companies and individuals have been asked to refrain from doing business with Israel, or with other American firms or individuals who do business with Israel, or with persons who have expressed support for Israel, or who are of the Jewish faith."

Moss declared it was the intention of the subcommittee "to find out what the effect of the boycott on our country has been." He added that ultimately the Congress needs answers to such questions as "How many companies have complied with boycott requests and why? What kinds of products are covered? Have firms which have refused to comply lost business? Have they suffered a competitive disadvantage? . . . What steps should the Congress take?"

Moss went on to say that the subcommittee needed those answers to "ascertain whether new laws are needed or whether the problem can be resolved by enforcing laws already enacted."

He wanted the information gleaned from the reports "which are required by law to be filed with the Secretary of Commerce concerning attempts to cause an American firm to engage in a boycott. At least up to this morning, the Secretary [Morton] has failed to furnish the reports in compliance with our subpoena," Moss said.

Moss reviewed the frustrating experience of his subcommittee. He recalled that President Ford had expressed grave concern about the Arab boycott in his February 26, 1975, press conference by referring to reports at that time "of attempts of the international banking community to discriminate against certain institutions or individuals on religious or ethnic grounds.

"There should be no doubt about the position of this Administration and the United States," Ford had said emphatically. "Such discrimination is totally contrary to the American tradition and repugnant to American principles. It has no place in the free practice of commerce as it has flourished in this country. Foreign businessmen and investors are most welcome in the United States when they are willing to conform to the principles of our society. However, any allegations of discrimination will be fully investigated and appropriate action taken under the laws of the United States."

Moss quoted Ford's words to Morton, and then expressed the intent of the Export Administration Act: "It is the policy of the United States . . . to oppose restrictive trade practices or boycotts fostered or imposed by foreign countries against any other countries friendly to the United States."

Moss also pointed out the laws administered by the Federal Trade Commission and the Securities and Exchange Commission that would be violated by any "unfair method of competition in commerce and unfair or deceptive acts or practices in commerce."

The intent of those and other laws would clearly make it unlawful for any firm to comply with the broad terms of the Arab boycott, and John Moss wanted to know if those laws were being properly investigated and enforced by the Ford Administration's Justice Department, the FTC and the SEC.

On July 10, 1975, Chairman Moss had written the Director of the Office of Export Administration in the Commerce Department requesting copies of the reports required under the Export Administration Act, which must contain "every instance in which a boycott request has been made to an American company, the number of transactions involved, and, most importantly, whether or not the company has agreed to comply with the boycott requests."

Was President Ford sincere in saying that the Arab boycott was contrary to American tradition and repugnant to American principles, or was he engaging in empty rhetoric while bending our laws to cater to the whims and arrogance of the oil-rich Arab nations?

The Commerce Department rejected the subcommittee requests, so Moss then asked that a subpoena be issued for Secretary Morton to produce them; this was met with a claim that the reports were "confidential."

Moss replied that the confidential designation applied to the public but could not under any circumstances apply to a proper committee of Congress operating within its proper jurisdiction.

It would be senseless for Congress to pass a law to exclude Congress from reports required by that law unless the exclusions were specific, such as Internal Revenue laws which barred all but certain congressional committees unless concrete permission to examine federal tax returns was defined under precise arrangements.

From the outset, Moss did not believe Secretary Morton would engage in an arrogant defiance of Congress. Nor did he believe that Gerald Ford would back such unreasoned secrecy unless prodded by Secretary of State Kissinger. Dr. Kissinger was then involved in secret negotiations with the Arab world on Middle East problems, prices and related matters. Kissinger did not want the technicalities of law to interfere with his international intrigue. He believed he could negotiate "a meaningful" settlement in the Middle East by forcing concessions from the Israelis and according gratuities to the Arabs.

Dr. Kissinger was not concerned by U.S. laws against the Arab boycott. The vital need was an early agreement in the Middle East to lay the groundwork for peace in that area, which would be beneficial to the Ford Administration and enhance Kissinger's own reputation as a miracle worker in international affairs.

Few Israelis trusted Kissinger because they believed his personal ego trips blotted out the long-term interests of Israel. Few Arabs trusted him because of his Jewish heritage. Representative Otis Pike, Chairman of the House Intelligence Committee, doubted that Congress should trust him to barter in secret with either the Soviet Union or the Arab world, particularly when the only evidence available indicated that Dr. Kissinger was disregarding the laws of the United States, the traditions of the United States and the longtime economic interests of the United States to make behind-the-scene settlements.

Harsher critics contended that Kissinger was only contriving to keep his floundering reputation afloat.

In the late summer of 1975, Chairman Moss decided a showdown was necessary on the vital question of access to the reports of the Arab boycott on file in the Commerce Department.

Moss would not believe that President Ford, who proclaimed as he was sworn into office that the hallmark of his administration would be "openness and candor," would refuse to allow access, but he also believed that an appeal to Rogers Morton for reason and logic would break the Kissinger influence.

Though disappointed by the initial responses of Presi-

dent Ford and Morton, Moss believed Attorney General
Edward Levi would spot the fatal flaw in this display of
executive branch arrogance—particularly in the wake of
Nixon's Watergate disaster. The California Democrat was
confident that Ed Levi, former Dean of the University of
Chicago Law School, former President of the University
of Chicago and a Democratic appointee in a Republican
administration, would be his own man and not be bound
by the political loyalties that enmesh most attorneys general.

Again his trust was misplaced and he was to be disillusioned once more. Commerce Secretary Morton presented a memorandum of law from the Justice Department supporting his still-adamant refusal to make the
Arab boycott records available to Congress.

Moss addressed Secretary Morton in stern tones as he
set the stage for a determined contempt of Congress action, "I now hereby order and direct that you comply
with the subcommittee subpoena and that you provide
forthwith the materials herein described."

In an effort to avoid contempt and also refuse the subcommittee's demand, Secretary Morton quibbled that he
was relying on the advice of Karl Bakke, general counsel
for the Commerce Department, who "advises me" that
the Attorney General "advises us that the committee cannot require us under the law to submit these documents."

Moss countered, "I recognize that the Attorney General
has drafted an opinion, and as the lawyer for the Executive
Department his advice should be given great weight, but
the actions and the determinations which are made on
behalf of the Department [of Commerce] are the sole
responsibility of the Secretary of Commerce, in whom

the discretion to release . . . information publicly is vested, and is not vested in the Attorney General."

Secretary Morton insisted that he had personally made the judgment that it was "not in the national interest" to disclose the contents of the reports of the impact of the Arab boycott on American firms. He protested that the term *boycott* was "somewhat misleading" because the Arab nations had made a request only for information relative to "commercial relations with the State of Israel, rather than a request that the U.S. firms boycott Israel.

"In virtually all transactions with most Arab countries, United States and other foreign firms are required to provide boycott-related information or certification as a condition for completing the transactions," Morton said, admitting the total requirement for information by Arab nations. He added,

"Failure on the part of the exporter to provide the requested information or certification will usually result in loss of the contract or sale. However, the fact that a U.S. exporter trades with Arab countries does not necessarily mean that it has boycotted Israel. There may be little or no market in Israel for the firm's goods or services. The firm may not be able to compete economically with other suppliers in that market, or any one of a variety of other business judgments may explain negative responses to the Arab questionnaires."

The Export Administration Act and implementing regulations of that Act require U.S. exporters to report to the Department of Commerce the receipt of boycott-related requests, even though the firm does not intend to comply with those requests. Morton explained,

"The reports describe the type of request received, the

country from which it originated, the name and address
of the party making such requests, the details of the transactions or trade opportunity in connection with which
the request was made—including a description of the com-
modities or services involved and other specific commercial data, such as quantities and prices, when available."

Morton objected that his refusal to provide the requested documents "has been construed by some [as] indicating tacit support within the administration for the
League of Arab Nations' economic boycott against the
State of Israel.

"I want to stress that such is not the case," he said. "We
are clearly on record in fully supporting the 1965 declaration of policy by the Congress, opposing boycotts by any
nation against another country friendly to the United
States and requesting U.S. domestic concerns not to take
any action that would lend them support."

But, Representative James Scheurer challenged Morton
on the effect of Arab countries' refusing to do business
with a firm dealing with Israel.

"It may or may not be legal under our anti-trust laws,
but assuming it is legal, isn't it contrary to the clear public
policy of the United States?" Representative Scheurer
asked.

"If it is clearly contrary to your [Morton's] instruction
to them and to presidential policy, State Department
policy and the policy of Congress, then if they insist on
flagrantly violating the declared public policy of this
country even though it may be legal to do so, why are
they entitled to a cloak of secrecy in making the choice
to cave in to the boycott threat and flout our national
policy?

"Under present law they have the right to make that choice, perhaps, but why don't their stockholders have a right to know of their choice? Why don't the consumers of America have the right to know of that choice and why doesn't the Congress of the United States have a right to know of that choice?" Scheurer summarized the issues.

Moss and Scheurer both conceded that to consider the filing of reports as surrendering to international blackmail would be misleading, but Scheurer insisted that the only way to separate the motivations of the complying firms was for Congress to examine the whole record and the record of enforcement by the various U.S. departments of government to determine whether there was evidence of illegality or impropriety.

Morton claimed arbitrary authority to withhold access to the reports from Congress because the Export Administration Act provided that the reports were "confidential."

Moss charged that unless Congress was specifically barred from reports, it was to be assumed that proper oversight committees should have access to all information. He opined that in those cases in which Congress expressly wished to bar availability to reports it had done so "with great precision."

"It has made, in the instance of the Internal Revenue Code, very clear that a committee . . . of this House" is the only one that can have access to tax-return information except by executive order of the President. Only by specific grants from Congress, Moss said, does the executive branch have a constitutional right to secrecy.

"The Congress has the only constitutional right to secrecy. You can search the Constitution and read every word and only in one instance is the word 'secret' used and this is Article I in connection with the right of Congress to keep its Journal secret. It is not given to anyone else."

Morton, aware of his own jeopardy, pleaded that he was "not a lawyer and perhaps, more than some other secretaries of commerce in a legal matter similar to this, must lean heavily on advice of counsel.

"I am put in a terrible spot if I change the rules of the game in the middle of it," Morton said, citing Attorney General Levi's opinion that declared a presumption of the right of an executive agency to refuse even "demands of congressional committees."

Relying on a flimsy legal position in the Export Administration Act, the Commerce Department and the Attorney General, intent on saving Morton from being the first cabinet officer in history to be found guilty of contempt, turned to a partial reliance on questionable rights to arbitrary secrecy, which they avoided labeling as the discredited "executive privilege."

Representative Moss, an expert on the misuse of executive privilege, immediately turned to recognized constitutional law experts from the academic world, including Professor Philip B. Kurland, of the University of Chicago Law School. Professor Kurland, a longtime close friend of Attorney General Levi, did not let that friendship interfere with his views on Levi's opinion in support of Morton.

After reading the entire record as well as the Attorney General's opinion, Kurland said, "I am of the opinion that, as a matter of law, they are wrong in their claim for executive immunity from congressional oversight in this matter."

He pointed out that the Department of Commerce continued to disseminate trade and investment opportunities from Arab countries, including those with the boycott clause. "It purports to satisfy the policy [announcements to the contrary] by a stamp affixed to such dissemination, which informs the recipient that the American policy is against supporting such boycott clauses, but that it is not illegal for any American firm to comply with such boycott demands.

"This stamp appears to be the extent of the total effect made by the Department of Commerce to secure compliance with American policy," Professor Kurland said. "Parenthetically I should say I have been informed this morning [October 22, 1975] that the statement about illegality of such performance has been removed at the direction of the Secretary of Commerce.

"There is no question raised and none could be raised that this committee has the right and duty to determine whether the administration of the law is in conformity with its objectives and to consider legislation that might be required to assure more realistic compliance with statutory policy, if that should prove necessary."

Professor Kurland observed that the Attorney General did not advise Morton not to make the reports available, but only provided a legal opinion after Morton had refused to surrender the reports and solicited legal support. "Such opinion is advice given to a client and not, in any way, authoritative or binding on Congress or the courts," Professor Kurland declared. Characterizing Levi's advice to Morton as "partisan advocacy," he said, "It is a brief, not a judgment; it does not weigh arguments, it makes them."

He said that neither Morton nor Levi had placed reliance "on so-called executive privilege, for good reasons. There isn't a semblance of evidence that any of the matters sought to be kept from Congress here involves either diplomatic or military secrets or confidential communications between government officials. Moreover, the concept of executive privilege is still in bad color as a result of its persistent abuse by recent executive actions. But attempts to frustrate congressional inquiry into executive action smells the same whatever the title given to it."

Kurland scoffed at the Attorney General's view that barring Congress from oversight was a "standard interpretation" of the law of Congress. "If such a construction were to prevail," he said, "Congress would indeed be, like Milton's Samson Agonistes, 'Eyeless in Gaza, at the mill with the slaves.'

"The Attorney General's contention that the legislative history of the statute supports his construction is also without foundation," Kurland testified. "He does not rely on any legislative history that occurred during the course of the passage of the 1969 law or its predecessor 1949 act.

"He purports to rely on the fact that in 1956 Senator [John] McClellan proposed an amendment that would, in effect, have precluded the assertion of executive privilege by the Secretary of Commerce in regard to foreign trade with Russia," Kurland said. "It had nothing to do with section 7(c), and the withdrawal of the amendment could not be construed as acquiescence by Congress in the Secretary of Commerce's interpretation of executive privilege."

Kurland labeled Attorney General Levi's conclusion "sophistical" and added, "Does the silence of the statute as to the accessibility of the data to Congress create a presumption that Congress was not to have access to the data? The Attorney General would indulge such a presumption, but solely on the basis that he and his predecessors, as counsel to the members of the executive branch, would prefer to exonerate their clients from congressional oversight."

Kurland declared that, in fact, the presumption "would go in the opposite direction," and described his own "syllogistic" reasoning:

"The major premise is that the congressional function of oversight and investigation is a power and duty of primary importance to our constitutional system of checks and balances. If judicial support for that proposition is necessary it is available in advance.

"My second proposition is that a legislature is not deemed to surrender its power in the absence of what the Supreme Court has called 'clear and unmistakable evidence of the intent to part with it.' "

After citing an abundance of precise legal authority, Professor Kurland commented, "I should think, however, that one need not resort to judicial authority but only to common sense, which is perhaps in shorter supply, to support the presumption that Congress is not deemed to surrender its authority to oversee the functioning of the Department of Commerce, itself, or that it be exercised solely at the discretion of the Secretary of Commerce."

He made one more point: "The Secretary of Commerce's reliance on the Attorney General is not exonerative of his contempt of Congress" and he cited the Supreme Court case of Sinclair v. United States, 279 U.S. 263,299 (1929) growing out of the infamous Teapot Dome scandal.

In conclusion, Professor Kurland encouraged Moss and his subcommittee "not to contribute to the continued destruction of congressional authority" but to continue to investigate and hold the executive branch accountable.

"The constitutional plan of checks and balances, an essential safeguard for American liberties, is constantly endangered by failure of Congress to assert its authority vis-a-vis the Executive. I trust that this case will not prove another instance of such surrender; the rights at stake are not rights of individual Congressmen, they are the rights of the American people whose representatives you are," said Kurland.

Raoul Berger, another constitutional law expert and Charles Warren Senior Fellow in American Legal History, Harvard Law School, declared that there was no more sound legal basis for Attorney General Levi's defense of Morton than there had been for the use of executive privilege to bar Congress from the Nixon White House tapes.

He declared that executive privilege and the arbitrary positions taken by Secretary Morton and Attorney General Leiv are "an occupational disease" of cabinet officers in Democratic and Republican administrations. He castigated Congress for permitting the executive branch to act arbitrarily to block Congress from information.

"The customary weight attached to an opinion of the Attorney General is considerably diminished when it pertains to a dispute between the executive branch and the Congress," Berger said, "for the loyalty of the Attorney General then runs to the President. He is an advocate with a client."

Berger referred to the cloak of confidentiality that President Nixon had tried to use to constrict Watergate investigations, and his warning that to disclose would destroy the presidency.

"I may remind you that there were those who thought it would utterly destroy the presidency to compel Mr.

Nixon to make the disclosure [of the tapes]. The court required disclosure. The presidency has kept rolling along just like Old Man River. The only one who was destroyed was an unworthy incumbent."

He emphasized that as the Vietnam war developed, various secretaries of defense and state had claimed the right to refuse Congress information in the "national interest" and that Congress did not resist.

"You have nobody to blame but yourselves," Berger said. "I would adjure you, whether you are a Republican or a Democrat, be as loyal to your institution as Nixon professed to be to the presidency in an unholy cause. You have a great institution.

"Theodore Sorensen said there is nothing wrong with executive privilege that a few contempt proceedings won't cure, and he is right," Berger declared.

Norman Dorsen, professor at New York University Law School, President of the Society of American Law Teachers and general counsel for the American Civil Liberties Union, also gave testimony supportive of the right of the House oversight subcommittee to receive the Arab reports, and he, too, was critical of the Attorney General's opinion.

Against that background, the Moss subcommittee voted 10 to 5 on November 11, 1975, to recommend that the House hold Secretary Morton in contempt for his refusal to produce the Arab boycott reports.

"If Secretary Morton's argument for not complying with a valid congressional subpoena is allowed to remain unchallenged, it will establish a dangerous precedent which could be more pernicious than the doctrine of executive privilege," Moss warned in a November 21 letter of transmittal to Harley O. Staggers, Chairman of the full House Commerce Committee.

"According to the Library of Congress report [to the committee], it appears that Congress would be precluded from access to information compiled pursuant to nearly a hundred statutes similar to the statute cited by Secretary Morton."

The five votes supporting Morton were from Republicans whose solidarity was induced by prodding from the Ford White House. If the issue received wide publicity and the public understood the arbitrary-secrecy issue involved, it would be difficult, if not impossible, to hold all the Republicans in line or to win the support of more than a handful of southern Democrats.

The penalty for contempt of Congress was a possible prison term. Even though President Ford could have granted another pardon, that too would have been recognized as an act of executive arrogance.

Secretary Morton scrambled to negotiate his way out of the contempt peril, and on December 8 he avoided the citation by agreeing to turn over the subpoenaed records to the Moss subcommittee, but with a proposal that he yield the records with a guarantee of confidentiality.

Moss rejected the proposal, saying he could not promise confidentiality on information he had not seen; but he permitted Morton and the Ford White House to save face by assuring him that the records would be treated "in consonance with their asserted confidentiality." However, it was understood by both sides that the Moss subcommittee would be free to make the information public by a majority vote of the subcommittee.

The agreement was finally reached on the evening before the scheduled vote by the full Commerce Committee on the subcommittee's recommendation to cite Morton for contempt. Morton thus escaped being the first federal official ever to be cited for contempt by either house.

It was a trying five-month tug-of-war lost by the Ford Administration. By supporting faulty legal principles for months, the President had relinquished more credibility. Secretary Morton was embarrassed and humiliated by being forced to take uncomfortable legal positions, by having to admit ignorance of the law and by contradicting his past image of openness.

But the big loser was Attorney General Levi, who had had a reputation for legal rectitude, independence and principle. He was now on record as just another "partisan advocate" for the Ford White House. The legal opinion he signed and supported on Morton's right to withhold the Arab boycott reports was difficult to distinguish from the partisan political whoring of John Mitchell and Richard Kleindienst on the question of Richard Nixon's accountability to Congress.

The Arab boycott reports were only the first of several issues to challenge the competency and the independence of the Justice Department under Edward Levi. Justice Department actions were to have a major role in further unfavorable reflections on the White House in matters dealing with the State Department and the Department of Agriculture.

The antitrust division's advice to President Ford regarding support of bipartisan legislation to require bonding of the meat-packing industry proved both the White House staff and the antitrust division to be politically inept and professionally incompetent.

16. Deregulation—Questions of Competence

WHEN PRESIDENT FORD criticized the federal government for engaging in much wasteful and expensive overregulation of business, his comments had broad appeal to big business, small-business men, farmers and the average citizen, all of whom were disenchanted with government regulations and the frustration of dealing with the Washington bureaucracy.

The United States Chamber of Commerce convention cheered when he told them on April 28, 1975, that he intended to deregulate business and would examine and improve the regulatory agencies.

"There are sound estimates that government regulations have added billions of unnecessary dollars to business and consumer costs every year," President Ford said. "To reverse this trend of growing regulation, my Administration is working hard to identify and to eliminate those regulations which now cost the American people more than they provide in benefits."

Democrats and Republicans alike agreed on the need

for reform, but their approaches to the problem differed widely. Those who were not demagogues realized that the pruning of unneeded regulations was a delicate job, requiring a thorough understanding of the reasons the laws were enacted in the first place, sound technical knowledge of the industry involved and a clear knowledge of conditions which had developed since the initial regulatory structure was established.

In short, decisions on deregulation would take skillful analysis by experienced, objective men. Neither novices in government or politics nor ideologues fascinated with the rhetoric of political budget cutting could be allowed to implement changes in the rules.

In May and June President Ford made additional comments on the high priority he was placing on deregulation in the battle against inflation and expanding government. However, in the summer of 1975, faced with an opportunity to demonstrate real understanding of the problems of regulation, the Ford White House bungled badly.

The issue was whether the Packers and Stockyards Act of 1921 should be amended and broadened to require bonding for meat-packing companies exempted from the initial legislation because they bought little livestock directly from farmers and ranchers. The bankruptcy of American Beef Packers Inc. in January 1975 stranded more than twelve thousand farmers and ranchers holding in excess of $22 million in worthless checks.

That catastrophic financial collapse of one of the biggest beef- and pork-packing firms in the country clearly demonstrated that the farmers needed guarantees that the checks they received for their livestock would be good when cashed.

Farm organizations, livestock organizations and eventually the packing industry itself exerted pressure for federal legislation to provide uniform packer-bonding requirements.

The four major farm organizations—the American Farm Bureau Federation, the National Farmers Union, the National Farmers Organization and the National Grange—for years had favored bringing the meat packers under the bonding provisions of the law, as had the major livestock organizations. But the packing industry, not wanting the additional burden, lobbied successfully in Congress that few meat packers were failing and that the problem was relatively insignificant.

The insolvency of American Beef brought quick action in farm-state legislatures, and within a few months more than twenty states enacted packer-bonding laws. The packing industry frantically tried to meet the requirements of the multiplicity of these state laws, which varied greatly, and it promoted federal legislation to assure uniformity.

The question of federal packer bonding was neither a political issue nor an ideological one. Senator Dick Clark, a liberal Democrat from Iowa, cosponsored packer bonding with Senator Carl Curtis, a conservative Republican from Nebraska. Likewise, on the House side, packer bonding legislation had the support of conservative Republican Representative Charles Thone, of Nebraska, and Representatives Berkley Bedell, Thomas Harkin and Neal Smith, all liberal Democrats from Iowa.

Dr. Gerald Engelman, veteran analyst for the Packers and Stockyards Administration in the Agriculture Department, Administrator Marvin McLain and Associate Administrator Glenn Bierman favored packer bonding as essential and long overdue. After consulting with Congressmen and Senators writing the legislation, they had

convinced Assistant Secretary of Agriculture Richard Feltner that such protection for the farmer was necessary.

With his experts favoring it, Agriculture Secretary Earl
Butz, an outspoken proponent of free enterprise, decided
the proposed law should be supported and made a recommendation to that effect to the White House.

James Lynn, Director of the Office of Management and
Budget (OMB), took note of the estimate of $500,000 to
$800,000 in cost and routed it to the Justice Department
for study.

At this point zealous amateurs took over, bringing more
enthusiasm than experience or judgment to the job in
their desire to display their knowledge of President Ford's
priorities on government deregulation.

The packer-bonding proposals landed on the Justice
Department desk of Robert D. Stewart, a twenty-six-year-
old honor graduate of the University of Iowa Law School
in 1974.

The young lawyer had no experience with the packers
and stockyards laws, nor with the practical problems of
marketing cattle, sheep or hogs. In fact, he had no farm
experience at all, having been reared in Chicago and completing his undergraduate work at the University of Illinois.

Another young lawyer, Donald Fitch, who had joined
the Justice Department only a few months earlier, was a
native of Washington, D.C., and a graduate of the University of Mississippi Law School. Only thirty years old,
he also lacked exposure to agriculture and to the problems
of the Packers and Stockyards Administration.

Fortified by their ignorance, they wrote a memorandum
recommending against support of packer-bonding legislation because it required spending additional federal funds

while imposing expensive red tape on the meat-packing industry in contradiction of President Ford's campaign for deregulation. They were proud when their recommendation went to the top of the Justice Department with few changes, was signed by a Deputy Assistant Attorney General in the Office of Legal Counsel and was returned to OMB Director Lynn.

As a matter of routine, Lynn turned it over to a subordinate and a copy was sent to the Agriculture Department, where it eventually reached the Packers and Stockyards Division. McLain, Bierman and Engelman were shocked at the decision to oppose packer bonding, but they were more shocked at the factual errors indicating how little the Justice Department understood of the history of the packer-bonding issue or the Packers and Stockyards Act.

Meetings were arranged to explain the meat-packing business to the young Justice Department lawyers, and after several hours McLain and his aides felt they had made progress. Stewart and Fitch acknowledged the limitations in their comprehension of the problem and of the extent of bonding requirements in the existing law.

McLain's aides did not press for assurance of a reversal because they assumed that, with explanation of the facts and corrections in the understanding of the law, a reversal of recommendation would be automatic.

Bierman and Engelman felt that the inexperienced lawyers now knew why it was vital that packers be bonded to restore the credibility of the packing industry in the wake of the American Beef disaster.

Stewart said later that "they [Bierman and Engelman] were pretty upset about our memorandum, and brought us all kinds of figures and statistics on how many firms had gone out of business in the last seventeen years and how much money had been lost by farmers and ranchers."

The figure showed that more than 150 meat-packing plants owing farmers and ranchers more than $45 million had gone out of business from 1958 to 1975, and that eight packing companies, including American Beef, had gone out of business since the first of 1975.

Stewart acknowledged that Engelman and Bierman had also stressed that there were between 75 and 100 "technically insolvent" packing plants at that time which must be monitored carefully by the Packers and Stockyards Administration.

"They were quite persuasive on many points, and I believe they changed the emphasis of our thinking," Stewart admitted later. He and Fitch learned from Engelman and Bierman that all of the stockyards, commission houses and dealers who bought livestock were already covered by bonding-law provisions and that only the packers had been exempted from the bonding law in 1921.

Stewart said they also learned of changes in marketing patterns that left 85 percent of the beef sales to packers unprotected by bonding.

But, in spite of this, he and Fitch still believed there was no need for bonding packers. "In the end, we did not feel they [Engelman and Bierman] made a case that there is an overwhelming need for packer bonding. It was a matter of trying to develop a longtime policy and not one of simply reacting to the American Beef collapse when it is an unusual bankruptcy coming in the midst of the worst recession in twenty-five years."

When Engelman and Bierman left the Justice Department the lawyers in the antitrust division notified the White House that there was "no reason to back away from the original position."

Only on the morning the House Agriculture Committee hearing on the packer-bonding legislation was due to start did Secretary Butz learn that OMB and the White House had directed the Department of Agriculture to give testimony in opposition to packer bonding.

Distressed at the overruling of his recommendation with no notice, Secretary Butz called President Ford. He was unavailable, but Special Assistant to the President James Cannon took the call of protest. Cannon told Butz that President Ford had been adamantly opposed and that Butz should proceed to arrange for the department to oppose packer-bonding legislation.

Since Butz had recommended packer-bonding legislation and Assistant Secretary Feltner felt even more strongly about it, it was necessary to find another witness to give the Administration's position. McLain and his aides were the most knowledgeable, but they had consulted with members of the House and Senate writing the packer-bonding legislation.

Therefore it was necessary to reach down to the third layer, to Deputy Assistant Secretary John Damgard, in order to find someone who could read an opposition statement and not contradict a position expressed to a Congressman or Senator. Though Damgard did not relish the job, he agreed to read the statement but insisted that a Justice Department representative defend the opposition to bonding of packers.

Bruce Wilson, a Deputy Assistant Attorney General in the Antitrust Division, was tapped to present the case for the opposition to packer bonding to the subcommittee

with less than two hours' notice. Understandably, Wilson
made error after error on the law, the history of the Packers and Stockyards Administration and the present conditions in the packing industry. He did not understand the
concern of the Congressmen who contended it was vital
that there be protection for livestock men whose cattle
and hogs were slaughtered within twenty-four to seventy-
two hours after sale and shipped to retail meat outlets,
making it impossible for them to retrieve their assets if
they were paid by checks that bounced.

House and Senate Agriculture Committee members
were appalled at Wilson's lack of knowledge of the livestock marketing industry and his factual inaccuracies, and
yet he was stating the Administration's opposition to requirement for bonds. Had there been press interest in the
hearings, the Justice Department and the Ford White
House would have been subjected to widespread ridicule.
As it was, only five or six reporters covered the hearings,
and most of them were less well informed on the livestock
industry than the Justice Department lawyers had been.

Fortunately for President Ford, only the *Des Moines
Register* and some farm-organization publications carried
comprehensive stories on the disaster of the foul-up on
the packer-bonding issue.

Senator Curtis, a longtime friend of the President, was
not consulted by the White House prior to the decision
to oppose his bill. He said he did not intend to protest
because "I am not sure there is anyone down there who
would understand what I was talking about."

The Nebraska Republican planned to work with Senator Clark and other midwestern Senators to pass legislation
and hoped to convince the President he should not veto it.

Representative Charles Grassley, an Iowa Republican,

protested to President Ford about the Administration's
opposition and pointed out that his packer-bonding bill
was "written with the assistance of the Department of
Agriculture."

"Responsible people in the management of packing
plants were consulted," Grassley wrote. "Farm organizations were favorable. Certainly the hundreds of Iowa farm
families who are holding collectively $6.6 million worth
of bad checks from one recent packer bankruptcy consider
this responsible legislation."

Senator Clark, upon learning of the role of the inexperienced young lawyers in Justice, declared that "the
decision-making process in this instance appears to be the
blind leading the blind," but he agreed with Senator
Curtis that the bill would pass the Senate and House by
an overwhelming margin despite White House opposition.

Senator Curtis commented, "I hope that by the time we
get the legislation through the Senate and House we will
have educated the White House and OMB on this subject."

Representative Neal Smith, a veteran Iowa Democrat,
said that it was "a shocking revelation" to learn of the
role of Stewart and Fitch as architects of the Ford Administration's position.

"But, the final decision on the packer-bonding legislation was no more incredible than have been a number of
other decisions in the agricultural field," Smith continued.
"Although President Ford took Agriculture Secretary Butz'
advice on the veto of the farm bill with increased prices,
he did not go along with the Butz suggestion to increase
the loan rates [on corn, wheat and cotton]," he said.
"Equally incomprehensible in my book is the acceptance
[by Ford] of the OMB opinions in opposing federal grain
inspection, and the abolition of the use of nongovernment

inspectors," Smith charged in referring to what he considered "unreasoned opposition" to reform demanded by the grain-inspection scandals.

A week later, White House Chief of Staff Donald Rumsfeld was still unaware of the blunders by the White House in disputing the need for bonding to protect farmers, but acknowledged the negative position as "a mistake" when the facts were related to him.

However, rather than acknowledge incompetence and reverse its position, Rumsfeld said the White House would wait until the Congress passed a packer-bonding bill and "just not veto it."

The White House hoped the problem could be glossed over without its having to admit publicly that a mistake had been made.

Fortunately for Ford and Rumsfeld, most of the newsmen were concentrating on Ford's meeting with ten major regulatory agency heads to urge the leadership to cut unneeded regulations. Ford cited four areas for agency action:

1. Assessment of the costs and benefits of major regulatory actions.

2. Reduction within six months of delays that prevent "a speedy and effective process."

3. Development of procedures more responsive and comprehensible to consumers.

4. Consideration of fundamental changes leading to deregulation where government interference "no longer makes sense."

While there was widespread agreement with President Ford's general intention to cut wasteful regulation, there was no evidence that the White House was following his blueprint for necessary regulation in the packer-bonding problem they were handling. In fact, the White House rejected the views of the experts in the Department of Agriculture who were conscientiously trying to "make procedures more responsive and comprehensible to consumers." The Ford White House demonstrated no depth understanding of the problem but was simply caught with an obsession to deregulate for the sake of deregulation.

In overriding Butz, the White House did not even extend him the courtesy of consultation before the decision was made and his request for a personal talk with President Ford was denied. James Cannon, who refused Butz' request, was as naïve and unknowledgeable about farm legislation and packers and stockyards laws as the twenty-six-year-old antitrust division lawyer had been. Two weeks after forcing Agriculture to oppose the legislation, Cannon still believed the proposed change in the law would have "put the Agriculture Department in the bonding business."

"There must be some way in which these packers can get their bonds through private industry," Cannon said, protesting the key provision in the packer-bonding bills. He was surprised to learn that the recommendation did not put the Agriculture Department in the bonding business, but merely gave the Packers and Stockyards Administration authority to insist that packers be bonded through private-industry sources.

They were the same inaccuracies that had shocked Senate and House Agriculture Committee members when stressed by Deputy Attorney General Bruce Wilson a few weeks earlier.

Fumbling of the packer-bonding issue documented the poor communications and lack of expertise in the White House organization under White House Chief of Staff Donald Rumsfeld. Many Republicans believed Rumsfeld was using his position to build his own political empire as a springboard to the vice presidency and eventually the presidency.

Conservative Republicans had accused Rumsfeld to his face of jockeying his men into control in the White House and into posts in the regulatory agencies and Cabinet departments to the detriment of the Ford Administration.

Rumsfeld blandly denied the accusations month after month, always ending up in the right place at the right time; yet his mentor, Ford, had to assume responsibility for all decisions and unfavorable political repercussions.

Don Rumsfeld had been a cheerleader on Ford's team for years, and Jerry Ford is loyal to old friends who expressed their admiration often. It seemed that every time Ford had a personnel shuffle, he dealt a winning hand to Rumsfeld.

17. "My Team"

WHEN NATO AMBASSADOR DONALD RUMSFELD hurried back to Washington after Richard Nixon's resignation to handle coordination of a four-man transition team, he denied any interest in a White House post and returned to Brussels. A month later the handsome, young, former Illinois Congressman was ensconced in the White House as a presidential counselor with Cabinet rank, an advantageous position on the ladder to his calculated goal of President of the United States.

The suave and ambitious Princeton man had ingratiated himself with Ford, and he saw the White House as a double opportunity to help the President and to take a giant step forward in the political firmament. At forty-two years of age, time was not pressing him for the final move. If the opportunity presented itself in 1976, Rummy was ready, but he could wait until 1980, or even 1984.

Don Rumsfeld's personal, longtime ambitions were explored by columnists and political writers and were the subject of increased political comment in Congress with each successful maneuver. From the outset it was perceived that Rumsfeld, to be a credible presidential candidate, wanted to round out his governmental experience with a major Cabinet post.

On the advice of then House Republican Leader Gerald R. Ford, Rumsfeld gave up what was considered a "sure House seat" to accept a job from Richard Nixon as head of the Office of Economic Opportunity (OEO). Displaying no outstanding success in that job, Rumsfeld nevertheless managed to wheedle a White House office out of Nixon and the title of Special Assistant to the President, with Cabinet rank.

In 1971 Rumsfeld used his White House connections to manipulate a move that made him Director of the Cost of Living Council while allowing him to retain his White House office and close proximity to power and politics.

After the 1972 election, Rumsfeld was appointed Ambassador to NATO, thus avoiding any taint of Watergate in the crucial cover-up stage that was enmeshing nearly everyone else in the White House in major and minor obstructions of justice.

The move to Brussels not only removed him from Watergate, but his nearly two years in that post gave the ambitious young man foreign relations credentials that widened the range of political moves possible to him, including, perhaps, a challenge to Senator Adlai Stevenson in 1974. Although Rumsfeld avoided personal involvement in Watergate, the damage it did to the Republican Party destroyed his chance for a successful challenge to Adlai Stevenson for the U.S. Senate seat in Illinois.

The resignation of Nixon and the elevation of Gerald Ford to the presidency was good political news for Rumsfeld. Although he had rapport with Nixon and Haldeman,

Rumsfeld knew that access to Nixon was contingent upon not displeasing Haldeman or Ehrlichman.

Rumsfeld's relations with President Ford were direct and welded by four terms in the House, where he had been an activist in the revolt that ousted minority leader Charles Halleck and boosted Ford to House Republican Leader in January 1965.

Rumsfeld had competition for Ford's favor from presidential counselors Robert Hartmann and John Marsh, but it was not necessary to go through them for access to the Oval Office, as had been true in Bob Haldeman's heyday. A quiet struggle took place in the White House structure as temporary Chief of Staff Alexander Haig was eased out to a NATO post as Supreme Commander, but Rumsfeld's strength became recognized when Ford's first shuffle was announced on December 18, 1974.

The move was theoretically to divide White House responsibilities and to make President Ford more accessible to all White House staffers; but on paper Rumsfeld emerged in a Chief of Staff position more powerful than H. R. Haldeman's had been under Nixon.

Significantly, it was Rumsfeld who announced that President Ford's reorganization was "to put his house in order" and increase top-staff accessibility to the Oval Office. The charts showed that Rumsfeld and three others—Hartmann, Marsh and White House Counsel Philip Buchen—appeared in lateral arrangements, but for purposes of administration Rumsfeld explained he was to be "the coordinator."

Rumsfeld revealed that in addition to the four of equal rank, five other White House staffers would have direct access to President Ford. On the surface it was a most democratic arrangement, but it had to "coordinate" through Rumsfeld.

Rumsfeld had the most intimate knowledge of who saw Ford, for how long, and the problems discussed. He knew firsthand of all developments within the White House staff, the satisfaction and the disenchantments. He could set the stage, pamper the star, Jerry Ford, and essentially be the director, producer and writer for any scenario Ford wished to present to the nation or to secure his political future. As long as the leading man's part was augmented, or protected, Don Rumsfeld could write his own ending.

If not the hero, he was definitely the victor; a victor who had manipulated the organization to flow, if not through him, at least within his reach. He could maneuver hand-picked aides into key positions in the White House and in agencies.

It was an open secret that Rumsfeld, while contriving quietly to solidify his power within the White House, was also interested in a future appointment as Secretary of State, Defense or Treasury "to demonstrate he could run a big government department." Knowing Rumsfeld's ambition, Schlesinger and even Secretary of Treasury William Simon were wary throughout the first ten months of 1975.

As Ford's December 1974 shuffle was being announced, reports surfaced that Transportation Secretary Claude Brinegar, a Nixon man, would soon resign and be replaced by John Robson, a forty-three-year-old Chicago attorney and former campaign aide to Rumsfeld. Robson, who served as general counsel to the Transportation Department under President Lyndon B. Johnson, also served as an under secretary of transportation in the Nixon Administration. Rumsfeld was Robson's major supporter and promoter early in the Nixon Administration when he was unsuccessfully pushed as Chairman of the Interstate Commerce Commission. Conservative Republican opposition to Robson developed because he was considered a Rumsfeld man and "too liberal." However, Robson was eventually nominated by Ford and confirmed as Chairman of the Civil Aeronautics Board.

Another straw in the wind indicating Rumsfeld's victory was the report that President Ford had decided to use Hartmann's office next to the Oval Office as a den for himself. Counselor Hartmann, speech writer and political confidant of Ford's for years, was being moved to a bigger, more remote office on the far side of the Executive Office Building.

"The President decided he would like to have an office as a study where he could relax," Rumsfeld explained. "Don't read anything into it. He wanted an office that is a bit less formal than the Oval Office."

Within ten and a half months after Rumsfeld announced the reorganization to put Ford's house in order, the young man from Illinois had solidified his hold on the White House and was recognized as the most powerful man in Washington, second to the President himself.

Rumsfeld was President Ford's major link with former Representative Bo Callaway, the Georgia Republican who headed the Ford campaign for the Republican nomination. Callaway's outspoken comments on Vice President Nelson A. Rockefeller resulted in Rockefeller's withdrawing his name on November 3, 1975, from consideration for the 1976 nomination as Ford's running mate. His stated reason was to give the President a "range of options" and simplify his campaign for the Republican nomination against conservative forces rallying behind former California Governor Ronald Reagan.

The same day, President Ford announced the highly controversial national security shuffle, including the firing of Defense Secretary James Schlesinger and CIA Director William Colby.

The chessboard strategy of Ford removed William Colby as head of CIA; brought George Bush, another potential vice-presidential candidate, to that post from Peking, where he had served as U.S. liaison representative; and moved Rumsfeld to Secretary of Defense.

Secretary of State Henry Kissinger lost his National Security Council chairmanship and his White House office to his deputy, Lt. Gen. Brent Scowcroft. This was a blow to Kissinger, who prized his second hat highly because it provided him immediate access to the Oval Office.

In the White House, Richard Cheney, thirty-two-year-old alter ego to Rumsfeld, moved up from deputy to become White House Chief of Staff.

On the surface unrelated, but taking place at the same time, was the shift of Elliot Richardson, Ambassador to London, back into the Cabinet to replace Rogers C. B. Morton, who was resigning as Secretary of Commerce. It was whispered that Morton soon would move into a White House post to direct the floundering Ford campaign. Richardson, a man for all seasons, had held three previous Cabinet posts in the Nixon Administration, and Ford wanted him available as a worthy Secretary of State in the event the temperamental Dr. Kissinger again threatened to resign over disappointment in the new power alignment.

President Ford explained that the changes would

strengthen the team for handling national security affairs, and stressed that he wanted "my team" in key positions. Still, it was difficult to see any gains, political or otherwise, from the complicated moves, except that he helped Donald Rumsfeld broaden his governmental experience. Rumsfeld, leaving the White House under control of his young protégé, Richard Cheney, went to Defense to replace Secretary Schlesinger, a move that upset Republican conservatives more than any of the other changes.

With Rockefeller eliminated as vice-presidential running mate for Ford, and Rumsfeld rounding out his experience in a top Cabinet post, he would now be available for the second spot on a national ticket. Why else remove Schlesinger, who was respected by Democrats and Republicans and who represented a strong counterforce against Secretary of State Henry Kissinger?

The timing of Ford's decision to remove CIA Director Colby made no sense. Colby was not involved in the scandals at CIA, and he had handled the difficult testimony before Congress in a generally satisfactory way. Was it reform, "Watergate style," to nominate a former Republican National Chairman, George Bush, to replace Colby?

Certainly there was no indication that Bush, a man with undisguised vice-presidential ambitions, wanted to be sloughed off to the political dead-end as CIA Director. A former Texas Congressman, he was a Ford favorite and was considered a possible vice-presidential selection at the time Nelson Rockefeller was nominated. He had served as Ambassador to the United Nations and then was sent to represent the United States in Peking, where he could have been drafted as Ford's running mate.

President Ford could hardly have expected the nomination and confirmation of Bush, a former Republican Party leader, to pass without a challenge in the wake of allegations of the Nixon Administration's political misuse of the Central Intelligence Agency. Rumsfeld himself couldn't have orchestrated anything better than the political fuss by Senator Jackson, Senator Robert Byrd and others which forced George Bush to eliminate himself from contention for the Republican vice-presidential nomination in 1976.

Carefully considering all of the moves of Ford's November massacre, Donald Rumsfeld was the only one to emerge unscathed.

Certainly the ouster was not intended to aid Schlesinger and Colby, although the manner in which it was accomplished won them considerable sympathy as well as praise.

Quick reactions to the firing of Schlesinger were regarded as a victory for Dr. Kissinger in their long, quiet struggle over defense posture and detente. But, on careful examination, it became apparent that Dr. Kissinger had been deprived of his White House office as Special Assistant to the President in charge of National Security Affairs, something he had resisted despite widespread congressional criticism of him for not yielding it when he assumed the post of Secretary of State.

Kissinger's dual role was regarded as too much concentration of foreign affairs power and responsibility in one man, but President Ford and Vice President Rockefeller defended it on the grounds of the unique qualities Dr. Kissinger brought to the job.

When Rumsfeld emerged as chief beneficiary of the shuffle, President Ford emphasized that he and he alone had made the decisions.

"Did you ask for suggestions, or did you do this largely on your own?" a newsman asked President Ford.

"I did it totally on my own," Ford responded. "It was my decision. I fitted the pieces together and they fitted excellently. It was my decision."

"With [regard to] Mr. Rumsfeld, who is involved in your decision," a questioner asked, "would he have had any input into the overall decision?"

"He did not," the President answered firmly.

The response was followed by another question as to whether the moves (Rumsfeld to Defense and Bush to CIA) would "give you a more directly responsive intelligence community than you have had hitherto?"

"Mr. Bush and Don Rumsfeld are long personal friends of mine," the President answered. "I have known of their fine record. I have an excellent relationship with them. I am certain that they will contribute very significantly, and these are my guys and the ones that I wanted and I hope and trust that the confirmation will be quick in the United States Senate."

"Does the nomination of Donald Rumsfeld as Defense Secretary, and the nomination of Mr. Bush as CIA Director, does that eliminate them as vice-presidential running mate possibilities?" another reporter asked, and Ford responded,

"They are first-class public officials. . . . I don't think they are eliminated from consideration by anybody—the delegates to the [Republican] Convention or myself."

The President was asked whether it was correct to assume that Secretary Kissinger's influence was substantially reduced by losing his NSC post and having to share access to him with Bush and Rumsfeld.

"Let me state affirmatively that Secretary Kissinger has

done a superb job as Secretary of State and as my Assistant for National Security Affairs. He will continue to handle the responsibilities of foreign policy, which I think has been not only successful but in the best interests of the United States. There will be organization changes, as I have indicated . . . but Secretary Kissinger will have the dominant role in the formulation of and the carrying out of foreign policy."

Then a reporter probed the possibility that Secretary Schlesinger was in conflict with Ford's and Kissinger's attitude on detente.

"There were no basic differences," President Ford said, glossing over some deep differences. "I wanted a team that I selected, and as President I think it is important that a president have that kind of a team on an affirmative basis, and I have it."

The President was further prodded to reveal his dissatisfaction with the dual roles of Secretary Kissinger, since Kissinger had stated publicly he considered them of great importance in the execution of foreign policy.

Still emphasizing that it was his decision, Ford responded: "I indicated that the team I put together will affirmatively satisfy the way I want an organization structure set up. That is the way I wanted it, that is the way it is, and I think it will work effectively."

It was an indirect way of saying Dr. Kissinger's wishes were no longer the primary concern of the Oval Office.

John Osborne, veteran White House correspondent for the *New Republic,* tossed in an important question to try to clarify precisely what President Ford meant:

"To follow up with a slightly repetitious question, are you saying and intending to be understood to say that neither personal nor policy differences between Dr. Kissinger and Mr. Schlesinger contributed to this change?"

"That is correct," President Ford said in a curt reply that was to raise the most serious question of his credibility in the days ahead.

It was possible though difficult to believe that Don Rumsfeld had no role in suggesting or guiding President Ford's thinking on moves so totally beneficial to Rumsfeld's political interests while creating political problems for Ford.

It was possible though difficult to believe Ford's assertion that "neither personal nor policy differences between Dr. Kissinger and Mr. Schlesinger had contributed to the change" at Defense, unless the motivation was simply to open a suitable Cabinet post for Rummy. Dr. Kissinger and Secretary Schlesinger differed on such fundamental questions as strategic arms negotiations, military aid to the Middle East and detente with the Soviet Union to the extent they had been the subject of congressional questions, news stories and columns.

"Secretary Kissinger and I have not always agreed on policy, but it's sort of natural given our varying responsibilities," Secretary Schlesinger had told a reporter only three days before he was fired. Kissinger was quoted as commenting only a few weeks earlier,

"If there should be a disagreement [on arms control talks] . . . then it will be settled by the President."

For months Schlesinger had been pressing for a $13.7 billion increase in defense spending for fiscal year 1976, coupling his request with statements that the Soviet Union was spending as much as 50 percent more on missiles, aircraft and other weapons than the United States.

Schlesinger termed the $7.6 billion House cut in the $97.8 billion Defense Department request savage and arbitrary and declared it would have a severe effect on the nation's defense posture.

These public comments by Schlesinger irritated Dr. Kissinger, who was seeking to work out a second-stage arms control agreement with the Soviet Union, and who wished compromise with the Soviet leaders to continue the spirit of detente.

Schlesinger, and many others in the Senate and House, believed that under Kissinger detente was a one-way street and that the United States was engaged in bargaining away the last segment of military advantage it had.

One issue that put Schlesinger and Kissinger on opposite sides was whether a new Soviet bomber, Backfire, should be included in the twenty-four-hundred ceiling on strategic nuclear weapons established in the Vladivostok accords in November 1974.

The Soviet position was that the Backfire, which had not been discussed at the Vladivostok meeting, was a tactical rather than strategic weapon and therefore should not be included in the arms ceiling.

Kissinger was willing to compromise on the Backfire bomber issue, but Schlesinger argued during a National Security Council meeting in September that the bomber had to be counted to compensate for Soviet advantages in missile size.

Also not discussed was another weapon system—the cruise missile—a low-flying, unmanned aircraft that can be adapted to carry nuclear weapons. The Soviets argued that U.S. cruise missiles should be counted in the overall ceiling, but the Defense Department insisted that only ballistic missiles that fly outside the earth's atmosphere should be counted.

The Defense Department suggested that both the Backfire bomber and the cruise missile be counted—in equal numbers, but at a level above the arms ceiling reached at Vladivostok.

While Ford accepted the Defense Department viewpoint on the Backfire bomber and cruise missile trade-off, Dr. Kissinger, who was to present the position to Soviet Foreign Minister Andrei A. Gromyko, resented the fact that it interfered with his efforts to reach an early agreement on SALT (Strategic Arms Limitation Treaty).

Schlesinger insisted on a firm bargaining stance and was skeptical of making military concessions to gain political agreements of short duration.

He also disagreed with Dr. Kissinger's reported promise to Israel during Middle East negotiations that the United States would study a request for Pershing missiles with a view to giving a positive response to the Israelis. Schlesinger publicly denounced Kissinger for giving assurances without consultation and warned, "It is unlikely that a near-term decision to provide Pershings to Israel is likely to be forthcoming."

President Ford's assurances were ludicrous in the face of the public disputes between Schlesinger and Kissinger, and his stance subjected him to severe editorial criticism and ridicule. Moreover, whatever President Ford hoped to accomplish in the changes were obscured by the emergence of Rumsfeld as the only sure beneficiary.

The shuffle damaged Ford in his political struggle with California Governor Ronald Reagan, and weakened his credibility at a time he was under attack by the AFL-CIO for breaking his promise to sign common situs-picketing legislation.

18. Lying to Labor

THE HIGHLY CHARGED issue of labor's demand for common-situs-picketing legislation had been before Congress in one way or another throughout most of Gerald Ford's twenty-five years in the House of Representatives. As a Congressman from Grand Rapids and as House Republican Leader he had consistently opposed the contention of the construction and building-trades unions that the United States Supreme Court had "misinterpreted" the Taft-Hartley labor law in barring them from picketing an entire construction site to protest a dispute with a single contractor working at the site.

The Taft-Hartley Act of 1947 forbade use of secondary boycotts, that is, action by a union against an employer other than the one against whom it has a direct grievance. In 1951, Gerald Ford's second year in the House, the Supreme Court had upset organized labor by ruling that a union with a dispute with one subcontractor at a construction site could not picket the entire site. The ruling came in the case of National Labor Relations Board *v.* Denver Building and Construction Trades Council.

President Ford did not stumble into the problem as a novice, for the battle raged periodically between the AFL-CIO and major employer groups. The specific labor groups with the greatest interest were the Building and Construction Trades Department of AFL-CIO and its seventeen member unions. They were supported by AFL-CIO President George Meany and many independent unions.

Leading the opposition were the Associated General Contractors of America, Associated Builders and Contractors Inc., the National Right to Work Committee, the Chamber of Commerce of the United States, the National Association of Manufacturers and a number of major corporations.

As a conservative Republican, Ford's natural constituency was the business groups with which he had sided over the years, and, the merits of the legislation notwithstanding, he had little to gain in bending to the demands of an AFL-CIO that would probably support a Democratic candidate for President.

Although labor's influence in Congress had been increased considerably as a result of the Democratic landslide in the 1974 congressional elections, organized labor still did not have the clout to insure the two-thirds margin required to override a presidential veto on the common-site-picketing issue.

But, when President Ford named Dr. John T. Dunlop Secretary of Labor, the hopes of the AFL-CIO building-trades unions rose. Dr. Dunlop, a Harvard professor and an expert in labor relations, had long sympathized with the building-trades unions' argument that construction workers were only seeking the right that every other union had to picket effectively in support of lawful goals in labor disputes.

Only a short time after Dr. Dunlop was confirmed as Secretary of Labor in mid-March, he testified in favor of common-site picketing legislation and over a period of months maneuvered President Ford into a position in which he agreed to sign a common-site-picketing bill if it included an amendment banning wildcat strikes and a specified package of collective bargaining reforms for the construction industry.

While some contractors as well as labor unions supported the Dunlop compromise, other business lobbyists attacked it as a fraud intended to disguise the extent of the AFL-CIO victory on the picketing issue.

A spokesman for Dunlop's Labor Department rejected that view, arguing that the measure was needed to bring stability to bargaining in a construction industry particularly hard hit by the recession.

President Ford probably did not intend to mislead labor, or to make a promise he did not intend to keep, but during the several months of persuasion by Dunlop, his comments on common-site picketing were such that they made him highly vulnerable to George Meany's later accusation that he had gone back on his word.

Whipsawed by Dunlop and the conservative constituency for nearly six months, President Gerald Ford had reached the point where he had virtually no credibility with anyone on the common-site picketing issue.

Disregarding President Ford's vacillation on the issue, Dunlop endorsed a common-site-picketing bill just before it passed the House by a vote of 230 to 178.

In a July 16, 1975, meeting at the White House, President Ford said that he would sign the common-site-picketing bill if it were amended or accompanied by a collective bargaining bill that would bring labor peace to the build-

242 THE MAN WHO PARDONED NIXON

ing and construction trade. House Republican Leader John Rhodes, of Arizona, recalled that President Ford said he would sign such legislation "if it had the support of both labor and management."

Representative Frank Thompson, a New Jersey Democrat, characterized Rhodes' version as "sheer unadulterated sophistry." Thompson conceded that "there were no details [discussed] except within those parameters" of the Collective Bargaining Reform Act that emerged as H.R. 9500.

"The bill was drafted by the Administration," Thompson told the House, "it was sent down in the name of the Administration by the Secretary of Labor [Dunlop] after consultation at the White House, and it did satisfy every request of the President."

"It is a fact that the President of the United States, in the presence of the gentleman from Minnesota, Mr. [Albert] Quie, Senator [Jacob]Javits, Senator [Harrison] Williams, myself and a number of others, stated without equivocation that if these two amendments to H.R. 9500 were adopted—and they were—if H.R. 9500 passed in the form generally as sent by the Secretary of Labor, and if it were enacted by both bodies and added to the conference report, every single bit of which has been done, without equivocation, the President said 'I will sign it.' "

Thompson reiterated that Ford had said, "If these conditions are met, I will sign it."

"They have been met," Thompson declared. "The President of the United States is a man of his word. I have no doubt whatsoever that he will sign this despite the attempts to fuzz it."

Although many Republicans and a few Democrats argued against passage of common-site picketing legislation in December when the report of a House-Senate conference committee was before the House, minority leader Rhodes, a longtime close friend of President Ford's, was the only one who contended that the President was not irrevocably committed to sign the legislation.

The conservative Arizona Republican argued that the conference report should not be adopted because it "is bad for labor, bad for management, bad for the consumer, and it is bad for the country.

"I think it is bad for labor because it will not result in labor peace but in more strife in the building trades," Rhodes told the House. "It will polarize organized labor against unorganized labor and it will polarize the contractors.

"It is not needed by labor," he said, "because anyone knowledgeable about the wage scales for the building trades is well aware of the fact that they are the highest wage scales in the country. It is not a downtrodden segment of organized labor."

Then Rhodes noted the number of comments by other speakers on the floor "as to just what the President promised to do or did not promise to do."

With the obvious intent of giving his friend President Ford a rationale for saying he had never approved the contents of H.R. 9500 as sent to the House by Labor Secretary Dunlop, Rhodes stressed that Ford had said he would sign the bill only "if it had the support of both labor and management."

"This bill does not have the support of management," Representative Rhodes said. "Quite to the contrary. I am told by people who were at the meeting at the White House that they never saw H.R. 9500 prior to its introduction and, consequently, had no input on the bill."

Rhodes declared that "the mandate which the President gave to the people who were supposed to work this out was not fulfilled."

"The President is not, in my opinion, either morally or legally or in any other way obligated to sign any piece of legislation which might come up looking like the one we have before us," Rhodes said. "So let us not have anybody misunderstand the President's position. He did not, and he has not said he would, sign this bill."

Obviously, by consultation or mutual understanding, President Ford had given John Rhodes the arguments for a veto that bore the impression he had gone back on his word.

The President backed himself into a corner by his efforts to be all things to all men—from his conservative Republicans to his labor-oriented Secretary of Labor.

The House passage of the conference report on December 11 by a vote of 229 to 189 was followed on December 15 by Senate approval by a 52 to 43 margin, and the ball was in President Ford's court for the next press conference on December 20.

Although the President said he had not decided what to do about the common-site picketing legislation, it was apparent he was beginning to equivocate and did not feel bound by what others considered his promise to sign.

"There is, of course, in the Administration differing views," President Ford said, minimizing the furious struggle which had culminated in Labor Secretary Dunlop's floating stories that he would resign if the President did not sign the bill. Whether or not Ford felt committed, Secretary Dunlop privately felt that the President had promised; he also felt that if Ford vetoed the bill, his own usefulness would be ended.

President Ford, following a normal pattern, avoided a forthright opinion: "The American people have very strong convictions on both sides of that issue and we have gotten a tremendous amount of mail in opposition to it."

"We are getting some mail in favor of it," he added.

"I am going to make an honest judgment over this weekend," said the man of candor, whose earlier comments indicated it would probably be a political judgment based upon the weight of the mail.

"Is there a difference in the mail, Mr. President?" a newsman followed up. "I mean the mail that is against . . . does it seem to be more from organized forces?"

"I can't tell," was the reply, "but the last count I [saw] showed there were something like 620,000 communications against the common-site picketing bill and something less than 10,000, as I recall, for it."

Another questioner referred to speculation around Washington that Secretary Dunlop "might resign if you veto the site picketing bill.

"I am wondering whether you and Secretary Dunlop have talked about that, whether he has raised that possibility with you and whether you think if you do veto the bill that might happen?" President Ford was asked.

The President said he "would not want to speculate on that aspect," but in typical Ford fashion he praised Dunlop for feeling "very strongly about the legislation."

"I feel very strongly that he is one of the finest members of my Cabinet," Ford went on. "We have had several discussions in depth as to the merits, the substance, of the common-site picketing bill. There has been no indication to me that he would resign, but since I have not made a decision on the legislation yet, I think any discussion is a little academic."

Since neither the Senate nor the House had approved the common-site picketing conference report with margins sufficient to override a presidential veto, the ultimate fate of the legislation was with President Ford.

Pressure mounted, with Secretary Dunlop privately urging Ford to sign against the advice of all the other members of the Cabinet. Publicly he said that unless the bill was enacted, "next year's [construction industry] negotiations will be unmitigated hell." Dunlop and his top aides spread the word that he had informed the White House he would consider resigning if the measure was vetoed.

Although the backstage tug-of-war continued to the end, it was no surprise when President Ford revealed on January 2, 1976, that he would veto the picketing bill.

"The collective bargaining provisions have great merit," the President declared. "It is [to] the common-site picketing title that I address my objection.

"I had hoped that this bill would provide a resolution for the special problems of labor-management relations in the construction industry and would have the support of all parties," said the President, wishing for a utopian consensus. "My earlier optimism in this regard was unfounded. My reasons for this veto focus primarily on the vigorous controversy surrounding the measure and the possibility that this bill could lead to greater, not lesser, conflict in the construction industry.

"There are intense differences between union and non-union contractors and labor over the extent to which this bill constitutes a fair and equitable solution to a long-standing issue," he said, stating the obvious. "I have concluded that neither the building industry nor the nation can take the risk that the bill, which proposed a permanent change in the law, will lead to loss of jobs and work hours for the construction trades, higher costs for the public and further slowdown in a basic industry."

While his veto was generally applauded by newspapers and organizations that had found little to approve in some of his earlier vetoes, he was criticized for creating his own problem by talking out of both sides of his mouth.

"Neither the President nor labor leaders are looking very good in the squabble over the 'common site' picketing bill," the *Washington Star* commented editorially. "The President worked himself into a corner by agreeing to sign the picketing measure if it were tied to an administration-sponsored bill to reform bargaining procedures in the building industry."

The editorial pointed out that President Ford obviously hoped for political gain with labor, but stated bluntly:

"Mr. Ford reneged on his promise to sign the bill after conservative elements in the Republican Party and potential important campaign contributors put pressure on him to veto it. With Ronald Reagan bearing down on him, Mr. Ford apparently concluded that it was more important to put first things first—that is, get the Republican nomination—and he vetoed the bill."

Newspapers reported that the President could have avoided the uncomfortable position of making a promise and then going back on it by sticking to his long-held position that such a picketing bill was "bad legislation."

"Mr. Ford was persuaded to go against the grain of his thinking by Secretary Dunlop," the *Washington Star* said. "Mr. Dunlop argued, erroneously in our opinion, that the advantages of reforming bargaining procedures in the construction industry would more than offset the disadvantages of common-site picketing.

"In the end, Mr. Ford made the right decision to veto the bill," the *Star* said. "But the trap he laid for himself has been costly."

George Meany and others from the AFL-CIO caustically commented about Ford's "breaking his word," being "a liar" and being "too weak to stand up to right-wing political pressure."

Meany declared he couldn't recall any U.S. president who had "publicly promised to sign a bill and then ran out in the manner of Gerald Ford."

Edward J. Carlough, President of the Sheet Metal Workers Union, declared that the Ford veto was done "with one eye on Ronald Reagan." Carlough declared that the nation and labor had discovered that "the word of Gerald Ford is no good."

In a speech before the International Ladies Garment Workers Union on January 19, Meany declared that "when the chips were down—when the right-wing threat of political reprisal became obvious, the President caved in. He proved his word is worthless.

"And this from the man who told America the truth would heal the wounds of Watergate," Meany added.

True to his threat, John Dunlop resigned on January 14th with a short, curt note of appreciation for "the opportunity . . . to try to be of service to the country and to you."

By trying to please everyone, President Ford lost all the way around. He equivocated to the point of frightening business interests by his flirting with labor on the issue of common-site picketing and his flirtation with labor led them down the primrose path. Jerry Ford's position throughout his political life on labor matters was forgotten. Business interests were now uncertain as to whether his word was good or if his principles could be pushed aside by the next political wind.

President Ford's dalliance with labor on common-situs picketing was costly politically, because in November and December of 1975 former California Governor Ronald Reagan was registering his most conspicuous gains in the polls.

The business community's uneasiness about Ford's commitment to conservative policies was not helped when he named W. J. Usery, Jr., as Dunlop's successor as Secretary of Labor against the opposition of the National Right to Work Committee.

Ford's clumsy handling of the common-situs-picketing bill problem had further damaged his credibility with both labor and management, and it allowed Ronald Reagan to emerge as a neck-and-neck contender for the 1976 Republican presidential nomination.

19. Politics as Usual

EVEN THE MOST enthusiastic boosters of Ronald Reagan would not have predicted that the former California Governor would be running neck-and-neck in the polls against President Ford by January 1, 1976. Conservative elements in the Republican Party who had backed the abortive Reagan for President campaign at the 1968 Republican Convention had pushed Reagan for the vice-presidential appointment which President Ford gave to Nelson A. Rockefeller in mid-August when his popularity was at its highest.

Initially, the conservative Republicans continued support for the feeble Reagan movement just to "keep Ford honest to his conservative image" and to pose a real threat to Rockefeller's nomination as the 1976 running mate. With each Ford fumble, from the Nixon pardon through the awkward handling of the common-site picketing issue, the Reagan forces gained momentum. But for the most part it was not based on a belief that Reagan could push aside an incumbent Republican president actively seeking the nomination.

Ronald Reagan, until November, was being groomed as understudy. Conservative Republicans, always wary of Rockefeller's ambitions to be President, wanted Reagan in the wings in the event Ford voluntarily stepped aside by prearrangement or was manipulated onto the shelf by the Rockefeller people who controlled the White House domestic council and influenced foreign affairs through Dr. Henry A. Kissinger.

Ironically, Ford's greatest plunge in popularity was in the aftermath of the Nixon pardon, an issue on which Reagan expressed mild agreement. From a high of 71 percent in mid-August, Ford's popularity dropped below 50 percent in one month. The wave of sympathy accompanying Betty Ford's cancer operation brought it up a few points in early October, but it plummeted further in the fuss over Rockefeller's gift giving and other controversial appointments indicating a continuation of Nixon people and Nixon policies. Ford's lack of leadership in connection with energy and economic matters also contributed, as did the stunning defeat Republicans received in the Senate and House races.

The Democrats picked up four seats in the Senate with victories over Republicans in Colorado, Kentucky, Vermont and Florida, but Nevada Republican Senator Paul Laxalt won the seat vacated by Democrat Alan Bible, for a net gain of three. It gave Democrats a 61 to 39 margin in the Senate, which was later increased to 62 to 38 by the victory of Democrat John Durkin over former Republican Congressman Louis C. Wyman in a special election.

Democrats gained 43 seats in the House, pushing their number past the two-thirds mark of 290 and with new members setting in motion the first major revolts against the establishment leadership. In theory the 291 Democrats provided a veto-proof House in the 94th Congress with only 144 Republicans. The 89th Congress had the only prior wider disparity between parties, with 295 Democrats and only 140 Republicans.

Congressional Quarterly reported that Ford won only 58.2 percent of the congressional votes on which he took a position during 1974. "This was the lowest level of support of any first-year president since *Congressional Quarterly* began keeping records twenty-two years ago," the authoritative publication stated. It revealed that Ford's support during his first four months in office was lower than what Richard Nixon had received in the first eight months of 1974. House Republicans supported former minority leader Ford only 51 percent of the time in 1974, compared with 65-percent support for Nixon. And House Democrats backed Ford only 41 percent of the time, while they had voted with Nixon 46 percent of the time.

President Ford's public support registered by the polls dropped below 38 percent in January 1975 and floundered slightly above and below that figure until May, when his handling of the *Mayaguez* affair brought a substantial boost in his ratings. Cambodian Communist troops off the disputed island of Poulo Wai in the Gulf of Siam set the stage for the President's brief moment of political triumph when they seized the American merchant ship *Mayaguez* and her crew of thirty-nine.

Ford moved swiftly to use U.S. troops to free the *Mayaguez'* crew under the War Powers Resolution of 1973, and on May 15 he reported to Congress on the armed intervention because the ship had been seized "in clear violation of international law." Three Cambodian patrol boats were destroyed by U.S. aircraft on May 13, and U.S.

Marines assaulted the island of Koh Tang on May 14 to retake the *Mayaguez* and recapture her crew.

Although two U.S. Marines were killed in the operation, it was a political success, with President Ford claiming his constitutional authority to protect American lives. The American people, fed up with the frustrations of detente and international talks that produced few measurable results, were in overwhelming support of the President.

Conservative Republicans cheered his action. Senator Carl Curtis, of Nebraska, declared that "the courageous and decisive action by President Ford will do more for the cause of liberty around the world than all . . . the conferences that have been held in the last few years and will be held in the next few years." Senator Barry Goldwater commented, "I thank God we have a President who has shown guts enough to do what he should have done."

Although Senator George McGovern and a few other liberal Democrats spoke of the action as "precipitous," most Democrats felt compelled to support Ford. Senator Hubert Humphrey said, "The President had to make a very difficult decision, but I think it was a right one."

The Senate Foreign Relations Committee, after being briefed on the *Mayaguez* incident, adopted a resolution of support for the actions taken by President Ford, and his popularity soared above 50 percent for the first time in eight months.

The cost of the operation was later estimated by the Defense Department to have been $9.5 million, including $6.3 million for three CH-53 helicopters lost.

Moreover the *Mayaguez* affair dimmed as a heroic military rescue as a House International Relations subcommittee headed by Representative Dante Fascell began to add up the toll in American lives. In addition to the $9.5 million price tag, the skirmish with the Cambodians cost fifteen U.S. servicemen their lives, and an additional twenty-three were killed in Thailand in a helicopter crash related to the *Mayaguez* rescue effort. Three additional servicemen were listed as missing and presumed dead.

The Ford Administration was beleaguered by charges of cover-up from Chairman Fascell and other members of his subcommittee when Robert H. Miller, Deputy Assistant Secretary of State for East Asian and Pacific Affairs, presented "the definitive" chronology on the *Mayaguez* incident. Fascell said his was one of at least three so-called accounts on the controversy, and declared, "I am concerned that we might not have all the facts in the chronology presented here."

Committee members inquired about the State Department's failure to warn the *Mayaguez* of possible danger in the Gulf of Siam because of earlier detention of two ships—one Panamanian, the other South Korean. Miller admitted State Department knowledge of those incidents and that "we did not warn our ships." But, paradoxically, he insisted that the warning system "works well."

Throughout the summer and fall of 1975, continuing frustrating debates on Turkey, Cyprus, possible Soviet violations of the Strategic Arms Limitation Agreements, energy policy and the economy plagued the Ford Administration. The stalemate on these issues between President Ford and the Democratic Congress was dissatisfying to the public and raised serious questions about Ford's ability to deal with his old friends in the House and Senate. Members of both parties still liked Jerry Ford personally, but they knew his limitations better than the electorate and resented his growing arrogance in the exercise of

Politics as Usual 255

presidential power, particularly the use of the despised
"executive privilege."

The Morton contempt citations grew out of the withholding of Arab boycott reports and was strictly a Ford
Administration action, but confrontations increased between the White House and the House and Senate Intelligence committees investigating the Central Intelligence
Agency and the Federal Bureau of Investigation. Most of
those matters involved intelligence blunders and misuse
of the power of both those agencies prior to the time
Gerald Ford became President, but often, too, they involved actions by Ford's Secretary of State.

Dr. Henry A. Kissinger had been "Mr. Intelligence" for
the Nixon Administration through his White House post
as Chairman of the National Security Council, Chairman
of The Forty Committee, which cleared all CIA covert
operations, and chairman of half a dozen other interdepartmental committees.

Because Dr. Kissinger formulated foreign policy and
directed foreign intelligence for the Nixon and Ford administrations, it was inevitable that he be responsible for
some of the ineptitudes in intelligence areas and the usur-
pation of power by the CIA and the FBI from 1969 on.
Serious questions were raised whether Dr. Kissinger had
perjured himself by denying he had "initiated" the FBI
wiretapping of newsmen and government officials, and
month after month new evidence surfaced indicating that
he had played the lead role in installing the taps and in
developing and transmitting the list of names from the
White House to the then FBI Director, J. Edgar Hoover.

President Ford made himself vulnerable to attack because he retained Dr. Kissinger as Secretary of State and
a White House adviser and because he backed Kissinger

to the ultimate by permitting use of "executive privilege" to obscure his precise responsibility for various intelligence failures in Cyprus, Portugal and Vietnam.

The impression of a massive cover-up for Kissinger was orchestrated in a series of long confrontations with Senator Frank Church, Chairman of the Senate Intelligence Committee, and with Representative Otis Pike, Chairman of the House Intelligence Committee. While President Ford managed to eke out a series of Pyrrhic victories over congressional access to testimony and records to save Henry Kissinger from contempt of Congress, the great price paid was President Ford's reputation for openness and candor.

With each confrontation President Ford had to take a stand, whereas former Governor Reagan could comment or not, as it suited his political purpose. Ideologically, Reagan was opposed to acceding to congressional demands for records, which Ford contended would expose the operations of the CIA and FBI and destroy the effectiveness of those two organizations in the battle against Soviet agents. However, Reagan was not forced into a position of having to defend specific withholding where the charges and the facts indicated that executive privilege was simply a cover-up for Dr. Kissinger.

Secretary of State Kissinger, despised by conservative Republicans as being Rockefeller's man, was popular with a majority of the American people when Ford took office, and even those in Congress who distrusted him most were forced to speak favorably of him, in much the same manner as they had voiced unsparing praise for the FBI and J. Edgar Hoover in earlier years.

The revelation that Dr. Kissinger had accepted $50,000 as a "gift" from Nelson Rockefeller just before assuming office as Richard Nixon's Special Assistant confirmed the worst suspicions of conservatives and raised questions of governmental ethics that honest liberals and conservatives could not defend.

As Kissinger lost popularity, foreign trips and foreign policy did not elevate Ford's prestige as they had for Nixon and former presidents. Ford's forays into foreign affairs did not project the image of a confident leader, but, rather, that of an amiable bumbler who didn't fully understand the issues and was totally dependent on the ever-smiling, ever-confident, and ever-present Kissinger.

Within four months after becoming President, Ford started to follow the Nixon foreign-travel route to get attention and win prestige and popularity in the polls. In November 1974 he visited Vladivostok for a summit meeting on arms limitation agreements with Soviet Premier Brezhnev. And he whipped through three foreign junkets in 1975, starting with an April trip to NATO headquarters in Brussels and side trips to Rome and Madrid. In late July and early August, he traveled to another summit meeting in Helsinki, Finland, stopping en route in West Germany and Poland. On his return from Helsinki, Ford visited Rumania and Yugoslavia.

In December he made a five-day visit to Communist China. On the return trip he stopped in Indonesia and the Philippine Islands, where he announced his "Pacific Doctrine." The Ford Pacific Doctrine drew yawns from Republicans, and most Democrats found it not even worthy of critical comment.

While President Ford was mired in seemingly insoluble problems, Reagan and his advisers, with a flair for the dramatic, waited until mid-November to make a formal announcement of Reagan's candidacy for the Republican nomination. While he waited, he kept before the public

with a weekly column published in two hundred newspapers, daily radio broadcasts on about two hundred sta-
tions, and more than one hundred speeches before
Republican audiences for expenses and fees of up to
$5,000.

To his Republican audiences he attacked Big Government, castigated welfare waste and frauds, spoke of his
own record in California and, with varying degrees of
acerbity, chided President Ford and Kissinger for making
"detente . . . a one-way street" for the Soviet Union.

"The Soviet Union would have greater respect for us
if they knew that we weren't fooled," Reagan declared.
"We must insist that we aren't going to be second to
anyone."

Such jibes brought down the house in Republican
groups at the same time Secretary Kissinger was defending
the Soviet Union against charges by former Defense Secretary Melvin Laird, former Chief of Naval Operations Elmo
Zumwalt and Senator Henry Jackson that the Soviet Union
had violated the SALT agreements. Although such defense
might have been necessary for Dr. Kissinger in order to
retain a working relationship with Soviet leaders, the
public deemed him a soft apologist for the Communists to
the detriment of the U.S. defense posture and U.S. economic interests.

President Ford's support of Kissinger on these and other
squabbles with Defense Secretary James Schlesinger did
not please conservative Republicans, and the demands for
a $100 billion defense budget alienated liberals as much
as did the revelations of U.S. financial military support
in Angola.

The financial collapse of New York City in the fall of
1975 was an unexpected advantage for former California

Governor Reagan, for it demonstrated that irresponsible fiscal policies, uncontrolled welfare and city employment policies can be catastrophic. These were the very points Reagan had stressed in his campaigning in California, where, whether by luck or otherwise, he had been able to deal with them in a reasonably effective manner. It also highlighted the sad financial plight of New York State, which had been under Nelson A. Rockefeller's guidance and control for a dozen years.

Ford was presented an opportunity to make political Brownie points for his conservative governmental and economic theories under attack by a Democratic Congress, but again he flubbed an issue that could have been a plus. Faced with pressure from the New York banking community, Vice President Rockefeller and the Democratic Congress, President Ford delivered the harsh threat of a presidential veto of congressional legislation to bail out the financially stricken city.

"I can tell you—and tell you now—that I am prepared to veto any bill that has as its purpose a federal bail-out of New York City to prevent a default," the President told a National Press Club audience on October 29. In the face of Senate and House initiatives for a federal guarantee of an $11.5 billion bond issue, Ford declared that it would set a "terrible precedent" for the federal government to aid faltering cities.

"Why . . . should all the working people of this country be forced to rescue those who bankrolled New York City's policies for so long—the large investors and big banks?" Ford asked. He then proposed to back legislation to provide for operation of the city after it had fallen into bankruptcy.

The tough rhetoric was popular in the rural states and

among the conservative Republicans flirting with Reagan, but it was obvious that the realities of New York City's plight would force a retreat from the tough talk, confirming once again his vacillating deportment and the uncertainty of his pledges, if they were not politically expedient.

President Ford was now diametrically opposed to Vice President Rockefeller, who had a few weeks earlier, without consultation, called for swift congressional action to save New York City.

Although the White House staff tried to minimize the differences between Ford and Rockefeller on handling the problems of New York City, it was apparent that the least of the existing difficulties was retaining Rockefeller as the likely running mate in 1976.

For months, Ford's campaign manager, Bo Callaway, had been saying bluntly that Rockefeller would represent a problem for the Ford candidacy. Although Callaway appeared to be winging it on his own, he was operating in direct contact with President Ford and Donald Rumsfeld, then White House Chief of Staff. Ford was supportive in acknowledging the problem but stopped short of a "dump Rockefeller" move.

It was moot whether the fault was Callaway's, Rumsfeld's or the President's, but the Ford campaign was in disarray by late October. Lee Nunn, a Nixon White House staffer and campaign aide, quit in disgust. A short time later former Deputy Secretary of Defense David Packard left his fund raising role with warnings that the campaign was just not falling into line, and speculation burgeoned that Reagan had built such strong political fences in New Hampshire and Florida that he could dynamite the Ford candidacy with big wins in those two early primaries.

Whether Nelson Rockefeller saw Ford as a loser and

bailed out, or whether he departed to help Ford win the Republican nomination, is open to conjecture, but Rockefeller made his final plans to get out in the days after Ford's tough speech on New York City on October 29.

His letter to President Ford of November 3 gave no specific reason: "After much thought, I have decided further that I do not wish my name to enter into your consideration for the upcoming Republican vice-presidential nomination."

While Rockefeller said he would continue to serve as Vice President and would support Ford's bid for the nomination, he refused to rule himself out or speculate as to whether he might be available as a candidate for the Republican nomination if Ford should flounder or voluntarily withdraw in the face of the Reagan threat.

In a press conference several days later, Rockefeller blamed party squabbles over his possible presence on the ticket for diverting the President's attention from the business of running the country.

The release of Rockefeller's letter of withdrawal came the morning before President Ford announced the controversial shuffle of his national security staff, which he asserted would strengthen his administration with "my team" and place him in a better posture to win the Republican nomination against the growing Reagan threat.

Donald Rumsfeld was the only figure to profit from the national security shuffle, and it was thoroughly destructive to Ford's image with the conservative elements in the Republican party. The firing of Defense Secretary Schlesinger, an outspoken advocate of a strong defense posture, was interpreted as a victory for Dr. Kissinger, the ultimate apologist for the Soviet Union.

President Ford became a sitting duck for Reagan's one-liner jabs before Republican audiences that "the President fired the wrong Secretary."

This series of events resulted in Ford's trailing Reagan with Republican voters. The first warning was a Gallup poll taken two weeks after the firing of Schlesinger. While it was admitted to be a smaller sampling than was usual with public-opinion polls, it showed Reagan leading with Republicans by a 40 to 32 margin—a sharp reversal of the 48 to 25 lead Ford showed only a month earlier. California pollster Mervin Field was quoted by *Newsweek* as saying, "It's a situation unparalleled in modern political history." Even in his worst moments, Harry Truman had never done so poorly in his own party.

That mid-November placement was obviously subject to substantial error, as the poll stated, but it was a high point for Reagan, who was formally launching his campaign; and it came before he suggested an unrealistic $90 billion federal budget cut, the political blunder that marred his first months of campaigning. Certainly Ford was at a low point because of his graceless handling of the Rockefeller withdrawal and the national security juggling, but Democrats, Republicans and political analysts agreed that it would be "a horse race to the wire" for the Republican nomination if Reagan were able to capture only a few of the early primaries.

John Rhodes, House minority leader and a longtime personal friend and political supporter of Jerry Ford, declared that Reagan was the more popular of the two with Arizona Republicans, but he believed the question would not be settled until the Republican Convention. In January, he predicted that President Ford would stick to the end regardless of primary results and that the power of an incumbent president would assist him in making a formidable bid.

Rhodes admitted that the wavering on the situs-picketing issue and the national security changes were the issues that had hurt Ford most in December and early January, but he believed that an upturn in the nation's economy and improvement in the unemployment picture could re-elect Ford if he won the Republican nomination.

A few early faux pas by Reagan, and fears among Republican moderates that a Reagan candidacy would be courting another disaster comparable to the Goldwater defeat in 1964, were the most potent forces moving for President Ford as he shifted former Commerce Secretary Rogers C. B. Morton into the White House in an attempt to bring some cogent direction to his campaign.

But, even that development brought a challenge from Thomas Curtis, Chairman of the Federal Election Commission and a longtime friend of President Ford and Morton. Curtis, a former Republican from Missouri with a reputation as a stickler for integrity, challenged the use of White House funds to pay the salary of Morton or anyone else whose duties would be primarily political. Although a compromise was worked out under which the Republican National Committee paid a part of Morton's salary, the incident had an unsettling effect on the Ford organization as Morton assumed control of the campaign.

More unsettling was Richard Nixon's sudden announcement that he was accepting an invitation to visit China in late February, just before the New Hampshire primary in which Governor Reagan and President Ford would have their first serious contest. The seemingly senseless antics and comments by Nixon as reported from China caused Ford's supporters to writhe quietly and led Senator Barry

Goldwater to comment critically on ABC television's "Good Morning America" on February 25:

"I don't think Mr. Nixon's visit to China did anything, and if he wanted to do this country a favor he might stay over there. He is violating the law. . . . The Logan Act prohibits any American—and that's all he is, he's an ex-President and a private citizen—the Logan Act says no one but the President and the Secretary of State can discuss foreign policy, and he made a tremendous mistake in doing what he did at the time he did it."

When Governor Reagan was asked for comment on Nixon's China trip, he declined with the quip, "Don't ask me . . . ask the man who pardoned him."

When John Sears, Reagan's campaign manager, was asked if this meant Governor Reagan was going to make Ford's pardoning of Nixon a campaign issue, he said that adherence to "the Eleventh Commandment" of Republican politics would keep Reagan from making the pardon an issue. But, Reagan's astute campaign manager added quickly, "We've noticed that all of the Democratic candidaltes have talked about the pardon."

Sears said he was "almost certain" that Ford's pardoning of Nixon would be an issue in the fall campaign if Ford received the Republican nomination for president.

Senator Sam Ervin recognized President Ford's high degree of political vulnerability on Watergate that started with the killing of Patman's investigation in 1972 and continued through the Nixon pardon controversy. Ervin told North Carolina audiences that Ford, as House minority leader, had "moved heaven and earth" to block Patman's investigation to trace the $114,000 in Nixon campaign funds to the Miami bank account of a Watergate burglar.

The assault on Ford by the highly respected North Carolina Democrat might well have been a factor in giving credibility and force to Reagan's lower key comments on President Ford's Watergate vulnerability, and to Reagan's unexpected win in the North Carolina primary.

Both Reagan and Ford knew that Sears' comments helped in making Ford's vulnerability on the Nixon pardon an issue in the remaining primaries even if they themselves didn't mention it directly. For even if the candidates were silent on the subject, bits of new evidence floated to the surface raising questions about the accuracy of Ford's explanation of his controversial decision. Mistakes of fact were a minor matter, but evidence of deliberate mistakes intended to mislead Congress or the public would indicate another presidential cover-up, and Representative Elizabeth Holtzman had a lot of unanswered questions pending in the House Judiciary Committee.

20. The Pardon Problem

By FEBRUARY 1976 the credibility of Gerald Ford had been severely damaged by his contradictory public statements and actions, his political pragmatism, his misuse of executive privilege and his outright misstatements of facts. His continued comments that his was an administration of openness and candor was insulting to the intelligence of the press and the public.

A year earlier, President Ford's unsuccessful effort to veto the Freedom of Information Act amendment was regarded as a blatant and cynical effort to align himself with federal bureaucratic cover-ups diametrically opposed to his promise to restore open government.

The House, by an overwhelming 371 to 31, voted to override the veto, and Democratic critics were joined by a wide range of Republicans from John J. Erlenborn, a liberal Republican from Illinois, to John J. Rousselot, one of the most conservative Republicans from California. The Senate override was by a vote of 65 to 27, and Senator Edmund S. Muskie rebuked Ford in his stinging comment,

"The same President who began his administration with a promise of openness sided with the secret-makers on the first test of that promise."

Through December 1975 President Ford had held twenty-four press conferences and more than fifty interviews, but an examination of the substance demonstrated that the man of candor could stonewall better than Richard Nixon. Ford simply disregarded known facts, but stated and restated the line he had decided to take without the deviations and embellishments that often landed Nixon in trouble.

One of the best examples was what a National Press Club report had called Ford's "press conference stonewalling." It dealt with his November 3 televised press conference in which he insisted that the Cabinet shake-up was motivated simply by his desire to form his "own team." In the face of widespread ridicule at his answer, Ford conceded that the shift had also derived from "growing tension" between Dr. Henry Kissinger and then Secretary of Defense James Schlesinger.

Skepticism about President Ford's flat assertion that he had no prearranged deal with President Nixon to pardon him continued to grow with each passing month. In October 1974 Representative Elizabeth Holtzman, a New York Democrat, was the only member of the House Judiciary Subcommittee with the courage to face Ford with the direct accusation of a pardon deal, and to continue in scornful disdain when he flatly denied it. She challenged him to make public all White House tapes of conversations between himself and Nixon on the Watergate matter, but he parried and dodged, completely rejecting their publication.

Even though Ford declined to produce the Nixon-Ford

tapes to clear up Congresswoman Holtzman's doubts, in October 1974 enough people still believed in him to accept his statement, "There was no deal, Period. . . ." The House Judiciary Committee, anxious to get on with other chores, permitted Ford to refuse to produce the best evidence of his conversations with Nixon in the crucial cover-up months in 1972 and 1973.

But, a number of reporters continued to probe and try to elicit new facts relevant to Ford's pardon of Nixon. It just did not make good political sense for Gerald Ford, the political animal, to wreck his reputation, become a liability for Republican congressional candidates in the 1974 election, and cripple his ability to deal with the Democratic Congress on energy problems, economic conditions and his "number-one priority," inflation, for no reason.

The number-one priority and his own political future had been sacrificed to pardon Richard Nixon precisely thirty days after Ford had assumed the presidency. Why? Was it possible that human compassion for his political friend and benefactor outweighed all his own stated political ambitions for himself in 1976, as well as the need for Republican gains to bar a "veto-proof Congress?"

It was not unreasonable for Ford's critics to question his explanation of the Nixon pardon. Had he promised Richard Nixon a full pardon within thirty days? Had it been a verbal promise directly or through someone else, or just a gentleman's agreement, understood without being specified, from the time Nixon tapped him for the vice presidency? What was the *quid pro quo*? Was it strictly Republican political partisanship? Was it a propensity to compensate the man who had bequeathed him an office above his highest dreams, and a $60,000-a-year pension for life in addition to his own congressional pension in excess of $35,000 a year? Or was there something on the Nixon-Ford tapes involving Ford in guilty knowledge of the cover-up when he was taking a lead role in stopping the House Banking and Currency Committee investigation in September and October of 1972?

Only Ford and Nixon knew the real answer to those questions, but there was other relevant evidence available. The tapes were obviously the best evidence, but it was possible that Nixon had made comments in conversations with John Dean, Bob Haldeman, John Ehrlichman, General Haig, Fred Buzhardt, Leonard Garment or others that would shed light on the crucial question of what Ford knew about Watergate and when he learned it.

In testifying before the House Judiciary Subcommittee that "there was no deal, period, under no circumstances," President Ford had said,

"I am here not to make history, but to report on history.

"If, with your assistance, I can make for better understanding of the pardon of former President Nixon, then we can help to achieve the purpose I had for granting the pardon when I did.

"The purpose was to change our nation's focus. I wanted to do all I could to shift our attention from the pursuit of a fallen president to the pursuit of the urgent needs of a rising nation. . . . We would needlessly be diverted from meeting those challenges if we as a people were to remain sharply divided over whether to indict, bring to trial, and punish a former president, who is already condemned to suffer long and deeply in the shame and disgrace brought upon the office that he held."

Had he intended that the pardon would help the nation

put Watergate behind us, he had been wrong—dead wrong—for it brought Watergate back to the front pages and destroyed his own credibility, his possibility of passing an energy program, his possibility of passing an economic program, his possibility of electing more Republicans in the Senate and House. That was all apparent by mid-October 1974 when he testified, and still he told his story as though it were otherwise.

"Yet, to forgive is not to forget the lessons of evil in whatever ways evil has operated against us," President Ford went on. "And certainly the pardon granted the former President will not cause us to forget the evils of the Watergate-type offense or to forget the lessons we have learned that a government which deceives its supporters and treats its opponents as enemies must never, never be tolerated."

These words came from the man who had already stretched his political power to the limit to shield Richard Nixon, who had deceived his supporters and treated his opponents as enemies. He protected Nixon from the indictment, conviction and imprisonment awaiting all of his top subordinates who had obstructed justice with Nixon's connivance and for Nixon's political benefit.

Referring to the broad power of a president to pardon, Ford quoted Alexander Hamilton envisioning its use in time of insurrection, "when a well-timed offer of pardon to the insurgent or rebels may restore the tranquillity of the commonwealth."

"When a pardon is granted, it also represents 'the determination of the ultimate authority that the public welfare will be better served by inflicting less than what the judgment fixed.'"

In emphasizing "the ultimate authority" of his legal

right to use the pardon as he damned well pleased, Ford said, "However, the Constitution does not limit the pardon power to cases of convicted offenders or even indicted offenders."

While reiterating his absolute right to grant a full and sweeping pardon to anyone, he declared that though people might differ on the subject, there was, in fact, nothing they could do about it.

In the same breath saying he had learned the lessons of Watergate, he stated the ultimate claim of "executive privilege" in terms not much different from Richard Nixon's throughout the two years of the Watergate cover-up, but softened his claim by saying, ". . . my own view is that the right of executive privilege is to be exercised with caution and with restraint.

"When I was a member of Congress, I did not hesitate to question the right of the executive branch to claim a privilege against supplying information to the Congress even if I thought the claim of privilege was being abused.

"Yet, I did then, and I do now, respect the right of executive privilege when it protects advice given to a president in the expectation that it will not be disclosed," said Ford, repeating Nixon's Watergate theme without any qualification of vital national security or any other limitation. "Otherwise, Mr. Chairman, no president could any longer count on receiving free and frank views from the people designed to help him reach his official decisions."

That claim was as broad a claim of an arbitrary right as any put forward either by Richard Nixon or by Attorney General Richard Kleindienst when he asserted in April 1973 that the Congress and the courts had a puny physical force compared to that at the disposal of the President as Commander in Chief of the Armed Forces.

While President Ford appeared voluntarily, he declared that he did not regard his appearance or his answers as setting "a precedent for responding to congressional inquiries different in nature or scope or under different circumstances.

"No references or discussions on a possible pardon for the then President Nixon occurred until August 1 and 2, 1974," Ford said. "You will recall, Mr. Chairman, that since the beginning of the Watergate investigation, I had consistently made statements and speeches about President Nixon's innocence of either planning the break-in or of participating in the cover-up. I sincerely believed he was innocent.

"Even in the closing months before the President resigned, I made public statements that in my opinion the adverse relations so far did not constitute an impeachable offense," he added, revealing he was either a poor lawyer or thoroughly negligent in examining the available evidence on the single most important issue before the country in the year from July 1973 through July 1974.

"I was coming under increasing criticism for such public statements [of Nixon's innocence]," Ford said, "but I still believed—I believed them to be true based on the facts as I knew them." It was an admission of gross negligence when the evidence of a prima-facie crime of obstruction of justice had been present and obvious to all but the politically blind if they had only looked. But it would not have served Ford's political purposes to inquire for himself or even to consider intelligently the summations of the evidence I had given him on at least two occasions to warn him against making "a damned fool" of himself with "an unwise defense of Nixon."

I had explained to Ford when he was Vice President that the prima-facie case of crime was made, that Dean's testimony was fully corroborated. I had not believed it would be necessary to explain to a Yale law graduate the meaning of "a prima-facie case" or the meaning of corroboration, or to have to go beyond the simple explanation that I judged it was "a stronger criminal case" than those upon which Jimmy Hoffa, Bobby Baker or Carmine De-Sapio had been convicted and imprisoned.

Vice President Ford had told me that others had made the same arguments to him, indicating he understood what I was saying but could make no acknowledgment of whether or not he agreed because of the sensitivity of his position as Vice President.

He told the subcommittee that his first conversations about a pardon took place following an early morning meeting on Thursday, August 1, 1974: "I had a meeting in my vice-presidential office, with Alexander M. Haig, Jr., Chief of Staff for President Nixon. At this meeting, I was told in a general way about fears arising because of additional tape evidence scheduled for delivery to Judge Sirica on Monday, August 5, 1974. I was told that there could be evidence which, when disclosed to the House of Representatives, would likely tip the vote in favor of impeachment. However, I was given no indication that this development would lead to any change in President Nixon's plans to oppose the impeachment vote.

"Then shortly after noon, General Haig requested another appointment as promptly as possible. He came to my office about 3:30 P.M. for a meeting that was to last for approximately three-quarters of an hour. Only then did I learn of the damaging nature of a conversation on June

23, 1972, in one of the tapes which was due to go to Judge Sirica the following Monday.

"I describe this meeting, Mr. Chairman," Ford explained, "because at one point it did include reference to a possible pardon for Mr. Nixon, to which the third and fourth questions in H. Res 1367 are directed . . . the substance of his [Haig's] conversation was that the new disclosure would be devastating, even catastrophic, insofar as President Nixon was concerned. Based on what he had learned of the conversation on the tape, he wanted to know whether I was prepared to assume the presidency within a very short period of time, and whether I would be willing to make recommendations to the President as to what course he should now follow."

Ford pictured himself as "shocked and . . . stunned . . . by this unbelievable revelation."

"First, under these most troubled circumstances; and second, the realization these new revelations and disclosures ran completely counter to the position I had taken for months, in that I believed the President was not guilty of any impeachable offense."

President Ford said that General Haig had outlined for him President Nixon's situation as he and others on the White House staff had assessed it. He recalled the following two general alternative courses:

"Some suggested 'riding it out' by letting the impeachment take its course through the House and the Senate trial, fighting all the way against conviction. Others were urging resignation sooner or later. I was told some people backed the first course and other people a resignation, but not with the same view as to how and when it should take place."

On the alternative to resignation a number of pardon

options were put forth by General Haig and reviewed by Ford. President Ford related those options as follows:

1. The President stepping aside temporarily under the 25th Amendment.

2. The President delaying resignation until further along in the impeachment process.

3. Trying to settle for a censure vote as a means of avoiding either impeachment or a need to resign.

4. Investigating whether the President could pardon himself.

5. The President pardoning various Watergate defendants, then himself, then resigning.

6. Ford pardoning the President subsequent to his resignation, should he resign.

President Ford continued, "General Haig wanted my view on the various courses of action as well as my attitude on the options of resignation. However, he indicated he was not advocating any of the options.

"I inquired as to what was the President's pardon power, and he answered that it was his understanding from a White House lawyer that a president did have the authority to grant a pardon even before any criminal action had been taken against an individual, but, obviously, he was in no position to have any opinion on a matter of law.

"As I saw it, at this point the question clearly before me was, under the circumstances, what course of action should I recommend that would be in the best interest of the country," Ford said. "I told General Haig I had to have some time to think."

Ford said he also wanted to consult with White House Counsel James St. Clair and with his wife, Betty. He said St. Clair came to his office at 8 A.M. the next day and reviewed the new evidence, and that "there was no question in my mind he considered these revelations to be so damaging that impeachment in the House was a certainty and conviction in the Senate a high probability."

President Ford said he asked St. Clair if there was any other new and damaging evidence and was told no. Then he reviewed "the various options mentioned to me by General Haig."

"He [St. Clair] told me he had not been the source of any opinion about presidential pardon power," Ford said. "After thought on the matter, I was determined not to make any recommendation to President Nixon on his resignation. I had not given any advice or recommendation in my conversations with his aides, but I also did not want anyone who might talk to the President to suggest that I had some intention to do so.

"For that reason, Mr. Chairman, I decided I should call General Haig the afternoon of August 2," Ford continued. "I did make the call late that afternoon and told him I wanted him to understand that I had no intention of recommending what President Nixon should do about resigning or not resigning, and that nothing we had talked about the previous afternoon [including the pardon option] should be given any consideration in whatever decision the President might make. General Haig told me he was in full agreement with this position."

The second conversation Ford had with Haig on the pardon option was the clearest indication that he believed that something in their conversation on August 1 might have been subject to interpretation as acquiescing in one or more of the options and that he wanted to reaffirm that he, Gerald Ford, true to form, had no suggestion or recommendation in mind.

Then Ford gave his rationale for feeling compelled,

despite knowledge of Nixon's guilt, to give speeches in
Mississippi and Louisiana on August 3, August 4 and
August 5 repeating his belief in Nixon's innocence even
though he had been told by Nixon's lawyer of the devastating evidence which had surfaced.

"Any change in my stated views, or even refusal to comment further, I feared, would lead in the press to conclusions that I now wanted to see the President resign to
avoid an impeachment vote in the House and probable
conviction in the Senate," Ford explained. "For that reason I remained firm in my answers to press questions
during my trip and repeated my belief in the President's
innocence of an impeachable offense. Not until I returned
to Washington [on August 5] did I learn that the President
was to release the new evidence late on Monday, August
5, 1974."

President Ford related that at a Cabinet meeting on
Tuesday morning, August 6, "I announced that I was making no recommendations to the President as to what he
should do in the light of the new evidence. And I made
no recommendation to him either at the meeting or at
any time after that. In summary, Mr. Chairman, I assure
you that there never was at any time any arrangement
whatsoever concerning a pardon to Mr. Nixon if he were
to resign and I were to become President.

"At no time after I became President on August 9, 1974,
was the subject of a pardon for Richard M. Nixon raised
by the former President or by anyone representing him.
Also, no one on my staff brought up the subject until the
day before my first press conference on August 28, 1974.
At that time, I was advised that questions on the subject
might be raised by media reporters at the press conference."

The details of all of the explanations were to be challenged by various revelations as the months went by. Newsmen's questions and the pressure of other problems provided the motivation for many of Ford's former associates to be more forthright in discussing Ford's role in killing the Patman committee, Ford's specific knowledge of Watergate events and Ford's conversations and actions in the crucial period between August 1 and August 28, when he admitted having discussed the several options with General Haig.

New York magazine carried an extensive article on October 14, 1974, by Frank Fox and Stephen Parker expounding the thesis that the Ford-Nixon tapes were a source of the continuing dominance by Richard Nixon over President Ford.

"Richard Nixon is out of office but not out of power," Fox and Parker wrote in the article, which was entitled "Is the Pardon Explained by the Ford-Nixon Tapes?" "We believe that the source of this power resides in over five thousand hours of secretly taped, candid conversations between Nixon, his aides, and the leaders of both political parties."

Gerald Ford's highest ambitions had been realized when he became House Republican Leader, and from 1969 until 1973 he had been Richard Nixon's most loyal and ardent minion. "No assignment which Nixon described as essential to the interest of the country or the party was too demanding or too distasteful," the authors wrote.

Calling attention to the evidence available in the tapes, they continued, "During the twenty-nine-month taping period, Gerald Ford met with Nixon on at least eighty-five separate occasions; during the same period, Ford spoke to Nixon over the phone well over a hundred times. By the

most conservative estimate, the White House tape recordings contain over twenty hours of candid conversations
between Gerald Ford and Richard Nixon." These vital
tapes covered the period between September 1, 1972, and
the November election.

The *New York* article stressed that the federal court
record revealed that access to the White House tapes had
been granted to White House Special Counsel J. Fred
Buzhardt on November 14, 1973—the day before Gerald
Ford was to testify before the House Judiciary Committee
in connection with his nomination for Vice President.
Court records show that Buzhardt obtained from John
Bennett, who kept records for the White House on access
to the tapes after July 1973, certain unspecified tapes
which he kept until November 19, when they were returned to the White House vault.

Again on Friday, November 30, Fred Buzhardt, presum-
ably at Nixon's direction, obtained the same tapes at 1:25
P.M. and returned them at 6 P.M. that day. On December 1,
Buzhardt requested and received nine tapes for the same
period, again presumably at the direction of President
Nixon, who was meeting with Gerald Ford.

No congressional committee has ever investigated the
reason for this flurry of activity by Buzhardt regarding
White House tapes during the period that the Ford nomination for Vice President was pending before the House
Judiciary Committee.

Buzhardt told me in February 1976 that his lawyer-
client relationship with Nixon would still bar him from
a full discussion of the White House tape editing and
other aspects of his dealings with Nixon and with Ford,
but that he could say he had never heard Gerald Ford's
voice on any of the tapes he had listened to at Nixon's

request. He admitted he did not listen to all of the tapes he took from the storage room, but only those parts of tapes designated for his review by Nixon. He could not remember all the tapes he listened to, but none were designated as Ford-Nixon conversations.

"I'm sure there are many Ford-Nixon conversations on those tapes, but I can honestly say I do not know of any tape that I obtained in November 1974 or any other time that had a Ford-Nixon conversation on it," the South Carolina lawyer said.

Buzhardt claimed that, as far as he knew, the tapes he obtained from the Secret Service for Nixon in November 1973 were in no way related to the Ford nomination hearings that were taking place at that time.

"We were getting tapes for review in connection with two or three court proceedings," he explained. "I listened to some of them, but not all of them."

Buzhardt said he turned the tapes over to Steve Bull, Nixon's appointments secretary, to be set up for monitoring by the President or others. "I would be the most surprised man in the world if it turned out that some of those tapes were of Nixon-Ford conversations," he added. "The only thing I know for sure is that I never heard Jerry Ford's voice on any of the tapes that I listened to in November 1973 or at any other time."

Fox and Parker also raised questions about whether H. R. Haldeman had knowledge of other information on the White House tapes that might be damaging to Nixon and others, including Ford.

According to the article, the record shows that Haldeman, on August 7, telephoned to demand a pardon of Nixon but that General Alexander Haig had taken the call. During this conversation Haldeman was reported by

Haig to have said he could "send Nixon to jail" if he didn't get a pardon. General Haig regarded this as a tactic designed to frighten rather than to blackmail Nixon. Haig was alarmed by Haldeman's threats and refused to continue the conversation until Nixon's attorney, James St. Clair, got on the line.

Significantly, Haig, Buzhardt and Washington lawyer Benton Becker have been identified as the individuals who carried out various administrative chores in connection with President Ford's pardoning of Nixon, yet none of them have been questioned by a congressional committee with regard to the important details of these duties.

Of equal significance is the agreement in the Ford-Nixon plan to eventually destroy the White House tapes, an agreement which was worked out and announced simultaneously with Ford's decision to pardon Nixon.

The magazine article speculated that a Ford pardon for Haldeman may be in the future if Haldeman has knowledge of Nixon-Ford conversations or other activities by Ford in conflict with any testimony Ford has given relative to the whole Watergate cover-up. Certainly, the trial balloons sent up by the White House press office the day after the Nixon pardon were more than a hint that Gerald R. Ford was searching for an opportunity to pardon other Watergate defendants. Any prospective pardons for Haldeman, Ehrlichman or Mitchell were dynamited in the firestorm of protest from the public and the Congress that greeted the suggestion of the pardoning of all Watergate defendants.

The fact that Deputy White House press secretary John Hushen was forced to accept responsibility for that suggestion did not deceive any thoughtful observer, for Hushen was too cautious a man to have announced that such a scheme was under consideration unless he had been directed to do so with the assurance that it was indeed President Ford's wish.

Hushen, after leaving the White House press office in January 1976, told me he "wasn't winging it on my own" when he had answered questions relative to the pardoning of other Watergate defendants and had said it was "under study" at the White House. He declined to discuss whether he had his authority directly from President Ford or from someone else who could speak with authority for Ford, but said "it was decided that we had come down a little too hard on them" by indicating in the first statement that they could never get a pardon. President Ford was interested in "softening the position a little" and wanted to indicate "that John Dean or Chuck Colson or anyone else would receive the same consideration as anyone else if they applied for a pardon."

The former White House press secretary said that the "unfortunate wording" had resulted in Congress' getting the impression "we were actively studying pardons" for Haldeman, Ehrlichman, Mitchell and the others. "That really brought down the roof," Hushen recalled.

On December 18, 1975, the *Washington Post,* in a story by Pulitzer Prize winners Bob Woodward and Carl Bernstein, reported on "apparent contradictions" in President Ford's account of events leading up to the Nixon pardon. The *Post* reporters stated that Ford granted the pardon "after hearing urgent pleas from the former President's top aides that he be spared the threat of criminal prosecution."

Although White House Council Philip W. Buchen was quoted as saying that the pleas did not figure in Ford's decision to pardon Nixon, Woodward and Bernstein found "several new facts" significant.

They quoted "a reliable source" as saying that President Ford gave General Haig "private assurances" that Nixon would be granted a pardon. Those assurances were given to Haig on August 28, 1974—the day of Ford's first presidential press conference.

"A second fact is an impassioned three-page memo written by former Nixon counsel Leonard Garment that same day, urging that Mr. Ford grant a pardon to his predecessor," the *Post* reporters wrote. "The memo, according to sources, indicated that Nixon's mental and physical condition could not withstand the continued threat of criminal prosecution. It implied that, unless he was pardoned, Nixon might take his own life, the source said."

The *Post* sources were "unsure if President Ford saw the memo, but said Haig used its argument in making the case for the pardon to Mr. Ford."

"In addition, former Nixon speech writer Raymond K. Price, Jr., drafted a two-and-one-half-page statement the same day for President Ford to read announcing the pardon at his first press conference. It was not used," the Woodward and Bernstein team continued.

On the day the *Washington Post* story appeared, William I. Greener, deputy White House press secretary, issued a public statement denying the implications of the story and saying, "The President has dealt with candor and truthfulness at all times on this matter."

Greener specifically denied the assertion in the *Post* story that Ford had assured Haig that a pardon for Nixon would be forthcoming, but he admitted there had been a discussion between Ford and Haig which Ford had failed to tell his own staff about until the *Washington Post* inquiries.

"Three reliable sources have told the *Washington Post* that the President and Haig had a substantive discussion that day [August 28] about pardoning Nixon, and that Haig received assurances from Mr. Ford that a pardon would be granted," the *Post* reiterated, and noted,

"Haig has refused to discuss publicly what was said at his meeting with the President. Buchen has said that he doesn't know exactly what was discussed by the two men."

That *Post* story said the new "facts" appear to conflict with President Ford's testimony before the Judiciary Committee when he said, "At no time after I became President on August 9, 1974, was the subject of a pardon for Richard M. Nixon raised by the former President or by anyone representing him."

The *Post* further pointed out: "In a telephone interview Wednesday, Haig—now commander of NATO forces in Europe—confirmed that he discussed the pardon with Mr. Ford on August 28. 'That's accurate,' Haig said when told that Buchen had acknowledged such a conversation."

In January 1976, Walter Pincus of the *Washington Post* wrote of an interview with former White House Counsel J. Fred Buzhardt in which he denied that he or any other White House staff member had originated the option of a pardon to President Nixon if he would resign.

"The significance of the disagreement lies in the fact [that] Buzhardt's version raises the possibility it was Nixon himself who developed the pardon-after-resignation idea and then sent Haig to discover Mr. Ford's attitude," Pincus wrote.

Buzhardt was quoted as saying, "It was obvious that a successor president has the pardon power . . . but it is something you could not explore very much. . . . It was a question of whether he chose to exercise it, and that would have been pretty difficult to speculate on.

"I don't know if Al [Haig] was rattling off every idea, every possibility. I would assume that he would have discussed with President Nixon this matter before going to the Vice President because it was my observation that he just didn't make decisions on his own without taking them up with the President, at this time or any other time."

Pincus noted that "Haig would not comment on Buzhardt's assertion. A spokesman at NATO headquarters in Brussels, where Haig is now commanding general, said the former Nixon chief of staff had 'consistently declined' to discuss his White House duties 'except in an official forum.' "

Buzhardt in his interview with Pincus had revealed that there were serious discussions of pardons for Nixon and other Watergate defendants long before the July 24, 1974, date the United States Supreme Court ordered Nixon to deliver sixty-four White House tapes to United States District Judge John J. Sirica.

On the day of the Supreme Court decision, Buzhardt said he suggested to Nixon by a telephone call to Haig and St. Clair that the entire issue could be "mooted" if Nixon pardoned all the Watergate defendants as well as himself and then resigned. This proposal was taken under advisement even though Haig, St. Clair and Buzhardt agreed it was "drastic."

Even while the press and a few Senators and Representatives continued to make restless inquiry into important details and seeming contradictions, the Judiciary committees of the Senate and House were content to let the matter rest and let unanswered quesions remain unanswered until some shocking contradiction became apparent.

On February 19, 1976, the House Judiciary Subcommittee headed by Democrat William Hungate, of Missouri, rejected an effort by Representative Elizabeth Holtzman to simply get the subcommittee to interview General Haig, Fred Buzhardt, Leonard Garment and others to try to resolve seeming conflicts. The White House was opposed to even the staff interviews and won a 4 to 3 decision in the subcommittee when two Democrats—Representative James Mann, of South Carolina, and Representative Martin Russo, a first-term Congressman from Cook County, Illinois—joined Republican Representative Charles E. Wiggins, of California, and Representative Henry Hyde, an Illinois Republican.

Chairman Hungate, Representative Holtzman and Representative Edward Mezvinsky voted in favor of engaging in low-key staff interviews with General Haig, Garment, Buzhardt and White House Counsel Phil Buchen to see if the apparent discrepancies in Ford's testimony could be cleared up.

"All should have been questioned under oath in the initial inquiry," Representative Holtzman said. "None have been questioned under oath or interviewed on these questions, and I had believed that a majority of the members of the subcommittee had indicated they would support that limited probe.

"It concerns me that the Ford Administration and the Republicans are opposed to clearing up these questions," she added.

But Representative Wiggins, one of the last-ditch defenders of Nixon, said the pardon is "a dead horse" and that Holtzman's resolution to reopen the pardon questioning "reeks of politics." He called the contradictions "trivia," but Representative Mezvinsky replied that questions involving the credibility of the President "are never trivia" when they have to do with the pardoning of a man involved "in the serious crime of obstruction of justice."

Representative Mann said he believed that the questions should have been cleaned up at the initial hearings and that the original investigation had not been a thorough one.

"We didn't question all the witnesses we could have at that time, and we didn't get in the legal experts we should have heard to make the record complete," Mann said. "I don't think it is the President's fault if we didn't do our job, and unless there are greater questions raised now than have been raised, I don't want to go back and plough over the same old ground."

Representative Russo told me that he had told Representative Holtzman he would vote in favor of the limited probe less than twenty-four hours before he reversed himself, but that at the time he made the commitment he "had not really examined the alleged discrepancies."

"When I got to looking it over last night, I saw that some of the discrepancy was because Bob Woodward had not quoted the President's testimony accurately," Russo said.

Mezvinsky countered that "there should be no objection to getting Haig, Buchen, Buzhardt and Garment on record as to precisely what took place.

"I would think that the President and the Republicans would want to clear these things up if they are explainable," he said. "This simply won't go away until the questions are raised and answered in a forum where the stories and documents are checked out in a responsible manner."

Mezvinsky added, "When they blocked the Patman com-mittee in the fall of 1972 they simply piled up more prob-lems for later. It appears they are intent upon doing it all over again."

Despite the rejection of Holtzman's request for a probe, Congress has made certain that the White House tapes will be preserved for historians so that future disputes may be resolved concerning the Ford-Nixon conversations during the Watergate cover-up era.

It is doubtful that President Ford finds much comfort in the continued existence of the tapes, especially since it is unlikely that he remembers the details of his many con-versations in the Oval Office.

21. The Credibility Chasm

And in all that we do, we must be more honest with
the American people, promising them no more than
we can deliver, and delivering all that we promise.

Gerald R. Ford
State of the Union Address
January 19, 1976

WHILE MANY PEOPLE were questioning whether President
Ford was a man of his word, February 1976 found him still
in close contact with two people who had every reason to
believe Ford was a politician who would keep his commitments.

Richard Nixon had been invited by the People's Republic of China to return on the fourth anniversary of his
triumphant opening of relations with that country. As a
private citizen, it was his privilege to accept "with plea-
sure," but as a former head of state, there were, of course,
political implications and the trip would receive heavy
press coverage.

It was also announced that John Connally, Treasury Secretary in the Nixon Administration, was to be appointed by President Ford to a post on the President's Foreign Intelligence Advisory Board.

Both incidents were indicative of Ford's forgiving nature, or unconcern, regarding the problems of his political friends.

On February 10 the President told a press group at a White House breakfast that Nixon had not informed him, Dr. Henry Kissinger or anyone else in government of his decision to accept the invitation from the People's Republic of China.

"I don't think anybody in our Government knew that he [Nixon] was going," Ford said. "I know that neither Henry nor I did. He made his decision to go without any consultation previously with us. I don't at the moment see any serious ramifications of his going, as far as my campaign is concerned, but only time will tell."

President Ford, thinking only of the impact on his political future, said he had not assessed the Russians' reaction to Nixon's trip, and added, "I am sure they were as surprised as we that he was invited."

He said he later had a conversation with Nixon relative to the trip and "in effect I asked him to let me know any communications or anything he wanted to divulge to me. I didn't ask him to make a special report. It is implicit when he comes back [that] if he has something to say he will."

A reporter asked President Ford the nature of his discussions with President Nixon in their periodic telephone conversations, and with his customary nonspecific reply he characterized them as "conversations between two old friends" that are "relatively short and cover a wide range of subjects."

"Do you call him or does he call you?" another reporter asked, and Ford replied, "I called him on his birthday and I think I called him at Christmas or New Year's, and on several occasions prior to that he had called me."

President Ford said he could think of no circumstance under which he would ask Mr. Nixon not to make his trip to China. "He was invited as a private citizen and he is going at their invitation, and I really have no strong feeling one way or another."

The President offered no apologies for continuing a personal relationship with the man he had said earlier had brought disgrace upon the office of the President and the nation.

From a technical standpoint, President Ford's pardon of Nixon was full and unconditional and had wiped out all legal taint. Apparently, as far as Ford was concerned, there was no stigma attached to maintaining the association, and he was trying to milk all political advantage from the small band of Nixon loyalists. Secretary Kissinger, who also maintained his association with Nixon, offered the suggestion that Mr. Nixon might someday return to public life as a United States Ambassador. There was no indication that this had been officially discussed between Dr. Kissinger and the President as a possibility were Ford to be victorious in the 1976 election, but President Ford was not one who needed formal agreements to reward old cronies.

Gerald Ford played the game of politics, applying the rule of allegiance to friends who still might have some value in any segment of the political organization. The effort to reestablish John Connally by appointment to an intelligence post was intended to demonstrate that President Ford believed Connally's acquittal on milk-support bribery charges had wiped out any blemish that the Senate investigations, the indictment by the Special Prosecutor or the trial testimony might have left on the Connally image.

Bribery and perjury indictments were returned against Connally and Texas lawyer Jake Jacobsen on July 29, 1974—one week before Ford became President. Pardoning Nixon had taken precedence over the pending criminal charges against Connally involving an alleged bribery conspiracy with Jacobsen and Dairy Industry lobbyist Harold Nelson to help secure higher federal support prices for milk products. Jacobsen, Nelson and David L. Parr, a former counsel for the Associated Milk Producers Inc. (AMPI), all entered pleas of guilty, were fined and served jail terms, but Connally pleaded not guilty and eventually was acquitted by an unprecedented secret jury panel in United States District Judge George Hart's court. Never before in our system of government had the names, addresses and identification of jurors been withheld.

Judge Hart imposed that order at the request of Connally's lawyer during the trial in April 1975, and it was not lifted when the jury returned its verdict of not guilty. Nine months after the trial, the press and the public could not learn the identity, background and economic circumstances of the men and women who acquitted Connally.

Of course Connally, as the defendant in the criminal trial, had a constitutional right to know the names of the potential jurors, to investigate them and to have his lawyer question them thoroughly about anything in their background that might create prejudices against Connally or anyone in his circumstances.

Judge Hart points out that the public interest was protected by the fact that the Special Prosecutor's office and the Justice Department had knowledge of the names, background and economic situation of each of the jurors, as well as the authority and responsibility to investigate any evidence of questionable actions involving any of them if it came to their attention. Judge Hart, who admits his secret jury was without precedent, overruled prosecution objections and press protests and kept a tight secrecy lid on the jurors' names "to protect them from being harassed."

While the federal criminal charges were pending against Connally, President Ford kept aloof from the prosecution of the handsome Texan, whom he referred to warmly as his old political friend. Although he expressed his own doubts about Connally's guilt by word and action, he did not exercise the ultimate power for compassion—the presidential pardon—before his trial as he had with his other "old political friend," Richard Nixon.

However, in the weeks just prior to Connally's trial, he and President Ford met privately at a Republican meeting in Texas, which was a signal to the political world that Gerald Ford was a loyal ally and that a federal criminal indictment would not affect their association. It particularly distressed the Special Watergate Prosecution staff, who were arguing in court that they had strong admissible evidence that Connally had accepted two cash payments of $5,000 each for his role in urging the boost of dairy price supports.

Most presidents, regardless of their compassion or per-

sonal opposition to actions by administration prosecutors
would have felt constrained to avoid personal contact with
a powerful political associate charged with serious political
crimes. But Ford brushed aside these personal risks, met
with Connally and used the prestige of the office of president to demonstrate his support.

In his own political life, Ford had felt free to criticize
and condemn the moral standards of the Truman, Kennedy and Johnson administrations on fragments of evidence before a specific crime was charged or an indictment
returned.

But, when his and Nixon's political friends were involved he cautioned restraint and developed a benevolence
and leniency not demonstrated when he charged corruption in the Truman tax scandals or the Bobby Baker case,
or when he attacked Supreme Court Justice William O.
Douglas as "unfit for office" and "impeachable" because
he had accepted annual payments from a foundation supported by the income of a Mafia-connected Las Vegas
gambling casino.

Whether the more compassionate view toward persons
charged with political corruption was strictly partisan or
whether it was indicative of a new, deeper understanding
of the rights of defendants, President Ford's fearless action
in associating with Connally when he was under criminal
charges was a forceful display of support that proved
helpful to Connally's public image in those dark days
before the jury acquittal.

While less advantageous at the moment than a presidential pardon would have been, in the long run Connally
was better off standing trial and being acquitted by a jury
of his peers, even though there were some uneasy moments
when his high-priced counsel, famed criminal lawyer

Edward Bennett Williams, was convincing the jury that
Jacobsen was lying when he told of delivery of two cash
payoffs of $5,000 to Treasury Secretary Connally. Even
though Connally made embarrassing admissions relative
to his meetings and dealings with an admitted Texas fixer
and briber, the jury acquittal was much more credible
with the public than a presidential pardon with overtones
of political favoritism and chicanery.

President Ford's overlooking of the Watergate-related
problems of Nixon and Connally established him with full
credentials as a tough political professional who did not
wince when the going was difficult but remained firm in
the best tradition of the machine politician doing all he
could for his friends.

The *Baltimore Sun* in mid-February confirmed reports
that President Ford was going to appoint Connally to the
Foreign Intelligence Advisory Board, with increased responsibilities in overseeing intelligence-gathering operations.

But the *Sun* also reported that Ford was considering
"Big Jawn" Connally as a vice-presidential running mate,
and in support of this White House sources were praising
Connally's "experience" and his "charisma" as a cam-
paigner.

The *Washington Star* commented critically that, despite
the acquittal, "one thing Mr. Connally can't shake is the
Watergate tar-brush.

"True, Mr. Connally was acquitted of bribery charges
in connection with a milk case, and he sometimes makes
the point that this makes him 'one of the few men in
America who was certifiably innocent,' " the article went
on.

It also made the remark that Connally's "certifiably

innocent" was comparable to George Wallace's explanations of his 10 percent disability pay for battle fatigue
suffered during World War II as making him "certifiably
90 percent sane, and that's more than most politicians
can say."

In a February 14 editorial, the *Star* commented, "Despite the not guilty verdict, and as much as he seems to
admire Mr. Connally's talent, we suspect that President
Ford would not want a constant reminder of Watergate in
his fall campaign, which is what Mr. Connally would be if
he were on the ticket."

The *Star* theorized that making a gesture to Connally
might be helpful politically to Mr. Ford for "stop Reagan"
strategy in Texas. "Mr. Connally is said to remain influ-
ential in Texas politics and it probably would not hurt to
have him in the Ford camp for the May 1 primary," the
Washington Star said. "After all, Mr. Ford won't even get
to the fall campaign unless he first gets by Ronald Reagan."

Use of the Connally ploy, if that was what it was, to win
Texas support was a perfectly legitimate tactic in pursuit
of the Republican nomination by a president who was running scared. If one believed the "confidential" information from so-called inside-White House sources on those
Ford was "really seriously considering" for the number-
two spot on the 1976 ticket, there was a list of at least
two dozen names and which was growing longer with each
succeeding week. It included nearly half the Senate Republicans, at least half a dozen governors and twenty to
thirty House members; even Nelson A. Rockefeller and
Reagan were reported "not ruled out completely."

Speculation had reached the point of absurdity, and
Ford and his supporters were throwing the bait out
blindly, hoping to get or hold backers who were moving

to Reagan. Nobody placed credence in Ford's leaked lists because even where sound and logical reasons existed for President Ford to select a specific young governor, Representative or Senator, there were doubts about his ability to bring it off.

Ford was truly "an accidental president," and his only accomplishments were combinations of accidents and non-action. The major success of his first nineteen months in office was the upturn in economic conditions.

"We have turned the recession around and we are starting, even more effectively than we anticipated, to come out of the recession more quickly," Ford told reporters on February 10. He characterized this as "our biggest success" domestically and credited it to "the fact that we kept our cool . . . by adopting a firm, and I believe constructive, policy."

In fact, Ford's policy had been criticized as "a do-nothing" policy in the face of dire forecasts of a depression comparable to that of the 1930's. His most spectacular actions were the nonactions following his vetoes of Democratic programs, and Ford could say with assurance, "The net result has been an economic recovery better and more rapidly than we ourselves predicted."

Although the economic issues were an important factor, and elections often turn on bread-and-butter issues, President Ford was being submerged in a political mire as bad or worse than what any other president had faced. His financial report and his income tax returns showed a modest net worth of $323,489, and no one could contend that Gerald Ford had enriched himself while in public office or had not paid a reasonable percentage of his salary and other income in federal, state and local taxes.

But, Ford, the man of candor, had destroyed his own

credibility, and the man of experience in government and politics had demonstrated he really didn't know much about running a government and had made a disaster of nearly every political problem he tackled.

President Ford had spoken of openness but had vetoed the Freedom of Information bill. He had spoken of political candor but had been duplicitous on his promises to labor on common-situs picketing, to the farmer on government farm price supports and to livestock producers on packer-bonding legislation.

He had promised "cooperation" with Congress on the intelligence blunders and abuses by the CIA and FBI, but had permitted the extreme use of "executive privilege" as a cover-up device for Secretary of State Henry Kissinger.

He had promised firm law enforcement policies but had pardoned Nixon. He had promised new standards of integrity in which his own conduct would be the measuring stick, but then disregarded well-documented records of conflicts of interests and displayed other questionable ethical conduct to push the nomination of Nixon men to a wide range of government posts, including regulatory agencies.

Ford spoke of the need for a strong defense but fired Secretary of Defense James Schlesinger when he pressed Congress for the defense budget Ford said he needed but would not fight for.

The final blowup came when Schlesinger declined to go along with the deception of a $7 billion budget cut, which President Ford termed only "a temporary cut" for cosmetic purposes in dealing with the public and Congress.

More than nineteen months of a Ford Administration had demonstrated that "Mr. Amiability" was a pushover for any lobbying group, and it was usually the man who saw him last who had the most influence on the final decision. But, having made a final decision in any area—domestic or foreign—President Ford was tenacious, some said "bullheaded," in his refusal to admit error and change direction.

He had more press conferences than President Nixon but was a better "stonewaller," in refusing to discuss facts or go beyond an unsatisfactory and superficial discussion of the issues.

In the field of foreign affairs, Ford had followed Dr. Henry Kissinger through fluctuating sweet talk of "detente" and belligerence from the Soviet Union, which had left our allies, our adversaries, our Congress and our public thoroughly confused with promises and then sellouts of the Kurds in Iran and various other groups in South America, Africa, Asia and Western Europe.

Dr. Kissinger, caught with the responsibility for past intelligence blunders and questionable covert actions by the CIA, resorted to secrecy as his solution to the Ford Administration's problems at home and abroad. Foreign policy was the province of the President and the Secretary of State, he declared, and Congress was fouling up his game plan for agreements with the Soviet Union on a Strategic Arms Limitation Treaty.

Kissinger's arrogant attitude toward Congress was comparable to Kleindienst's theories on "executive privilege" at the height of the Watergate cover-up. And Ford, in following Kissinger's lead, was as destructive of executive branch accountability as Richard Nixon had ever been, although the professional compromise rhetoric used by President Ford was less offensive. The results were much the same, and were potentially more destructive to the operations of democratic processes in the United States.

Without the power to compel the production of testimony and documents from the executive branch, Congress is a weak and toothless tiger. The Ford-Kissinger theories on the right of the executive branch to hide its actions, records and testimony from properly authorized committees of Congress would accomplish the ultimate destruction of checks and balances if permitted to become practice.

If Gerald Ford is nominated by the Republican Party and elected in November as President of the United States, it is likely that he and Dr. Kissinger will view that election as a mandate to continue the programs and policies they have pursued since August 1974.

It is difficult, even impossible, to predict what that would mean to the nation. Even if Gerald Ford or Dr. Kissinger were to reveal the policies they intend to pursue in promoting our general welfare at home and abroad, only a fool would believe them in light of the Ford Administration's record.

President Ford has demonstrated that he sees what he wants to see, and sees it in the light in which he wants to see it. He is a waverer who can find political rationalization to reverse himself on almost any promise. What more can one expect from the total political man who pardoned Richard Nixon after having told a congressional committee that the American people would never stand for a president to pardon a predecessor who had appointed him?

"I was asked a hypothetical question," Ford explained. "In answer to a hypothetical question I responded by saying that I did not think the American people would stand for such action."

Whether he was right or wrong will be demonstrated by the 1976 election returns.

Index